PRAISE FOR *SACRED WOUNDS*

"Dakota Hauck has an extraordinary gift for asking tough questions and untangling nuanced answers. He is both a compatriot and a guide, a wise leader and a friend-in-arms. We want him on this road with us. *Sacred Wounds* is a beautiful road map, offering thoughtful, compassionate guidance on how to understand a world of hurt and a God who restores all things."

— Kimberly Stuart, author of *Star for Jesus (And Other Jobs I Quit: Rediscovering the Grace That Sets Us Free)*

"*Sacred Wounds* is a beautifully written, deeply honest, and hope-filled invitation to see our pain through the lens of God's redemptive love. Dakota reminds us that our wounds are not the end of our story—they are the very places where Jesus meets us, heals us, and makes us whole. A must-read for anyone searching for beauty, goodness, and truth in the midst of suffering."

— Brandon Janous, author of *Just DO! Stories about Discovering Purpose, Gaining Perspective and Being Present.*

"*Sacred Wounds* is a disarming invitation to a new generation of those deeply hurt, the walking wounded that search social media for answers they can never find. It is deep but accessible, insightful but not overwhelming and a bit threatening, (talking about pain always is) and yet engagingly inviting.

Dakota takes a very difficult subject and skillfully walks you into it. Before you know it you're up to your ears dealing with your pain and finding not only are you not alone in your pain there is a God who loves to journey in it with you and that it's actually possible to grow in your pain."

— Dan Carroll, Founding Pastor of Water of Life Community Church in Fontana California

"The book you hold in your hands is a profound gift to suffering souls everywhere. Dakota Hauck provides a sacred space to explore our sacred wounds. To be human is to suffer. Let this book provide a nuanced and compassionate testament to the unshakable truth of Christ's love enduring in the midst of our earthly sufferings."

— Katherine Wolf, author and disability advocate

"While I have learned a great deal from blessing and abundance, I have learned even more through struggling, disappointment, and pain. What you believe about struggle, its purpose, and most importantly, our attitude towards it will determine how you face it, grow through it, and triumph over it. Dakota masterfully leads us on a journey discovering the beauty, goodness, and truth that can be found in the midst of pain. He will challenge your thinking, shake your theology a little but ultimately, give new and lasting hope."

— Dan Sneed- Pastor, author, international bible teacher, and conference speaker.

"Pain is our unwanted story, and without help, it weaves a future filled with lies and heartbreak. Amid our pain though, there is another story of hope and redemption. *Sacred Wounds* tells that other story. What Dakota has written is more than a book; it's a journey towards the heart of God paved through his own sufferings. Remarkably poignant yet practical, Sacred Wounds is a vision of true transformation in a secular age, and offers a genuine discipleship invitation that is rarely found. I can't recommend this highly enough."

— Phil Manginelli, Author and Senior Pastor of the Square Church in Smyrna, Georgia

"In *Sacred Wounds*, readers are invited into an honest exploration of the complexities of life in a broken world. With pastoral sensitivity and theological depth, the book reveals how grace meets us in our pain and reorients our disappointments in light of God's redemptive purposes. This is a compelling and hopeful read—one that is both intellectually engaging and spiritually nourishing."

— Darrell L. Bock, Executive Director for Cultural Engagement, Senior Research Professor of New Testament Studies, Hendricks Center

"This book is a gift to anyone who has ever asked, "Why is there so much pain in the world?" and longed to believe that their own story could be part of a redemptive narrative. With biblical insight, poetic reflection, and courageous honesty, *Sacred Wounds* will not only comfort your soul but commission your pain for purpose. It's a timely and timeless message for a weary, fractured world."

— Davey Blackburn, Founder of Nothing is Wasted Ministries, Host of the Nothing is Wasted Podcast, Author of *Nothing is Wasted: A True Story of Hope, Forgiveness, and Finding Purpose in Pain*

"*Sacred Wounds* tackles the conversations many Christians tend to avoid, and Dakota addresses them head-on with honesty and biblical wisdom. We need voices like his—willing not to tiptoe around hard truths, but to sit with them, wrestle through them, and walk with us into what God might be forming through them."

— Zacharay Maakreebs, Pastor in Residency at Asbury Theological Seminary, Author of *Lower: Igniting Spiritual Awakening through Radical Obedience*

"The question of pain echoes throughout human history. Why does it exist and if God is good, why does he allow it? Weaving together profound Biblical truths, personal antidotes, and contemporary examples, Hauck paints a compelling picture of not only the usefulness of pain, but the beauty that can be found within it. His convivial and authentic voice will leave you avidly considering how you can partner with God to create a more beautiful world through your pain."

— Emily Manginelli, Co-Founding Pastor of the Square Church in Smyrna Georgia, Director of the School of Biblical Studies Atlanta

Foreword by
BOB GOFF
New York Times
Bestselling Author

SACRED WOUNDS

Finding the Beauty, Goodness, & Truth in Our Pain

Written by
DAKOTA HAUCK

Sacred Wounds
Finding the Beauty, Goodness, & Truth in Our Pain
Copyright © 2025 by Dakota Hauck

This book is a work of nonfiction based on the author's personal memories, interpretations, and experiences. While every effort has been made to ensure accuracy, certain details, events, and conversations may have been reconstructed or adapted for narrative purposes.

The publisher and author disclaim any liability or responsibility for any actions taken or not taken based on the information in this book. The views expressed herein are solely those of the author and do not necessarily reflect the views or opinions of the publisher or any affiliated parties.

No portion of this book may be reproduced, stored in a retrieval system, or transmitted in any form or by any means—electronic, mechanical, photocopy, recording, scanning, or other—except for brief quotations in critical reviews or articles, without the prior written permission of the publisher.

Scripture quotations are taken from the Holy Bible, New International Version® (NIV®), unless otherwise indicated. Used by permission of Biblica, Inc.® All rights reserved worldwide.

Scripture quotations are from the ESV® Bible (The Holy Bible, English Standard Version®), copyright © 2001 by Crossway, a publishing ministry of Good News Publishers. Used by permission. All rights reserved.

Scripture quotations marked (NLT) are taken from the Holy Bible, New Living Translation, copyright © 1996, 2004, 2015 by Tyndale House Foundation. Used by permission of Tyndale House Publishers, Inc., Carol Stream, Illinois 60188. All rights reserved.

Scripture quotations marked (CEV) are from the Contemporary English Version, copyright © 1995 by American Bible Society. Used by permission. All rights reserved.

Requests for information should be addressed to:
info@bluehatpublishing.com

Hardback ISBN: 979-8-89514-025-3
eBook ISBN: 979-8-89514-008-6

Cover design: Jon Arriaza
Interior design: Jessica Arnett

Printed in the United States of America

"May the Lamb that was slain receive the reward of His Suffering" (Which is you and me.)
— *The Moravians*

For those who have been overwhelmed by the immensity of their pain, may you come to know the even greater depth of Jesus's kindness, compassion, and unwavering mercy; and may you become overwhelmed with the immensity of His love for you.

To my mom,
who sacrificed everything for Isaiah and me.
You carried your own pain while raising two sons, and your sacrifice shaped me in ways I can never fully express. Thank you!

To Kennedi & JD,
I love you both more than words can say.
I wrote this book with you in my heart, knowing that life will bring you pain, challenges, and moments of doubt. But I pray the words of this book will remind you that you are never alone, that your faith is worth holding onto, and that your dad has walked through struggles too.
I am proud of the people you are becoming, and I will always be in your corner. I love you!

To Bren,
Thank you for standing by me through my hardest moments, for believing in me, and for being a physical reminder of God's grace in my life. Your presence has been a gift, and I couldn't have done any of this without you.

CONTENTS

Foreword	11
Letter to the Reader	13

PART ONE: THE PROBLEM OF PAIN

Chapter 1: Not How It's Supposed to Be	19
Chapter 2: God's Great Goof	27

PART TWO: OUR WOUNDED WORLD

Chapter 3: A Broken World	39
Chapter 4: Catastrophic Coincidence	53
Chapter 5: Beautiful Disaster	65
Chapter 6: Understanding Our Problem	79
Chapter 7: Hope You Guess My Name	93
Chapter 8: God's Idea or Ideas as God	109

PART THREE: OUR WOUNDED LIVES

Chapter 9: Self-Made	131
Chapter 10: A Redefining Culture	147
Chapter 11: Disordered Loves, Disordered Lives	159
Chapter 12: Lost in Masquerade	173
Chapter 13: More Similar Than Expected	183

PART FOUR: SACRED WOUNDS

Chapter 14: The Path Forward: Beauty, Goodness, & Truth	205
Chapter 15: Revolutionary Stubborn Love	225
Chapter 16: Real, Near, and Satisfying	243
Chapter 17: Sacred Wounds	255

Thank Yous	273
End Notes	275

FOREWORD

I love how life has this wild, unpredictable way of taking us places we never thought we'd go. Some of those places feel like standing on top of a mountain, where everything seems possible. But if we're honest, a lot of those places feel more like valleys, where the walls close in and we're not sure we'll find our way out. The thing about Dakota is, he's not afraid to meet us right there—in the middle of the mess, the questions, and yes, the pain—and point us to the One who's been there all along.

Dakota writes a thoughtful and timely book about how pain influences and impacts our lives. But he doesn't leave us staring at the wound. He lifts our eyes, helping us see what God sees: the sacred ground where *wounds* turn into something *sacred*—a place where we discover hope and healing not just for ourselves but for others, too.

In *Sacred Wounds,* you're going to find more than words. You'll find a friend. Someone who's walked through the dark and can show you the light. Someone who'll remind you that God doesn't waste a single tear, a single setback, or a single moment of pain. Instead, He transforms those places into solid ground where others can stand and find Him.

Here's the thing about Dakota: he's not interested in making you more like him. He's got his own quirks and adventures, and he'd be the first to admit he's still figuring it all out. No, Dakota's goal is bigger and bolder than that. He wants to help you see how Jesus shows up in every broken and beautiful piece of your story so you can be more like Him.

For some of you, that's going to mean giving yourself a little grace—the kind of grace Jesus gives so freely—to walk through the hard stuff without pretending it doesn't hurt. For others, it'll mean finding the strength to keep going, to persevere when life feels impossible. And for all of us, it's about letting the life of Jesus transform us into His image through pain.

Here are four takeaways from Dakota's book:

1. **Hope:** Because even in the hardest times, God's promises never waver. He's with you, and that changes everything.

2. **Joy:** Not the kind that ignores the pain but the kind that sits with it and still finds a reason to smile—because joy in Jesus is untouchable.

3. **Empathy:** The kind that softens our hearts and helps us see others not as projects to fix but as people to love. It's about learning to carry each other's burdens like Jesus carries ours.

4. **Mission:** God didn't call us to sit on the sidelines. He invites us to be part of His beautiful, redemptive plan—the renewal of all things—even when we're still a work in progress.

Here's what I know: Dakota lives what he writes. He's the kind of guy who'll stop whatever he's doing to remind you that you're loved, you're seen, and you're not alone. He's been a friend to me and a trusted voice on the journey of turning wounds into worship. And I'm confident he'll be the same for you.

So, as you turn these pages, I hope you laugh a little. I hope you cry a little, too. But most of all, I hope you walk away reminded that the God who heals broken hearts and binds up wounds is writing a story of redemption in your life. And trust me, it's going to be beautiful.

Bob Goff

LETTER TO THE READER

Dear Reader,

If these words have found you, then I believe—truly believe—it's not by accident. Perhaps you're holding this book because pain has found its way into your life, or into the life of someone you love. However you've come, I'm grateful you're here. Before you begin reading, there are a few things I'd like to say to you personally.

First, I've been praying for you—long before I ever typed a single sentence. My deepest hope for this book has never been recognition or reach, but rather that it would land softly, yet powerfully, in the hands of the ones God intended it for. That means you. Your presence here is an answer to that prayer. And I believe with all my heart: God has something in these pages meant just for you.

Second, this book was born from Isaiah 43—a chapter that has carried me, steadied me, and reminded me of the nearness of God in seasons of ache. It is a passage where God speaks to His people with tenderness and strength, calling them back to their identity, their belovedness, and His faithful presence in their suffering.

> **"You are Mine."** (Isaiah 43:1–7)
> God begins with these words of comfort: *"Fear not, for I have redeemed you; I have called you by name, you are mine."* He does not promise ease, but He promises presence. Whether you're walking through fire or deep waters, you will not be alone. He sees you. He values you. He loves you.

> **"I Alone Save."** (Isaiah 43:8–13)
> God reminds us that no idol, no substitute, no other name saves—only He does. *"I, I am the Lord, and besides me there is no savior."* He is steady when all else fails. He is faithful when everything else falls short.

> **"I Am Doing a New Thing."** (Isaiah 43:14–21)
> God recalls the great rescue of the past, but then gently urges us to lift our eyes to what's ahead: *"Forget the former things; do not dwell on the past. See, I am doing a new thing!"* He is not done. Not with you. Not with your story. Even here, even now—He is making a way.

This book may stir things in you. It may touch tender places. There will be moments that feel heavy. But I believe—more than anything—that Jesus wants to meet you there, not to harm but to heal. If ever the weight feels too much, return to this letter. Return to Isaiah 43. And most of all, return to Jesus. He is gentle. He is near. He cares deeply for you. And yes, He is doing a new thing in you.

You are His beloved. Sacred. Chosen. And most Cherished. Let Him into your wounds. Trust Him with the broken pieces. He will breathe life into what feels beyond repair.

One more thing.

Before you dive in, there are a couple of things I want to say—just to help you as you read.

First, throughout this book, you'll come across the phrase "good, true, and beautiful." A lot. Like, more than once or twice. You'll also see it used in a few different ways—and that's on purpose.

The original phrase is: what is good, true, and beautiful.

It's not something I made up. It's old. Ancient, actually. Plato and Aristotle both talked about it. They believed that to live a virtuous life, you needed all three. But here's the thing—they didn't see them as one inseparable whole. They saw them as distinct, individual virtues.

Later on, people like Augustine and Aquinas picked it up. Augustine connected it to the Trinity. Aquinas used it to talk about how God reveals Himself. Over time, others used it too—philosophers, theologians, cultural critics. People trying to make sense of what matters most.

I guess I'm just one more voice in that long conversation.

In this book, I mostly stick with the order: good, true, and beautiful. But you'll notice I change it up sometimes. On purpose.

LETTER TO THE READER

At one point, you'll see: truth, goodness, and beauty. That's because I'm talking about how those first two—truth and goodness—are at the center of a lot of tension in our culture right now. Especially when we talk about ethics, politics, religion. You know, the dinner-table minefields.

Later, the phrase shifts again: beautiful, good, and true. And I explain why when we get there. It's not just a stylistic choice—it has everything to do with how we make sense of pain, suffering, and the long, slow path of healing. So don't skip that part. It matters.

Okay—almost done. One last heads-up.

You'll notice most of the references in this book are tucked into the endnotes. That includes Bible verses. So when you read something like "scripture says…" and then see a little number at the end, and you're wondering, "Where exactly does it say that?"—flip to the back. It's there.

I did this for a reason. Most of us skim over references. We treat refrences like background noise. But that's not what I want for you. I want you to pause. To actually sit with the verse. To let it speak louder than my writing ever could.

This book isn't meant to be rushed through. It deals with some heavy things. Deep wounds. Real questions. And healing doesn't happen fast. So this is one small way I'm inviting you to slow down. To listen. To reflect.

Please don't hate me for it.

Okay, that's it for now…

Thank you for being here. I carried you in my heart as I wrote every word. My only prayer is that by the final page, you would know—truly know—that you are loved, that Jesus sees you, and that He is for you.

With all my love,

Dakota

PART ONE:
THE PROBLEM OF PAIN

"Is pain God's great goof?"

— *Philip Yancey*

"I have told you these things, so that in me you may have peace. In this world you will have trouble. But take heart! I have overcome the world."

— *John 16:33*

1

NOT HOW IT'S SUPPOSED TO BE

"This is not how it's supposed to be!" The cry echoed off the walls.

Deep anguish. Rage. Grief. It all roared from Randy's office. Standing down the hall, outside his door, I had no idea what I was walking into.

Randy owned my favorite coffee shop in Townsville, Australia—my home during that season. Five days a week I'd show up for a flat white and a pastry. If you know anything about Australians, they tend to be witty, sarcastic, and sharp. Randy was no exception.

But today, something was different.

I stepped closer, peeking my head into his office. His head was buried in his arms, shoulders shaking as he wept.

"Randy, what's wrong?"

Brushing his tears away, he forced a half-smile. "Nothing, mate. I'm all good."

I hesitated. I didn't want to push, but I also didn't want to pretend I hadn't seen the wreckage in his eyes. "Clearly, you're not. What's going on?"

He lifted his head, his face raw with sorrow. "My wife passed a couple days ago."

Silence.

What do you even say to that? I muttered something about how sorry I was. How much that sucked. Then I asked if I could just sit with him. And for the next two hours, that's what we did.

Between sobs, Randy started talking. About his wife. About her dreams—how she had always begged him to work less and live more. About the trips they never took, the memories they never made. He had been so focused on building for "someday."

And then, while he was at work, she died of a heart attack.

As I listened, Randy uttered a phrase I had said myself just eight months earlier:

"This is not how it's supposed to be."

WHAT'S GOING ON?

We're not the only ones who have felt this tension in the world.

In 1971, Marvin Gaye released *What's Going On*, a Motown hit born from the chaos and pain he saw around him. He once said, "With the world exploding around me, how am I supposed to keep singing love songs?" The world he saw was unraveling:

- Racial injustice
- Police brutality
- Unnecessary wars
- Political polarization
- Systemic oppression
- The war of ideas

Sound familiar?

It feels like we're facing the same tensions now—maybe worse. Wars break out every day. Israel and Palestine. Russia and Ukraine. Civil wars in Africa and Syria. Some even say the US is on the verge of its own civil war.

And then there's the ideological battlefield. The 2024 election wasn't just about policies—it was about rights. If Kamala won, some feared parents would lose their rights. If Trump won, others feared for women and LGBTQ+ communities.

Meanwhile, divorce, suicide, and cynicism are at an all-time high. Many of us wake up with a low hum of anxiety, wondering if hope is even worth it anymore. Even Christians—the ones who are supposed to carry hope—have resigned themselves to: *Well, it's just a sign of the end times.*

So, we do what Randy did. We build toward *someday*, hoping to squeeze in a few happy moments before the inevitable catches up to us.

Yet, deep down, we know this isn't how it's supposed to be.

THE COMMON DENOMINATOR

There's one thing every human being shares:

Pain.

And pain leaves us with more questions than answers. It messes with how we see the world, others, and God. It isolates us. It makes us wonder if we've been abandoned. It steals our hope and leaves us whispering the same phrase:

"This is not how it's supposed to be."

You don't have to be a Christian to feel this. You don't have to be religious at all.

You can be Republican or Democrat. A Dutch king or a Papua New Guinean villager. Pain doesn't care. It comes for us all.

And yet, when pain strikes, something strange happens.

You ask someone how they're doing—just a casual "Hey, how's it going?"—and they say, "Actually, my mom has cancer" or "My grandparent just died" or "I just lost my job."

And suddenly, you feel it. A lump in your throat. A strange connection. It doesn't matter if they voted for Trump or Kamala. If they're pro-Palestine or pro-Israel. In that moment, all that matters is their pain. And, somehow, you feel closer to them than before.

Pain unites us in a way nothing else does.

But it still leaves us asking:

Is there a purpose to my pain?

Did God *cause* my pain?

How do I see myself, others, and God in light of my pain?

If you grew up religious, maybe you've been told, "It's all part of God's plan" or, my personal favorite, "God gives his toughest battles to his strongest soldiers."

But those lines don't land when you've lost a loved one to cancer.

Or when your newborn dies at 35 weeks.

If you grew up in a secular home, maybe you were told pain is just random. It happens. There's no meaning to it. Just get through it.

Either way, the result is the same: pain comes. It doesn't discriminate. It doesn't care about your race, gender, sexuality, or religion. It just shows up.

And even though we've grown familiar with it, even though we've accepted that pain is a part of life, there's still something in us that resists it. Something that *knows* pain wasn't meant to be part of our story.

Why?

Because we live in a culture where comfort and happiness are gods.

Now, if you'll allow me, let's dig a little deeper into that.

HOW IS IT SUPPOSED TO BE?

Part of the frustration of being human is that we—at least I—didn't ask to be born.

I wasn't just hanging out in heaven, looking at Jesus, and saying, "Put me in, Coach!"

No, like you, I'm here because my parents had sex, and nine months later, baby Dakota showed up, screaming and confused. I didn't arrive with a theological framework or a philosophical outlook on life. I didn't have a preloaded sense of good and evil, right and wrong. I was just born.

My mom was sixteen. My biological dad left shortly after I was born. Eventually, my mom married my stepdad, which meant I didn't just have two sets of grandparents—I had five.

You might be thinking, "This guy sucks at math." And you'd be right. But not about this.

My stepdad's parents were divorced—two sets there. My mom's parents were divorced—two sets there. And, surprisingly, my biological dad's parents stayed married—so one set there.

That was my norm.

For me, this was just how families worked. Divorce? It was normal. Remarriage? Normal. Five sets of grandparents? A little weird, but also ... more Christmas gifts.

It wasn't until later that I realized: this isn't how it was supposed to be.

Divorce isn't just a legal process; it's a tearing. Families rip apart. Hearts split open. And that pain trickles down—into the lives of children and grandchildren.

You've probably felt it. Maybe around the holidays, deciding whose house you're going to first—Grandma's or Grandpa's. In my family, arguing over Christmas dinner plans was a tradition.

As kids, we don't always realize we're growing up in the wreckage of something broken. We just adapt. We normalize pain because, well, what else do we do? And over time, that pain starts shaping our definition of what's good, true, and beautiful.

Since we don't get to choose when or where we're born, most of us default to the same goal in life: avoid pain. Maximize comfort. Chase happiness.

If suffering is inevitable, the least we can do is try to dodge as much of it as possible.

And this, I think, is why so many people wrestle with the idea of God.

In Romans, Paul writes, "In all things God works for the good of those who love him."[1]

But what does that actually mean? Because "things" are different for everyone.

For me, it's rejection.

For my wife, it's a dad who wasn't present.

For others, it's grief.

Depression.

Anxiety.

The list goes on.

And if we define the "good life" as comfort and happiness, then how does God work all things for good? Because rejection doesn't feel good. Grief doesn't feel good. Anxiety sure as hell doesn't feel good.

So what is the purpose of life? What is good? What is true? What is beautiful?

Pain will shape your answer to each of those questions.

But then Paul furthers his point by saying: "For those God foreknew he also predestined to be conformed to the image of His Son."[2]

Let's unpack that.

1. "For those God foreknew"—This is talking about humanity. God knew us before ... but before what? Before the fall. Before sin cracked the world open.

2. "He also predestined to be conformed to the image of his Son"—The Greek word for "predestined" (*proorizō*) literally means "to design beforehand." Like blueprints before a house is built.

    And then there's "conformed" (*summorphos*)—not just imitation, but deep, intrinsic union. So before time itself, God's design for humanity was to share in the nature of Jesus.

3. "That he might be the firstborn among many brothers and sisters"—The Greek word for firstborn (*prōtotokos*) is where we get "prototype." Think of the very first iPhone. When

Apple decided the prototype was good, they made every iPhone after it to match.

Jesus is the prototype.

And our purpose? To be formed into His image.

Which means the goal of life isn't to be comfortable or happy—though those things are good. The goal is to be shaped into the likeness of Jesus.

Jesus, the man of sorrows. The one who wept. Who grieved over cities. Who mourned for the brokenness of the world. Who felt pain in His bones and still pressed forward.

Jesus doesn't minimize our suffering. He shares in it.

But the world tells us something different.

"How can God be good if He allows kids to be abused?"

"How can God be good if there's war and genocide?"

"If God existed, why wouldn't he save my mom from cancer?"

Pain has become the loudest voice in our culture—the lens through which we view goodness, truth, and beauty. And in order to define those things on our own terms, we first have to remove God from the conversation.

I remember sitting across from Randy when he asked me, "You believe in God, don't you?"

"Yes."

"And you think He's good?"

I knew where this was headed. I exhaled. "I do. But He doesn't seem too good right now."

Randy looked up, surprised. "How can you say that? Aren't you a Christian?"

"I am," I said. "But that doesn't mean I understand how God operates."

"Then why believe in Him?" he fired back. "If you can't count on Him to protect you from all this?"

I smiled. "Randy ... if I had that answer, I probably wouldn't be sitting here with you. I'd be rich." (I joked. Risky move—Aussies are lighthearted, but still.)

He laughed. Wiped his nose. Then leaned in for a hug.

And as I held him, I whispered, "I can't tell you why God allowed this. But I can tell you that He feels your pain with you. You asked why I'm a Christian? Truth is ... I just got tired of carrying my pain alone."

Randy was an atheist. He didn't believe in God. But pain is tricky like that. On one hand, we want to blame someone for it. On the other, we just don't want to bear it alone.

And when pain goes unchecked, unnoticed, untreated it forms us into people we never wanted to be.

So what if the brokenness in the world isn't just evil—but misplaced, untreated pain?

What if Putin's thirst for power comes from a childhood wound? What if Derek Chauvin became a cop because he was bullied as a kid? What if the person who abused you ... was first abused themselves?

As John Mark Comer puts it, "Wickedness is tied to woundedness."[3]

I'm not minimizing your pain. The things that happened to you, the things that happen in this world—they are not okay. But what if pain isn't the enemy?

What if pain, though awful, could be the thing that heals the world?

What if pain is actually a gift?

A hard, holy, painful gift.

I guess what I'm asking is . . .

Is pain God's great mistake? Or His great mercy?

2
GOD'S GREAT GOOF

In the first half of the 20th century, Pepsi and Coca-Cola were engaged in a rivalry for the title of "America's Drink."

For many, Pepsi was seen as the second-class option. It was dubbed the "kitchen drink," a symbol of the working class. Coca-Cola, on the other hand, was the "living room drink," enjoyed by the elite—those who had the luxury to sit back, relax, and entertain guests.

To keep up with the Joneses, people would buy Pepsi for its lower price, but then pour it into Coca-Cola bottles when hosting, hoping to create an illusion of higher status. It's funny, isn't it? People stay the same through the ages.

Then came the 1950s, during the rock 'n' roll revolution. Pepsi made a bold move to capture the younger generation with a new marketing strategy. One of their slogans was, "Cause Pepsi helps 'em come alive." The message was clear—Pepsi would energize you, unlike the stodgy, old Coca-Cola.

And it worked. Pepsi quickly became a sensation in the U.S. But their overseas campaign? Not so much.

In China, the slogan was translated a bit too literally, turning "Cause Pepsi helps 'em come alive" into the belief that Pepsi could *bring your ancestors back from the dead*.

Whoops.

The Chinese bought Pepsi in droves, hoping for some mystical reconnection with their ancestors, only to be disappointed when the drink didn't deliver on its promise. The result? Pepsi's popularity tanked.

I can only imagine what it was like for the marketing strategist trying to explain that one to the CEO.

It's moments like these that make us think about how we respond to God in our pain.

Philip Yancey asks a tough question: "Is pain God's great goof?"[4]

Is pain God's "whoops" moment?

Why, we wonder, would a loving God create a world where pain exists?

This is where our theology and our lived experience collide. In our culture, the gods of comfort and happiness reign supreme. They shape how we see God far more than we realize.

In the West, we suffer from a kind of *John 10:10 theology*.

JOHN 10:10 THEOLOGY

Jesus says in John 10:10 that He came to give us "life and have it abundantly" and that's true.[5] He offers us a life full of abundance. But we often misinterpret this abundance through the lens of our Western, consumer-driven worldview.

"Abundance" sounds distinctly American. In the US, we're never satisfied with "large." No—everything must be *extra-large!*

And, of course, no one can tell me how to live my life. I'm American. I'm free!

At its core, the American gospel assumes that if we experience pain, hardship, or trial, it can't be from God. Instead, we view pain as something to avoid, something that's more about spiritual warfare than spiritual formation.

Under this framework, we struggle to reconcile pain with a loving God. And so, we have a gospel that promises wealth, health, and comfort—but it doesn't prepare us for the brokenness of life.

This is how the *prosperity gospel* was born.

When we think of the prosperity gospel, we often picture preachers promising financial blessing in exchange for a generous donation.

"Give $100, and God will bless you with more money." That's a well-known version, sure. But there's another, more subtle version of the prosperity gospel that has deeply influenced us all.

John Mark Comer describes the prosperity gospel as the *Health and Wealth Gospel*—or the *Word of Faith Gospel*.[6] It teaches that financial blessing and physical health are always God's will, and that pain, poverty, and sickness are signs of a cursed life from which Jesus came to rescue us. The promise is clear: If you have enough faith, pain will be replaced with happiness, poverty with riches, and sickness with health.

You've probably heard people say, "You just need more faith" or "Speak life over yourself" or "God loves you, He's for you, you're His child, and your victory is coming."

And here's the thing: I'm not condemning these phrases. They are not inherently heretical. But they often reflect only a partial gospel. They focus on emotional health and relational flourishing—but they don't prepare us to navigate life's storms and deep pain.

The tricky part? There's some truth here.

Jesus does love you. He is for you. He wants to help you in the midst of your suffering. Faith in Him and the flourishing He offers are good and biblical.

But here's the problem: When it comes to handling pain, loss, loneliness, and despair, the prosperity gospel offers no real answers. It sets people up for disillusionment and fails to reflect the life and teachings of Jesus.

Jesus lived a life marked by *the Spirituality of Descent*. He left the glory of heaven to descend into our broken world. He embraced pain, suffering, and loss. He was a man of sorrow, acquainted with grief. Scripture teaches that Jesus was perfected through His pain—and it was through His suffering and death that He inaugurated His reign as King of the world.[7]

Let's compare **John 10:10 theology** with the **life of Jesus**:

	JOHN 10:10 THEOLOGY	LIFE OF JESUS
Goal of life:	Happiness & comfort	Accomplish salvation through pain
Deal with pain:	Avoid	Embrace
Formation:	Name it & claim it	Refined by pain
Warfare:	Positive thoughts	Sorrow & grief
Truth:	Based on happiness level	Trust in the Father's plan
Goodness:	Desire & circumstances align	Obedience despite pain
Beauty:	Lifestyle	Wounds

If we want to become more like Jesus, we can see how the prosperity gospel—or the John 10:10 theology—fails to teach us how to navigate pain.

I get it: There's something appealing about a theology that avoids pain. It gives us hope that maybe, just maybe, we can live a life free from suffering. For centuries, people have tried to curate, manipulate, and declare a pain-free existence. But the truth is … it doesn't exist.

ANALGESIC CYNICS

Now, let me introduce you to the other side of the aisle—*the Analgesic Cynics*.

This is where I often find myself.

Analgesic means "relieving pain," [8] and *cynicism* is the distrust that follows pain, loss, or disappointment. Analgesic cynics use cynicism as a protective shield against further hurt.

How do you become an analgesic cynic?

Maybe you prayed for your mom to be healed from cancer, but she passed away.

Or you asked for financial provision, and your house was foreclosed.

You prayed for your marriage, and your spouse left.

You felt God leading you in a certain direction, but it led to heartbreak.

Or maybe your spiritual mentor fell, and you realized that pastors are no different than anyone else.

And so, over time, disappointment turns into cynicism. We lose hope, and our experiences with pain and loss become the loudest voice in our lives.

Jamil Zaki, in his book *Hope for Cynics*, argues that people often mistake cynicism for wisdom. It's tempting, isn't it? To act as if we know how things will turn out before they even happen.[9]

Cynicism masquerades as discernment.

Ever had someone take the wind out of your sails?

I remember when I was saving to buy a car that I really wanted, a Lincoln Aviator if you were wondering. My friend was going to sell it to me for $12,000, which was a great deal. All spring and summer I worked, saved, and took up any odd end job I could think of to save and buy the car.

I remember getting my paycheck after working 120 hours in two weeks, and in my excitement, I ran and showed my parents and excitedly said, "Only four more checks like this, and I can get my car!"

And my parents looked at me and said, "Don't count your chickens before they hatch."

Wind out of my sails...

In their mind they were just protecting me from possible disappointment. Because you never know—what would happen if the restaurant burned down or my friend sold it to someone else or I broke a bone playing basketball? For my parents, nothing is a sure thing until it's finished.

It's this same mindset that makes us cynical when we see people praying for healing

or

fasting for spiritual breakthrough

or

giving generous amounts of money to someone in need because you know God is faithful to honor you back. (All my prosperity people just shouted AMEN!!)

Christians are called to be a hopeful people amongst a cynical culture.

God promised those who renew their hope will also renew their strength to live in a cynical world.[10] That if we focus on Him, He is faithful to fill us with abundance (AMEN PG people) with hope, joy, and peace.[11] Scripture warns us that life is going to be hard, there will be moments in life that attempt to pull you away from hope, but we are to hold fast to the hope that we have.[12]

Jamil Zaki writes, "Hope is not a matter of looking away; it's a matter of looking more closely and more clearly."[13]

The temptation is to avoid pain, to look away from grief, but Jesus shows us that growth happens when we embrace, endure, and accept the pain, loss, and grief.

Because for Jesus, pain is a gift.

THE GIFT NOBODY WANTS

One morning, my wife and I were enjoying a quiet cup of coffee together, and I asked her a simple question: "If you could only have one superpower, which would you pick—super strength or never feeling pain?"

She didn't hesitate. "Super strength, are you kidding me?"

I was taken aback by her answer. She's not someone who likes discomfort. In fact, she even associates being tickled with pain. So, I asked her why she chose super strength.

She looked at me, as if it were obvious, and said, "Don't you know the value of pain? Pain protects you from hurting or damaging yourself further."

I paused, then responded in my best bro tone, "Yeah, I knew that. I was just testing you."

But here's the truth: I had never really thought about pain that way. To me, pain was something to avoid at all costs. I've avoided difficult relationships, surgeries, extreme sports—even running from God in an attempt to sidestep pain.

Like you, I hate pain.

For me, it's the opposite of comfort, of happiness.

But Brenda sees it differently.

Philip Yancey once wrote, "Pain is the gift that nobody wants, but the gift everybody needs."[14]

Why?

Because pain does two essential things:

1. Pain is the gift that protects us from losing the things we enjoy.

    Think about the last time you took a bite of something fresh out of the fryer—maybe I'm speaking from experience here—and burned your tongue. That pain protected you from a far worse consequence: losing your ability to taste that delicious food.

    Or imagine touching a hot stove. Without the pain of the burn, you wouldn't just be at risk of injury—you wouldn't have the ability to enjoy the warmth of another person's touch, the cozy comfort of a soft blanket by the fire, or the joy of petting a puppy's ears. (I know, this may seem random, but I love all those things.)

2. According to William J. Cromie, a scientist at Harvard, pain and pleasure are processed in the same part of the brain. Without experiencing pain, we can't fully grasp the depth of joy.[15]

3. Pain is the gift for countercultural living.

   In a culture of go, pain forces us to stop.

   In a culture of distraction, pain forces us to examine and contemplate.

   In a culture of "authenticity," pain forces us to acknowledge what's wrong.

   In a culture of apathy, pain forces us to respond and take action.

   In a culture of self-deification, pain forces us to realize we can't heal ourselves.

   In a culture that elevates self-sufficiency, pain shows us our need for something greater than ourselves.

C.S. Lewis said, "We can ignore even pleasure. But pain insists upon being attended to. God whispers to us in our pleasures, speaks in our conscience, but shouts in our pains: it is His megaphone to rouse a deaf world."[16]

Yancey further observes: "We moderns, in our comfort-controlled environments, have a tendency to blame our unhappiness on pain, which we identify as the great enemy. If we could somehow excise pain from life, ah, then we would be happy."[17]

One more thing I want to point out:

Our culture knows pain is inevitable. We don't seek it, but we certainly strive to avoid it at all costs. Yet, even as we try to outrun it, pain is something we still have to manage in some way.

Here's another story about Brenda:

My wife, who's Dutch, had her first experience living abroad when she roomed with American girls. She was shocked by how "medicated" we are as a society.

We have pills to help us sleep,

pills to lose weight,

pills to control our emotions,

pills to make us happy,

even pills for our pills.

She often jokes, "Americans have medication for everything."

I didn't even realize how medicated we are—this just seemed normal to me.

If you're on medication, this isn't a critique of you. I believe in the importance of medicine when it's needed. I was thankful for pain meds after I had my wisdom teeth removed. But here's the thing: We've become a culture that runs from pain. We treat its symptoms but rarely address its source.

Think I'm wrong?

Let me give you an example:

One night, while watching a football game—about two hours long—I decided to count how many pharmaceutical commercials came on. Want to guess how many?

58!

And what were they all advertising? Something to take away your pain. Not to heal the source of your pain, just to numb it.

It's almost as if our society says: *Who cares if you're sick, as long as you don't feel the pain?*

Our culture capitalizes on this. If you look at the other ads during the game, you'll notice something strange:

Car commercials promise an adventurous lifestyle—*Just five easy payments of $300, and you too can own this truck and live a life of freedom.*

Credit card ads focus on freedom—*What's in your wallet? Don't wait for payday to get what you want.*

Jewelry commercials sell love—"Every Kiss begins with Kay."

Alcohol ads offer relief from hardship—*Forget your troubles, unwind with a cold beer.*

Tech commercials promise sacred moments—*Trade in your old phone for the latest model, capture memories like never before.*

Clothing ads sell status—*Wear these Nike shoes and run faster than Usain Bolt.*

What are they really selling?

Ways to numb pain.

James K. A. Smith, a theologian and philosopher, writes that, in the West, we attempt to numb our pain through consumerism. Consumerism, he argues, is the modern form of therapy: It temporarily numbs the pain, but to keep it working, you have to keep consuming.[18]

Without saying it outright, we've made it culturally acceptable to numb our pain by:

- Going into debt
- Taking medications
- Getting drunk
- Shopping excessively
- Overeating
- Sleeping around—so long as it's consensual

These are all ways of managing symptoms, not healing the root cause of pain.

So what's my point in all this?

Pain demands our attention if we're going to heal. When we simply medicate it away, we miss out on its generosity.

As William Faulkner once said, "It's hard believing, but disaster seems to be good for people."[19]

This mindset—that pain is something to avoid or simply mask—has contributed to the broken, wounded world we live in today.

PART TWO:
OUR WOUNDED WORLD

"We all live in a house on fire, no fire department to call; no way out, just the upstairs window to look out of while the fire burns the house down with us trapped, locked in it."

— *Tennessee Williams*

"Jerusalem, Jerusalem, you who kill the prophets and stone those sent to you, how often I have longed to gather your children together, as a hen gathers her chicks under her wings, and you were not willing. Look, your house is left to you desolate."

— *Matthew 23:37-38*

3
A BROKEN WORLD

During the course of writing this book I was living in the Netherlands, home of the stroopwaffle, clogs, windmills, and tulips.

Netherlands means "the lowlands" because there isn't a hill or mountain to see. Speed bumps are the highest elevation in the Netherlands. But one of the more beautiful things about living in such a flat country is that you can see so much of the beauty of the land and historic buildings.

Recently, my wife and I were driving to visit my brother-in-law's father. He lives in a small village called Hoogeloon. No, I didn't make that up. In order to get to his house, you need to drive through other small villages with names that look like a linguistic obstacle course. (Here are some more examples: Oirschot, Huygevoort, Heieind.)

While driving I noticed something interesting. We knew we were approaching a new village when in the distance you could see the spire of a church building. As you continued to get closer to the village you would be able to see all of the houses, businesses, and restaurants surrounding the local church. Town after town the layout was the same: everything was built around the church.

Now, I'm a city boy. I grew up in southern California, just 40 minutes from downtown LA. One thing that you notice in modern cities is that the tallest buildings in most cities are the financial and governmental district buildings. This is also the case in more modern cities in the Netherlands, like Rotterdam and Amsterdam. These buildings tower over every other building around, much like the churches do in small Dutch towns.

This difference in city layout represents a massive cultural shift.

If we were able to rewind 300 years, it would be nearly impossible to find someone who didn't believe in God. Meaning that most people believed that they were held under the authority of something greater than themselves. Therefore, at the very center of people's lives, homes, and towns was belief, honor, and respect to God.

This is why at the very center of each village in more rural parts of the Netherlands is a church. The organizing principle or the very thing that was at the center of each person's world was God, and the physical church building represented that.

As time moved on, belief in God started to decrease in prominence in the public arena. During the Renaissance period (1400-1600) the idea of humanism was born, which meant that human flourishing was the top priority over all things. Out of the Renaissance was born the Modern Age, where scientific research was prized above all.

From there, the Industrial Revolution took off, and as my friend Phil Manginelli says, "societal decline of religious importance and participation emerged. From 1800 to 1960, this 'age of mobilization' moved forward . . . simply said, God became less and less important."[20]

THE SHIFT IN OUR SKIES

The Industrial Revolution gave birth to the first "skyscrapers."

The term skyscraper is relatively clear, referring to a building so tall that it metaphorically scrapes the sky.

The symbolism is quite remarkable because with skyscrapers pushing to the heavens and humanism on the rise, this was the cultural shift from God being the organizing principle of society to financial and government buildings being the center, both of which represent freedom and rights.

Genesis 11 tells a similar story. The people of Babel wanted to make a city for themselves, and in this city would be a tower that "reached the heavens, so they could make a name for themselves."[21]

Their goal also increased freedom and sweeping rights.

But freedom from what?

Well, God.

For the people of Babel, freedom was about self-deification, they wanted to be their own gods. For those living in our modern society, many believe that religion is actually the reason for the issues in the world, not the solution to the issues.

This was the reasoning of some of the most influential philosophers who shaped our modern thinking.

For Voltaire, religion was limiting human reason by blind faith. He believed humans can be self-sufficient.

For Nietzsche, religion was hindering culture from evolving, so he believed God must be removed from society.

For Freud, religion was wishful thinking and intellectual inferiority.

For Hume, it was the problem of evil.

But even more interesting is that all viewed *pain* as a reason for God's non-existence.

Hume is famous for saying, "If God is all powerful, and wholly good, why evil? If God wills to prevent evil but cannot, then He is not all powerful. If He can prevent evil but does not, then He is not good. In either case He is not God."[22]

Before Hume, Voltaire made a similar statement in his works *Candide*[23]. Freud would make similar points in his case against God.[24] Nietzsche would elaborate how the senselessness of pain is proof of the senselessness of God's existence.[25]

Many of us ask the same questions, wondering if God is good, then how can he allow_____?

Pain and the lack of understanding of how it works in our lives is one of the reasons God has been pushed to the sides. The question then becomes: who takes His spot in society?

Each of the four philosophers mentioned above would offer slightly different answers, but we can summarize their answers. The replacements for God are reason, intellect, and the individual.

But how does removing God from society affect our lives?

Well, in several ways.

1. **Shifts from The Transcendent Frame to the Immanent Frame**

    The Transcendent Frame was a time where everyone believed in God, the era we explored earlier in this chapter. We no longer live in that world. We live in what Canadian Philosopher Charles Taylor calls the Immanent Frame.[26]

    Simply said, the Immanent Frame means "here and now, this is all that there is" as opposed to the Transcendent Frame which meant that you were part of something bigger than yourself. The Transcendent Frame implies there is a higher order and a grander narrative that you are a part of, ultimately God and eternity.

    All of the existential questions that we long to answer are unknowable, and therefore our attention shifts from, *I will give an account for my life* to *the only thing that matters is my life*.

    We are stuck in the here and now. The concerns in life are: who is following me on Instagram; where is my next vacation going to be; what is the latest trend on TikTok.

2. **We experience a loss of answers to existential questions.**

    Since there is no "higher power" and humans have now replaced the role of God in society, it's now humans who have to determine what is good, true, and beautiful. If there is no God, then there also isn't a "higher" meaning to the pain and struggles we face on earth.

    This is where the term "Critical Theory" is born from.

    Slavery isn't a result of sin, it's a result of white supremacy.

    Domestic violence isn't a result of sin, it's a result of toxic masculinity.

    Poverty isn't a result of sin, it's because of broken power structures.

    War isn't an issue of sin, it's because oppressors are dominating the oppressed.

The religious explanation for what is wrong with the world is now irrelevant, ultimately leading culture to mask the sins of brokenness by blaming people, institutions, governments, and religion as the problem.

3. **Humans lose their sense of meaning.**

   Humans have always found their sense of meaning by answering the question, "Who is God?" We have always found our identity based on the answer to that question.

   Now with religion being pushed to the margins all that is left is the "inner way." The inner way remains since there is nothing "up there" or "out there," so the only way to find meaning is *inward*. The individual now holds the key to meaning, freedom, and unity.

   German sociologist Helmut Schelsky spoke about the modern age as a time of "continuing reflection."[27] Instead of a transcendent authority telling us how to think and what to do, this "continuing reflection" has entered into the center of human experience. Dogmas are now hidden realities that humans have to discover in their inner consciousness as the sources of self-understanding.

   The modern mind, Schelsky says, is in a state of constant "self-reflection" trying to penetrate deeper and deeper into the core of its own individuality.

   The goal of life is material comfort and the immediate gratification of existing needs and desires.

You may or may not recognize the effects of this in your life, but I am sure you can recognize the effects of God's removal from society in our culture.

Youth suicide is at an all-time high.

Mental illness and burnout have gone viral.

Depression and anxiety have become normalized.

We have come to just accept these realities as part of life, and in our frustration and anger with the realities of life, we have come to blame God for His lack of engagement in our broken world. Leaving us to doubt His very existence.

But I think there are some important questions we need to answer in our heart about God and how He engages with our world.

Do you think God is ignorant to the fact that the world is broken?

Do you think He even cares that the world is broken?

I do, and I think there is something beautiful in the brokenness.

And I believe God views brokenness differently than we do.

BEAUTY IN BROKENNESS

There is a Japanese saying, "*Everything that has a shape breaks.*" In Japan even the earth shatters. There are roughly 1,500 earthquakes in Japan every year because of their geographical location. Japan is located on the Circum-Pacific belt which is responsible for 90% of the world's earthquakes. Because of their familiarity with cracks and breaking, the Japanese have attached meaning to them. For the Japanese, cracks and things that are broken are viewed as having character, stories to tell, and hope to be found.

We in the West have this idea that we need to cover our scars or our cracks. I mean, how many of us put in our Instagram bio:

Dakota Hauck
Husband & Father of 2
Habakkuk 3:2
I struggle with rejection that stems back to when my biological dad abandoned me.

None of us!

The Japanese however view cracks and brokenness as a beautiful component of your life's journey. Our cracks and brokenness, rather than being hidden or suppressed, are brought to light as a part of a life lived.

Life is delicate and precious, yet sometimes events occur that leave us cracked, broken, and wounded. The Japanese believe that by accepting and valuing these imperfections, we can find peace amidst the uncertainties and challenges of life.

This is what the Japanese art of kintsugi represents.

Recently, I went to a kintsugi workshop in Los Angeles. This class was an introduction class that only had 3 broken pieces, and they gave us artificial materials to use because the real materials are so expensive.

As my uncle and I were working on our kintsugi, I asked the instructor who barely spoke a word of English, "How long does it take to become a kintsugi master?" Through her translator she said, "No one ever becomes a master in kintsugi because we are all kintsugi."

What she meant was because we are all a work of art, none of us can truly say that we have mastered life—beautiful.

I followed up my question by asking, "How long does it take to become an instructor of kintsugi?" Her response blew me away. Traditionally, it takes about 5 years before someone can teach remedial classes.

I asked her how long she had been doing kintsugi and she said her entire life. She even lived on a urushi (the lacquer that is used as glue for the broken pieces) tree farm. She was someone who grew up with kintsugi, and she would never dream to call herself a master.

This humility had me so intrigued that I continued to bombard her with questions. "What do you think about before you start a new kintsugi project?" I asked. She responded in a way that moved me to tears, looking at the broken fragment in her hand she said, "I stare at the pieces until I begin to see myself in the broken pottery."

The job of the kintsugi craftsmen is to be patient and cautious with the broken fragments, not rush to *fix* the brokenness. The craftsmen contemplate every ridge of the broken ceramic piece for a long enough time that he or she begins to see themselves in the broken artifact, holding the broken piece in their hand tenderly and thinking of the possibilities and outcomes for this broken pottery. The process of mending the broken pieces is not something that is a quick fix, it's something that is done with kindness, patience, and tender care.

One of the misconceptions of kintsugi is that it aims to make the broken pieces "as good as new."

How many of you have heard that expression?

I remember one time my brother and I were playing with our WWE (back then it was WWF, so I just showed my age) action figures and the arm of my favorite wrestler broke off (Jeff Hardy if you were wondering).

I took Jeff Hardy to my dad crying, and he looked at the arm, performed a surgery on him, and relocated the arm back in the socket and said, "There you go, good as new."

The philosophy of kintsugi isn't to make something "good as new." It's not about popping something quickly back into place and trying to make all evidence of the injury disappear. It's about making something new, not new in the sense of preserving as much of the past but uniting the past with the future.

Creating a new newness.

Elizabeth Spelman says, "Repair is the creative destruction of brokenness."[28]

The beautiful thing that kintsugi teaches us is that we can repair. We can survive a fall. A physical, emotional, or spiritual setback will not and does not define our future. Breaking does not mean the end; it's an opportunity to mend and become new.

In a time of political unrest, mass information, and civil upheaval, it's easy to grow sorrowful and cynical. Kintsugi reminds us to take every opportunity to instill hope and beauty into the cracks of the world. If you are someone who has a passion for keeping things fracture-free in life, you might find life a quite stressful experience. As our Kintsugi Master says, "For whoever wants to save their life will lose it, but whoever loses their life for me will find it."[29]

Jesus is in the Art of Healing business.

He is the world's great Kintsugi Master.

He is the beautiful artist behind creation, the intentional heart that created the beauty we see in everyday life, and His heart breaks at what has happened to His masterpiece.

His whole mission was to restore and renew the broken fragments of people's lives.

WEEPING ARTIST

The *Mona Lisa* is widely regarded as the best known, the most visited, the most written about, the most sung about, the most parodied work of art in the world. The Italian artist Leonardo da Vinci painted the portrait of Lisa del Giocondo for her husband, Francesco del Giocondo. The term "Mona" is an old Italian way of saying "ma'am." An English translation of the painting's title would be "Ma'am Lisa" or "Madam Lisa."

Anyway, one of the world's most beloved pieces of art and history has been the target of attempted vandalism on four different occasions.

Now, I am far from an art connoisseur, but could you imagine the outrage of those who love art if something happened to the *Mona Lisa*? One of the most invaluable pieces painted by one of the most renowned artists completely vandalized and ruined forever

Even I, a novice, would be completely saddened by the destruction of this timeless piece.

And what about Leonardo da Vinci? If he were alive, and somehow able to see how his art would impact the lives of millions, how do you think his emotions would reel to witness someone destroy his sacred art?

Sure, he could probably paint something similar, but the replacement would never have the same place in his heart as the original.

This is what we see about Jesus in Matthew 23:37-38, where He is weeping over Jerusalem. Jesus was an artist whose most treasured work has been completely vandalized. One might say or argue that most of Jesus's ministry was Him repairing and restoring the broken pieces of His art—humans—through healing.

Jesus was not just a man or great teacher; He was God incarnate.

Jesus, through parables, teachings, healings, dinners, and long walks, was trying to get people to come to this revelation that He is God on their own, that He was the intentional heart behind creation.

That is why the main question Jesus asked of people was,

"Who do you say that I am?"

Because who He was had giant ramifications for the lives of people and the world.

If Jesus really was who He said He was, then that didn't just mean that He was Israel's long-awaited Messiah, but He was in fact the loving heart and divine artist behind all of the earth's beauty.

As Jesus journeyed with His disciples for three years, teaching them who He was and what it meant to be a follower, everything led up to a moment recorded in Matthew 23.

Matthew 23 was Jesus's last public speech before He ultimately was beaten, killed, and crucified.

The context of Matthew 23 starts in Matthew 21:23 where Jesus's authority is being questioned by the religious leaders of His day. The religious leaders of the Pharisees and Sadducees (who hated each other, by the way) joined arms to attempt to trap Jesus with a series of questions in their attempt to find a reason to legally kill Jesus.

I guess the saying is true, the enemy of my enemy is my friend.

Jesus in His sage-like mastery, answered every question that left the religious leaders speechless.

Now, it's Jesus's turn to ask the questions!

Matthew 23 begins with Jesus's challenge of the religious leaders and how they have failed to care for God's people like they were supposed to do. Echoes of Ezekiel 34 now vibrate through the ears of the religious leaders. Ezekiel 34 is God's judgment against the religious leaders of Ezekiel's day. He tells them how they have failed to care and nurture His people and instead have only looked after themselves and their own selfish gain.

God then makes a beautiful statement in Ezekiel 34:11-13, that He will ultimately be the new shepherd of Israel, and He will be the one who will selflessly take care of His people. Israel will be rescued from exile and be brought back to God's glorious mountain where they will be safe from danger, rest for their souls, and find food to nourish them. God will be their shepherd responding to their every need. But most importantly, God will "search for the lost and bring back the strays. I will bind up the injured and strengthen the weak."[30]

Jesus begins by acknowledging that the scribes and Pharisees carry a certain level of legitimate authority. They sit, metaphorically speaking, on "the seat of Moses."

Jesus doesn't tell the people to rebel against these leaders. Rather, He warns Israel not to imitate their hypocrisy. This is the beginning of a systematic take-down of their heart motives and spiritual blindness leading us to the "seven woes."

A "woe" is a term that the religious leaders of Jesus's day would have been extremely familiar with. Throughout the Old Testament, whenever God would express His heartbreak, accusation, and judgment on Israel, He would speak through the prophets, saying, "Woe to . . ."

We see this in the opening verses of Ezekiel 34 as well. "This is what the Sovereign LORD says: *Woe to* you shepherds of Israel who only take care of yourselves! Should not shepherds take care of the flock?"[31] If you were "Woe'd" by Jesus or a prophet, you might want to listen to what they have against you—it was a call to repentance and an expression of grief.

The "woes" of Jesus are a list of charges against the religious leaders.

First, they are hypocrites.

Second, they are "converting" people to Judaism, but since the Pharisees themselves are hypocrites, they are also making their converts hypocrites, making them "children of hell."[32]

Third, Jesus calls the Pharisees "blind guides," an allusion to shepherding. Blindness in scripture is often used as a metaphor to the rejection of God's message. Jesus's charge against the religious leaders was creating loopholes so "some vows" they made could be broken. Jesus says integrity matters.

Fourth, Jesus says, just because you "tithe" does not make you good with God! What about justice, mercy, and faithfulness? They only obeyed the laws that are convenient for them.

Fifth & Sixth, Jesus is saying that outward actions don't mean anything when you're dead and rotten inside. The religious leaders may be ceremonially "clean" on the outside but they are morally "unclean" on the inside—as a matter of fact, they are dead.

Seventh, Jesus is showing that the religious leaders may claim to care about the prophets of old, but they are just as guilty as those who murdered the prophets of old.

Ouch.

Jesus then turns and looks at Jerusalem, perhaps thinking to Himself the same words that Randy and I uttered, *This is not how it was supposed to be.*

He weeps.

"Jerusalem, Jerusalem."[33]

Whenever you see two expressions repeated, there is an emphasis implied. It is a Semitic style of writing. It denotes close intimate friendship or knowing.[34]

Beautiful.

So, what is Jesus saying?

Jesus is weeping because of what Jerusalem was supposed to be and represent. Jerusalem was supposed to be the place where the nations and the world gathered to worship God.[35]

It was supposed to be the sacred city that was a light to the world.

It was supposed to be the place where the people came face-to-face with the living God.

It was supposed to be a place where people could find rest and salvation!

Instead, it had become a dark and corruptible place where people were neglected, taken advantage of, and the corrupt place where God's final judgment would rest (Jesus's death).

It went from blessed to cursed, sacred to corrupt, and a place for community and celebration to empty and desolate.[36]

I can just see Jesus's lips quiver, uttering the words "Jerusalem, Jerusalem."

As Jesus and the disciples are walking away from the temple, the disciples, who just witnessed a first century "eight-mile diss track," start commenting on the beauty of Jerusalem and the temple. "Some of his disciples were remarking how the temple was adorned with beautiful stones and with gifts dedicated to God."[37]

Jesus, with death in His heart, is haunted by the future events of His life and Jerusalem's. Jesus looks at His disciples and tells them in just forty years Emperor Titus would destroy the temple and Jerusalem. The beauty which they see will be no more. The words of Jesus should chill us to the bone because they remind us that even after His death and resurrection, there will still be pain, loss, destruction, loneliness, death, and uncertainty in the world.

Jesus, the Creator of the Universe, acknowledges the cry in our hearts that the world is not what it's supposed to be. Something has gone very wrong, but Jesus gives us a promising answer to hold on to.

"I have told you these things, so that in me you may have peace. In this world you will have trouble. But take heart! I have overcome the world."[38]

What we see in Jesus's words isn't some blind or naïve faith that is ignorant to the pain of the world. His words are both an invitation to and an affirmation of the trouble that we see in our everyday world.

The question remains, are we going to be like Voltaire, Nietzsche, Hume, and Freud, who let pain dictate their story and how they see the world?

or

Are we going to believe Jesus's story of the world, and though we don't understand it, trust that His story is the one that leads to life?

4
CATASTROPHIC COINCIDENCE

"An idea is salvation by imagination."[39]

We live at the expense of our ideas. Our ideas are not just fairytale-ish utopias that live in our mind. What we believe about God, life, and ourselves dictates our entire way of living and has a tremendous impact on how we view the story called life.

Much of what we attempt to unpack, understand, and comprehend in our modern world are the effects of ideas from the people who came before us.

As I talked about in the previous chapter, Voltaire, Nietzsche, Hume, and Freud all believed that in order for humanity, or better yet, society to move forward, culture had to remove God from the center of its life.

The postmodern world is the first time in the history of human existence that humanity has attempted to eradicate God from the center of society. Even the most pagan kingdoms of the past still believed they were subjected to the "gods."

The question we must now face is, *what now*? What is the impact on society now that we have removed God from culture?

In his famous work, *The Gay Science,* Nietzsche writes, "God is Dead. God remains dead. And we have killed him."[40] But even Nietzsche was worried and even unsure as to what society would look like without the belief in God. He goes on to say, "We thus face a long, daunting task of dismantling our now foundationless values to rebuild them in healthier, life-affirming ways."[41]

Christian philosopher Nancey Pearcy echoes Nietzsche's uncertainty of how we proceed without God at the center of human existence.

She writes that our modern world is one giant experiment, "a new social construction, something we are making up as we go along."[42]

We now live in a world that has never been seen before.

Or, as theologian Carl Trueman calls it, a "strange new world."

Things that used to be a universal belief or things that people once held to be concrete and true are now deemed as weird, strange, or even the source of the problems in our world. Trueman writes, "Things once regarded as obvious and unassailable virtues have in recent years been subject to vigorous criticism and even in some cases come to be seen by many as more akin to vices."[43]

With God pushed from the center of society, who is now at the center?

Well, humanity.

Humanity now holds the highest office in the cosmos, and the tension that we see, feel, and know in our world is because humanity is in a war with one another. Not a war that is filled with bombs, guns, and drones (even though in some cases those are used), but we are in a war of ideas.

David Patrikarakos, a British author and war correspondent, argues that modern wars are no longer about conquering territories, but ideas.[44]

One look around our communities, local, national, and global alike, and we can see Patrikarakos is right. Most of the tensions we are observing and feeling are because we are in a war of ideas.

MAGA's vision of democracy versus the Left's vision of democracy.

Pro-life versus pro-choice.

Marriage as a covenant versus marriage as a social contract.

Blue lives matter versus black lives matter.

Israel's land was stolen, or Palestine's land was stolen.

Gender is binary versus gender is fluid.

You see the point.

Frank Lloyd Wright, an influential American architect, famously said, "An idea is salvation by imagination."

The word salvation in Hebrew is *yesha*, which means "freedom from what binds or restricts." In Greek, salvation is *soteria*, which means "to provide recovery or rescue."

So, Frank Lloyd Wright's statement means that an idea is a way to find freedom from what is binding or restricting you, and an idea can provide a way to freedom by imagining *what could be*.

A world where you're free from the oppressions of God, familial expectation, governmental overreach. But what we need to realize is that ideas carry weight. They wield power. There is a sobering reality about living in a world where ideas are the most valuable currency. As Dallas Willard once wrote, "We are truly at the mercy of our ideas."[45]

IMAGINE

1971 was a year of chaos and uncertainty. One didn't need to be a political analyst to see that the world was on the verge of a third world war, which would have been its third in 57 years. The West was also in the midst of massive cultural shifts, the ideas that had been conceived in the '60s were now giving birth in the '70s.

The sexual revolution was in full swing, antiwar protests were at an all-time high, drug culture expanded into college life, distrust in authority, including those in government, church, and family, started to rise, the US was facing an economic crash, wars broke out in India, Pakistan, Brazil, Cambodia, and Israel, and fear of communism continued to strike fear in America.

In March 1971, in a world unraveling with war, division, and uncertainty, John Lennon sat down to write what would become one of the most famous anthems of modern history; you might know the song: *Imagine*.

It was a vision—a dream of a world set free. In his eyes, the root causes of humanity's pain were clear: religious and nationalistic ideologies. The way forward? Strip it all away. No heaven. No hell. No borders. No possessions. Just people, here and now, living as one.

It struck a chord. Decades later, the song is still sung as an anthem of hope and an ideal utopia for humanity. A vision of peace, a better world—one where the things that divide us no longer exist.

And yet, that wasn't always Lennon's perspective.

Lennon grew up Anglican, was part of the church choir from the ages of eight to fourteen, and most likely had the most religious background of all the Beatles.[46] As he grew up and began writing music, Lennon became more agnostic than atheist. However, when he met his wife Yoko, he became an atheist and in his first album after separating from the Beatles he wrote a song called "God." It was a song that Lennon wrote as a "declaration of personal independence" from his past.[47] Today we would call that "deconstruction."

On this journey of self-discovery, Lennon had to rid himself from the past naivety he once believed. In the first line of the song he writes, "God is a concept by which we measure our pain."

In other words, the belief in God was more so a way to help in one's personal pain. The belief in God or something "out there" gave hope and was a means by which to escape from the world and the pain. For Lennon, faith was a private and subjective belief, holding no cosmic or universal truth.

His journey of self-actualization led him to the conclusion, where Lennon declares, "I only believe in me, Yoko, and me," asserting his rejection of outside influences in favor of self-reliance.

The emancipation of his past was a journey of personal awakening and authentic self-expression, and yet this journey still came up empty for Lennon. In 1977, Lennon became friends with evangelist Oral Roberts and became a "born-again Christian." After a year of trying out Christianity he lost interest in Jesus and went back into "curious spirituality."

In 1980, Lennon stated that there was no single truth. He interpreted Jesus's teachings as: "You are here. Be true to yourself. Try to love people. Love your neighbor. Help someone if they're down."[48] For Lennon, Christianity, or more importantly Jesus, was not someone who could explain pain and chaos that we see in the world. Jesus was more of a means one could use to be a good person. (If that is the religious preference or guide *you* chose of course.) But, in his mind, Jesus was not the answer the world needed.

Lennon believed Jesus's teachings on heaven, hell, idolatry, and pain are all metaphorical at best, and at worst, the very things that are causing pain and wounding in the lives of people and the world around us.

Imagine was an idea to bring salvation by imagination.

In Lennon's world, the way to escape pain or live a life where pain wouldn't be the dominant voice in our world, was to remove the one person who can turn pain into something beautiful.

Lennon's ability to summarize what so many people feel and hope for has given a voice to the imagination and ideas of what the world could be, ultimately birthing a new reality in our modern world.

THE ABSENCE OF A FOUNDATION

You don't need to have written a song like Lennon or a book like Nietzsche to realize that you have taken on a lens that has formed how you think and view God, creation, and humanity.

When God was at the center of society, humanity had a starting point of origin, meaning, value, and purpose. But now that God has been removed from culture, what is the meaning behind our origin story?

Is there value to humans? If so, why are humans valuable?

Do we have purpose? Or is life just about "eat, drink, and be merry for tomorrow we die?"[49]

And, how do we view the brokenness of the world?

Without the answers to these questions, we are left with nothing to build our life on. Creation and humanity are just some catastrophic coincidence.

Pastor Mark Sayers says, "In the absence of a story or foundation that gives hope or meaning, life has become a never-ending quest for pleasure and experience. Instead of being good, people want to feel good."[50] One of the leading ideologies when it comes to creation and human purpose is an ideology called secular humanism. This is a movement and belief system. Secular humanists even have their own website explaining who they are and what they believe.

> Secular humanism is comprehensive, touching every aspect of life including issues of values, meaning, and identity. Thus, it is broader than atheism, which concerns only the nonexistence of god or the supernatural. Important as that may be, there's a lot more to life . . . and secular humanism addresses it.

> Secular humanism is nonreligious, espousing no belief in a realm or beings imagined to transcend ordinary experience

> Secular humanism is a life stance, or what Council for Secular Humanism founder Paul Kurtz has termed a eupraxsophy: a body of principles suitable for orienting a complete human life. As a secular life stance, secular humanism incorporates the Enlightenment principle of individualism, which celebrates emancipating the individual from traditional controls by family, church, and state, increasingly empowering each of us to set the terms of his or her own life.[51]

Simply put, Secular Humanism holds to the following:

First, secular humanism is a life stance, something that one can build their whole life around. In other words, secular humanism declares that it can satisfy all the questions in your heart.

Second, the transcendent doesn't exist, which means nothing created the world. Therefore, beliefs such as Darwin's big bang theory or evolution are primary beliefs when it comes to creation. In other words, whatever science can determine as fact is what a secular humanist deems as true. Here is how SecularHumanism.org explains it:

> Secular humanism provides a cosmic outlook—a worldview in the broadest sense, grounding our lives in the context of our universe and relying on methods demonstrated by science. Secular humanists see themselves as undesigned, unintended beings who arose through evolution, possessing unique attributes of self-awareness and moral agency.[52]

That is, since there is no Creator behind creation, you're just an accident. There is no greater meaning to your life, story, or pain. Life is just one big game of chance.

Third, since there is nothing "above" or "below," all that is left is the individual. Now the individual can set the terms of his or her own life. Pursue whatever is in your heart, you are the creator of your destiny, life, and circumstance—you are the god of your life.

However, the previous point isn't fully true. What makes humans unique is that we have "self-awareness," we are free to pursue the things we deem as valuable and happy.

Fourth, you set the ethics of your own life. Family, church, or state do not hold the authority over you; therefore, you are able to create the laws, ethics, and the path for "eternal life" for your own life. Again, this is how SecularHumanism.org would describe it:

> Secular humanists hold that ethics is consequential, to be judged by results. This is in contrast to so-called command ethics, in which right and wrong are defined in advance and attributed to divine authority. "No god will save us," declared Humanist Manifesto II (1973), "*we must save ourselves.*" Secular humanists seek to develop and improve their ethical principles by examining the results they yield in the lives of real men and women.[53]

In plain English, they are saying don't worry, no one has the right to tell you what to do or how to live your life. You're free!

The gods of this story are freedom, comfort, happiness, and self. Or better said, you...

The oppressive structures of the past that were rooted in "blind faith" are now stories of history and no longer dictate your future. You are free to be whoever you want. Your value comes from your ability to make yourself whatever you want to be. You are the god of your own life.

We should be asking ourselves, does secular humanism answer all the questions that are in my heart? Does it answer:

Why am I on earth?

What is my purpose?

What is truth? Is there even such a thing as truth?

What about goodness? What is good?

Who do we blame for the world's issues? Ourselves? Our neighbors?

How do we experience that salvation that Frank Lloyd Wright was talking about?

How does secular humanism answer those deep questions that are in our heart?

The ones of identity, purpose, and pain?

Well, the answer to those questions is one big "*IDK.*"

You are responsible to become the best version of yourself. You are responsible for creating purpose in life, you must now determine what truth is, what goodness is, what beauty is, and the pain you experience has no grander meaning to it, at best pain is just unpleasantness that must be avoided at all costs, and at worst the pain you experience is someone with more power enforcing their truth on you.

Um, how scary is that? Who would want to live in a world like that?

Well, this is our world. We are living in it. Right now.

And we see the impact of secular humanism in our everyday life. Secular humanism has birthed:

1. The most anxious generation to ever live.

   You are responsible for creating, dictating, and fulfilling your own salvation and story. You must determine what is right from wrong, good from evil, and what the purpose of pain means. You are the creator of your own cosmos.

2. Rise of the self as god.

   Since God is no longer the authority, you are in charge of creating your own narrative. You are left to fill the gaps in which God formally gave answers to. David Wells puts it this way: "Theology becomes therapy . . . righteousness is replaced by a search for happiness, holiness by wholeness, truth by feeling, ethics by feeling good about oneself. The world shrinks to the range of personal circumstances."[54]

   There are 7.9 billion gods roaming the earth.

3. The genocide of ideas.

   What happens when my "right" is my neighbor's "wrong?" Whose right stands? If Secular Humanism's main purpose is to liberate you from those holding you back from expressing yourself, what do we do when your expression of self is someone's greatest sin? It leaves people at war with one another and ultimately isolates themselves from one another.

   Hello, cancel culture.

4. Loss of purpose and identity.

   No matter how much we attempt to answer those existential questions, we too become like John Lennon, just hopping around from ideology to ideology, hoping that one of them will quench the thirst of the question that your soul longs the most to answer: *"What on earth am I here for?"*

   American poet Jason Kirkey beautifully affirms, "Our identity is intimately tied to the stories we tell about ourselves and the world, both consciously and unconsciously."[55] With no fixed identity, we are wanderers.

Is it any wonder our culture is obsessed with identity? What pronouns to go by? What your sexual preference is? With God moved from the picture, we are lost trying to cling to anything that will give us a sense of hope, meaning, and purpose.

Okay, I know that was a lot to take in.

Take a deep breath.

Let me show you an example from my life how the secular narrative forms our lives.

I grew up in a Christian home. My parents did their best to talk about Jesus and bring us to church every Sunday. We prayed before every meal. We even had our own law that if you took a bite of your dinner before praying, then you'd have to be the one to pray. (This practice taught us self-control, patience, and praying as a punishment, but I understood their intention.)

We were taught the morals of "what Christians do and what they don't do." We did our best to listen to what my parents deemed to be good, bad, right, and wrong. But Jesus wasn't in my heart. Sure, we got baptized as a family and said the "Romans 10 sinner's prayer." But I had zero desire to follow Jesus. Indeed, he was the roadblock in the way of my happiness.

From a young age I always knew what I wanted to do when I grew up. I wanted to be a police officer. The three shows that I binge-watched back in the day were *CHiPs*, *COPS*, and *America's Most Wanted*. (My parents didn't let me watch those shows, but my grandparents let me get my fix in.)

Becoming a police officer was a dream that haunted me since I could remember. I don't know why; I just remember thinking how cool they were—real-life superheroes.

Growing up I did my best to stay out of trouble. Not because I wanted to obey my parents or Jesus, but because I wanted to be a cop.

When I was 21 years old, I got hired by LAPD. I was the youngest one in my academy class. I remember showing up on my first day to the academy. It was a cool October morning, still dark out, with 120 recruits standing outside of the academy building and waiting for our drill instructors.

All of a sudden, a giant scream: "Get in line recruits!"

"WHAT ARE YOU DOING JUST STANDING AROUND?!"

The instructors were swarming us like bees, picking and choosing random recruits to do push-ups or some other form of rigorous calisthenics.

In the first hour, fifteen recruits quit. But I loved it! This was my dream! Twenty-one years in the making, and I had finally made it. With zeal in my heart, I would boldly shout "Yes, sir!" or "Yes, ma'am!" to any challenge they presented.

Have you ever felt like you were doing the very thing you were put on earth to do?

CATASTROPHIC COINCIDENCE

That was me! Ironically, when I was in the academy, I started to go back to church. Somehow my sense of purpose was tied to my desire to know God.

But just like all of us, I had my issues. I was very arrogant, insecure, not teachable, and most importantly, I lacked integrity. Not very good qualities for a cop.

Needless to say, I drove my academy instructors crazy.

Two weeks after I was sworn in as a police officer, I was forced to resign for a lack of integrity. A 21-year dream lost in seven months.

I remember walking out of my drill instructor's office to my car thinking, "I will rise from this." Like a first-round draft pick who tore his ACL, I would be back!

I applied to various police agencies, 27 to be exact, and all of them turned me down because of how recently I got fired from LAPD. What I didn't realize at the time was that after each rejection I was slowly rejecting my belief in God.

In other words, when I lost my sense of purpose, I lost God.

Over the years I have questioned and thought about how closely intertwined our sense of purpose is to our belief in God.

In our culture, the societal belief in God is becoming less and less every year. Could this also be tied to the rises in depression, anxiety, and suicides that our culture is facing?

Secular humanism's belief that creation and humanity are just a catastrophic coincidence leaves us without a sense of meaning and purpose. Without meaning and purpose, everything is vain, left to chance, or frankly, doesn't matter.

That means there is no greater meaning to your pain, that you are just a victim in a twisted game called life. In other words, every day you are held hostage at the expense of the next coincidence.

I remember one day I was praying for a young man whose dad shot and killed his mom, leaving him to take care of his two younger sisters all alone. He was 17 years old. As I was listening to him describe how he felt like his life was over, and how he felt overwhelmed with the pain from the death of his mom and burdened with the insurmountable pressure of taking care of his two younger sisters, he looked at me with grief in his eyes and said, "I guess life just dealt me a bad hand."

This is what secular humanism does, it disguises itself as freedom, but it enslaves us to coincidence.

There is no greater meaning to your suffering, pain, or hardship.

There is no greater meaning to life.

There is no greater meaning to the world.

This is your story, or at least the story that the world is telling you to live by . . .

But is there a *different* story?

Is there another story that doesn't give cheap answers for the pain and suffering we see and face on earth?

What if there is a story that says, "You are valuable regardless of what you do or what you've done?"

What if there is a story that holds the space and tension of recognizing the wounds of the world while also holding to the face the world is beautiful? And behind the scars of the world there is a loving heart?

Is it possible to find our lives in the hands of a Sacred Author who holds true your feelings of doubt, insecurity, and pain, that takes the responsibility of dictating your story so that you don't have to? So that you can live a truly free and hopeful life, with a better ending?

5

BEAUTIFUL DISASTER

I have never been one who has a deep love for kids. You know those people who just loooove kids, the kind of people who don't mind screaming children, the smells, the mess, or playing with kids' toys?

Whenever friends of mine would have kids, they would send me photos of their newborns and in their awe and excitement, they would ask me the dreaded three words: *"Aren't they cute?"*

I was always taught not to lie, but I was also always taught to be nice. That three-word question has made me a liar and a jerk more times than I'd like to admit. I mean, I never understood it. Newborns look half-alien and half-blob. "Cute" isn't exactly where I go with that combo.

You guys are probably thinking so low of me right now...

For the longest time I wasn't sure if I wanted my own alien-blob. Tied up in my uncertainty was the fact that my biological dad left me when I was a child, and I knew what his abandonment did to me. Luckily, at the age of two my mom married an awesome man. Brock is technically my stepdad, but because of the way he cared for me and my family, I consider him to really be my dad. He took care of me, taught me, fed me, disciplined me, and taught me what it is to be a man. Nevertheless, even with his best efforts to be an amazing dad (Which he is! The best!), there were still things he did that really deepened the fractures of my heart.

So when I considered being a dad myself, my fear was that I just didn't want to mess up any more humans.

The other reason I didn't want to be a parent was that I was too selfish. I wanted to live my life on my own terms, and even with all I still had to learn, I at least had the awareness that being a father would mean I couldn't live my life on my own terms anymore.

What tied both of those things together—selfishness and awareness—was fear. The invisible foundation that lay behind all of my hesitancies was the fear of failing and the awareness of what my chaos brought to other people.

But when I met my wife, the voices of fear and hesitancy started to slowly fade away.

It was mostly because of my trust in her being able to "hold down the fort" rather than a boost in my ability. Soon there was no more time for me to indulge in my wariness of becoming a parent. After two years of marriage, we were pregnant with our first, a daughter. All nine months I waited in anticipation, anxiously praying, doing the best I could to "perfect" myself before Kennedi's arrival. I spent hours and hours praying, fasting, and attempting to bribe God to give me some supernatural power to be a "good dad."

On a summer day in June, my beautiful daughter Kennedi was born.

The best day of my life.

Right when she was born my heart melted away, I looked at her, and I was flooded with an immensity of love and tenderness, all at the same time realizing that I was standing on holy ground.

As I examined Kennedi, who was laying on Brenda's chest, I uttered to myself, *Beautiful*.

I knew at that moment that there was nothing she could ever do to get me to not love her. I was already so proud of her, and she didn't do anything. It was as if God allowed me to feel what He felt towards Jesus at His baptism.

"This is my Son, whom I love; with him I am well pleased."[56]

Before Jesus did anything in ministry—before the healings, teachings, and becoming an "influencer,"— the Father declared how proud He was of Jesus. And I felt the same of Kennedi.

Brenda and I locked eyes with one another, and we agreed. Kennedi was perfect.

Obviously deep down we knew she wasn't.

We knew there would be moments where the romanticism of that moment would fade. I knew there would be moments where Kennedi would disobey us, lie to us (funny how you never have to teach kids how to lie . . .), test us, yell at us, respond out of hurt to us. But I knew there was an unwavering commitment that I would have to her. No matter what and no matter where, I was going to be there for my daughter.

How did this change happen? Where was the guy who thought newborns were just about as cute as aliens? Had I become more mature than I gave myself credit for?

I don't think so. I believe that being a parent reveals something about the transcendent that can't be articulated with words but only by creating.

Brenda and I together created Kennedi.

Out of our love, something that bore our image came alive.

Kennedi would possess half of me and half of Brenda. She would gain both the best of mine and Brenda's qualities and unfortunately our worst as well. There would be moments when Kennedi would act like a disaster, but our love would be the mode which prepared us to handle those moments of unpleasantness.

This is the story of Genesis.

IT WAS GOOD

Genesis is probably one of the most misunderstood and misinterpreted books in all of the Bible. The first question that often comes to mind when we think of Genesis is: "*Did God really create the world and universe in seven days?*" or "*Why are there two different creation accounts in Genesis 1-2?*"

Those are valid questions, but we're already missing the good stuff.

We often come with our own preconceived notions about the book that we have heard from our pastors, theologians, and favorite podcasts. The problem is that in doing so, we have lost the profound beauty of the book of Genesis. For the people of the Ancient Near

East, the book of Genesis would have been considered controversial, scandalous, and completely unheard of.

The book of Genesis is less concerned with *how* things happened and instead is focused on *why* things happened. *How* questions are about the process, method, and manner in which something occurs. Whereas *why* questions are about the reasons and motivations behind the occurrence.

Genesis explains *why* humanity and creation have purpose, meaning, and value; but it also explains *how* the world got to its current state. If we read Genesis through the wrong lens, we will miss out on the reason God gave us this book in the first place.

Let's take a look at what I mean. Oftentimes in our modern world we view the first two chapters as a literal description of what happened at creation. We then take what we know to be true of scientific discovery and use those findings as a means to debunk the first two chapters of Genesis.

For example, dinosaurs.

Where are those in the Genesis account? Does their absence mean we kick the entire story to the curb and label it as irrelevant myth?

No, I don't think so.

But what if the opening chapters of Genesis were a story that God gave to answer the deepest longings in your heart?

For some, dinosaurs might be the longing in their heart.

Nonetheless, when we compare the Genesis account of creation to other creation accounts, we can see how the other creation accounts of the Ancient Near East have a similar worldview as those who believe the world is just a "catastrophic coincidence."

I will share brief creation accounts of the Greeks, Babylonians, and Egyptians to compare.

The Greek creation narrative believes that the world started with chaos (something was already there) and from that chaos came the female Gaia (the earth) and male Uranus (the sky). Uranus and Gaia waged war against one another when Uranus imprisoned Gaia's children. Gaia sought revenge by telling her son Cronus to castrate Uranus.

When Uranus approached his wife to have sex, Cronus came out of nowhere and castrated Uranus and threw his testicles into the sea.[57]

Out of that came humanity.

The Enuma Elish (Babylonian narrative) describes creation as a victory of Marduk over the goddess Tiamat, with the help from the sky gods Anshar and Nudimmund. From the fighting and the bloodshed, humans were created. In this myth, the natural state of humanity was one of chaos and conflict that needed to be subdued by the royal family.

The Egyptian narrative asserts that multiple gods were responsible for creation. The world came about through spitting, fighting, and masturbation. The main god, Ra, was conceived from the chaotic world. From Ra came the gods Shu (air) and Tefnut (moisture), who had multiple wives Geb (earth) and Nut (sky). Geb and Nut had the children goddess Osiris, Isis, Set, and Nephthys.

In this story, Osiris was murdered by Set, which caused an all-out war between the gods for power and control.

One thing that is important to notice about all three of these narratives is that the gods were created by some external force. Also, there is a consensus that the world is a chaotic and dangerous place and that all the world's problems stem from grasps of power and control. This ancient posture mirrors secular humanism. Finally, all three of these creation narratives contain statements with explicit tones of violent sexuality.

Comparatively, in the Biblical account we see no conflict in creation, no murder, and no sexual assault.

There is peace, order, and most importantly, God isn't created by some outer force. God is already there, and He creates the world as an extension of His beauty. In the Genesis story, we can see God's heart.

Genesis 1 shows us what matters to God. Genesis 1:2 says, "Now the earth was formless and empty, darkness was over the surface of the deep, and the Spirit of God was hovering over the waters."

In Hebrew, *"formless and void"* is *tohu wa-bohu*. In other parts of the Bible, those words are used to describe a state of chaos (Isaiah 24:10, Jeremiah 4:22). This gives us an insight to the Father's heart: formlessness and emptiness are not good things.

Yet our culture values it.

Think about the modern worldview of escapism; belief systems like New Age, yoga (religious kind), and Buddhism are all about emptying yourself and escaping the world and the problems we face. The goal is to become "nothing" or feel "nothing."

Comparingly, what we see in Genesis is that God bridges the gaps of formlessness and emptiness with the forming of creation and the complementarian pairs that fill the earth. Let's have a look. In our story, there are six days of creation that are divided into two groups of pairs.

God creates the Heavens to go with Earth.

Day with night.

Land with Sea.

But the beautiful part is that God doesn't just create these spaces, He creates the species to *fill* the void, leaving nothing empty.

He goes on to create:

Sun and moon to fill in the sky, both day and night.

Fish and birds to fill the waters and sky.

Animals and humanity to fill the land.

Christopher Watkins says, "In the first three days, God creates the form, and in the second three he brings the fullness. So, God does not simply create an indeterminate or empty form but gives that form a determinate content."[58]

Not only that, but God created with diversity and abundance, making the world not just beautiful but enjoyable.

IT WAS BEAUTIFUL

Last Thanksgiving Brenda and I went to visit my parents in Friday Harbor, Washington. Brenda loves to go for walks, and we ended up walking on a trail not too far from my parents' house. On this crisp clear morning we were walking, enjoying the beauty of the fall trees, and I could see the vapor of my breath with every exhale. (I love that!) Hand in hand, I got an urge to go and smell the pine trees. (I love that too!)

I pulled a branch off the pine tree, and the needles smelled like oranges! Blown away I ran to Brenda.

"Smell this!"

She looked at me, hesitant. I had obviously played too many jokes on her. I looked at her and said, "Trust me."

She looked at me, still wary, but she leaned in to smell the pines.

As soon as she did, her eyes opened wide and a smile crept onto her face. I asked her what she smelled, and she said, "Orange!"

We continued our walk, and I was holding the branch in my hand, smelling it on and off. Eventually the smell went away so I walked up to another tree and pulled off another branch. This time . . .

The pine smelled like . . . lemon!

The exact same scene played out.

When I got home, I shared our excitement with my parents, and they gave me this look like "Yeah? Those are called citrus pines . . ."

In my heart I was thinking *What kind of God would make two trees that look identical and yet, smell different? What is the purpose of that?*

I believe the answer to that question is that God is a loving God who provides in diverse and abundant ways so that His creation can enjoy creation. In Genesis 1, God says to Adam, "Behold . . . I have given you every plant yielding seed that is on the face of all the earth, and every tree with seed in its fruit. You shall have them for food."[59]

God could have just created apple trees. Instead, he created red apples, green apples, and golden apples.

He created orange trees,

Banana trees,

Lemon trees,

Strawberry bushes,

Grape vines,

And so on!

I can just see God calling Adam and Eve to observe what He made, standing in front of the proverbial curtain, eager to reveal His creation to them and saying, "Behold! Look what I made for you!"

I'm not sure what Eden looked like, but I can imagine the feeling Adam and Eve had when they first laid eyes on creation. They probably had this deep sense of awe and wonder; just think of the feeling you get when you first see the mountains of Yosemite or when you see the raw power of Niagara Falls or when you try some exotic fruit for the first time in Papua New Guinea. It leaves you feeling bewildered, curious, and excited!

That's the point, the world is filled with beauty and abundance!

Think about the minerals we have in the earth: diamonds, gold, silver, emeralds, onyx, pearls, and rubies. God didn't have to do that! Think about it; we take these minerals and use them as gifts to show our love and affection for one another. We take these stones and display them in our homes for other people to marvel at.

Or what about reproduction? God could have created any way to reproduce humanity. Instead, he created something intimate, fun, exciting, and pleasurable so we could procreate.

But that's not all . . .one of the most beautiful and controversial aspects of the creation story found in Genesis is that the world is deemed as *very good* and human beings are made in the image of God.[60]

In other Ancient Near Eastern origin narratives, the world is dangerous and human beings were not made in the image of the gods; humans were an accident.

How many of you have heard that you were an accident? I know that I was. My mom had me at sixteen years old.

It doesn't feel good to be called an accident.

Not only that, but in these ancient stories, humanity's main purpose in life was to serve the gods. Humanity needed to make the gods' lives as happy and fruitful as possible, and when humanity failed to do that, the gods would bring harm and pain on humanity.

Not here. Not in the Biblical account of how humanity began.

In Genesis, God gets on His hands and knees and forms humanity with His hands. Holding the face of humanity in His hands, He blows life into humans, and it is there that humans come alive. Humans are not just some cosmic coincidences but are beautifully designed.

But . . .

One of the biggest differences in the Biblical narrative is that God's blessing to humanity came *before* God's call on their lives.[61]

We often get this backwards.

We believe if we do a good job we will be blessed. This is the same worldview as those from the Ancient Near East and even some belief systems today, like Karma. And every major world religion. And legalistic Christianity.

Genesis is the story of blessing *before* achievement.

You are loved because of whose image you bear, not because of your doing or what you can bring to the table.

It's important to notice that creation doesn't declare itself "good." Adam and Eve aren't "speaking life" over themselves or "speaking things into existence." They don't have to plead their case to God on why they are good or worthy. Creation, and more importantly humanity, are declared good by God himself!

You are good!

The earth has value because God created it. Humans have value because they are made in His image. Just like a new dad looking at his daughter. When Kennedi was born, I felt a small glimpse of what the Father feels for us—she was good, accepted, valued, and I knew I would remain committed to her no matter what she did.

This is why we can't view Genesis as a book to argue facts; because Genesis wasn't written to argue facts, Genesis was written to show what God *values*—in other words, God does not merely create facts, he creates *values*.

Whereas secular humanism wants to argue facts and diminish values.

To a secular humanist, values are considered individual and privatized, while facts are universal.

And what Genesis shows is that value is based on the facts. The two can't be separated.

It's important to remember that when the book of Genesis was written, the Fall (Chapter 3) already occurred. God inspired the author of Genesis to tell the story of Genesis 1 and 2 because that is how the church is called to live.

We all struggle with finding our "calling." (If I had a dollar every time I said that I could probably buy X.)

Genesis answers that profound question. Genesis gives us our calling. Your calling is to live out Genesis 1 and 2 in a Genesis 3 world.

What is a Genesis 3 world?

It's the world you see around you.

A world of pain, chaos, and fractures, formlessness.

Last point, something to take note of is that Adam and Eve are not traditional Hebrew names. As a matter of fact, no one else in the Bible is named Adam or Eve. Just like most biblical names, their names describe something beyond themselves. Adam, in Hebrew means "*human*" and Eve's name means "*life*." Adam and Eve are the archetype, the meaning of their names tells the story of humanity and life.

The Hebrew language is poetic and picturesque in nature. The Hebrew alphabet was originally composed of pictographs, which were stylized pictures representing words or concepts. Each letter in the ancient Hebrew alphabet had a pictorial meaning that contributed to the overall understanding of words and phrases. The language plays a huge role in how the story of Genesis is told.

You may be asking, "So? What's the point?"

Remember the original question we asked in the opening chapter of this book?

It was, "What is wrong with this world?"

And everyone is attempting to answer the question, but no answer seems to hold both the beauty of creation and the disastrous state in which creation is in.

This is what the names Adam and Eve answer for us. In the very first book of the Bible, God gives us the answer to our question without removing the value from creation.

The story of Adam and Eve describes how humans and all of life got into its present state of evil, pain, and chaos.

As you may have noticed, Genesis 1 and 2 don't mention pain, chaos, and the fracturing of the world. That's intentional. That's because there wasn't any pain, chaos, or fracturing yet. Humanity lived in complete wholeness with one another, creation, and God.

But something has gone terribly wrong.

This is where we turn our attention to Genesis 3.

THE TRUTH

We all know the story of Genesis 3; there are two trees, a talking snake, and a poisonous fruit that changed the fate of the world.

But again, I think we have become too familiar with the story that we are missing the point. Remember earlier when I said Genesis 1–2 wasn't arguing *how* creation was made but *why* creation was made, and we discussed *"how"* questions are about the process and *"why"* questions are about the intent.

Well Genesis 3 gives us the *how*.

How did the world come into its current state of chaos, darkness, and evil? The pain, chaos, and fracturing of the world came in not purely by human rebellion but by Satanic temptation. (We aren't going to talk about the Devil in this chapter, we will soon, but not now. Right now, I want to show you what is affecting our world.)

The goal of Satan was to distort goodness, truth, and beauty in such a way that it would entice humanity to seek independence from God. The key word here is *distort*. Satan didn't rid the world of beauty, goodness, or truth—we still seek and value them—but now beauty, goodness, and truth are no longer defined by God, but by us. Satan understood if he could alter how we relate to God then he would alter how we "rule and subdue the earth."[62]

Let's take a look.

To recap, Adam and Eve are made in God's image and share a perfect relationship with God, each other, and creation. God blesses Adam and Eve and commissions them to rule over the world in the same manner in which God rules over them, which is to bless and then care for creation's needs, and God's only law is not to eat from this one tree. This seems simple enough.

One day as Adam and Eve are relaxing and enjoying a flat white while taking in the scenery, a talking snake walks over to them and says:

> "Did God actually say, 'You shall not eat of any tree in the garden'?" And the woman said to the serpent, "We may eat of the fruit of the trees in the garden, but God said, 'You shall not eat of the fruit of the tree that is in the midst of the garden, neither shall you touch it, lest you die.'" But the serpent said to the woman, "You will not surely die. For God knows that when you eat of it your eyes will be opened, and you will be like God, knowing good and evil." So when the woman saw that the tree was good for food, and that it was a delight to the eyes, and that the tree was to be desired to make one wise, she took of its fruit and ate, and she also gave some to her husband who was with her, and he ate. Then the eyes of both were opened, and they knew that they were naked. And they sewed fig leaves together and made themselves loincloths. (Genesis 3:1-7)

The Snake (who is later identified as the Devil) goes right after God, challenging Eve (life) with the same question that we ask every day: "Did God really say that?"

The premise of the question is: *Is God good? Is He restrictive?* The question is about goodness.

Eve, who feels the need to defend God says, "He's not restrictive. It's just that if we eat or touch this tree we will die."

The Snake's response to Eve is, "You won't die. God just doesn't want you to be like Him. But if you eat this, then you will really be like God." The premise of this statement is trust. Is God trustworthy? Or is He withholding something from you?

That simple question of "Did God really say?" led Eve into contemplation, questioning the goodness and trustworthiness of God. Where does the Serpent's question lead her?

"The woman saw that the tree was *good* for food, and that *it* was a *delight* to the eyes, and that the tree was to be desired to make one *wise*." (emphasis added)

She saw that the tree of good and evil was, in fact, *good*.

The tree was desired to make her wise, *truth*.

The tree was a delight to her eyes, *beautiful*.

Somehow the Serpent was able to ask one simple question that challenged the three core questions in every human's heart.

1. Who is God, if there is one at all?
2. Who are we in relation to God?
3. How do we live in light of the first two questions?

Another way to put it,

1. Why listen to God when you can be god?
2. You're already made in His image; might as well live independent from Him.
3. Now you can determine what is good, true, and beautiful for yourself.

This decision from Adam and Eve birthed disaster into the cosmos. The blessing that God gave, the authority to rule and to reign on the earth, had now been handed over to the Serpent.

Ignatius said that the "deadliest sin is ingratitude."[63]

Living as if life is something we're owed, rather than a gift we've been given. As if we're entitled to a certain kind of life, instead of living in gratitude for the life and abundance we already have.

The blessing to be made in God's image and to rule and to reign like God wasn't good enough. The first humans wanted independence and autonomy to make decisions for themselves.

What was once good, true, and beautiful has now become an evil, chaotic, and painful place. The world hasn't ceased to be beautiful; it just spews pain and chaos instead of goodness and truth.

This darkness that we feel and the pain that shadows our lives has a name: Sin.

Sin is everywhere and it infects everything in our human experience. The cry in your heart that is reminding you that the earth is not what it's supposed to be is right.

Sin is the issue.

6

UNDERSTANDING OUR PROBLEM

Growing up my favorite superhero was Superman.

There was nothing he couldn't do; he was strong, he was fast, he could fly, and you couldn't kill him unless you had a special kind of rock from another planet known as kryptonite.

One of the secret powers that I always wanted to have was the ability to fly. So as a kid when I would play Superman, I would grab my cape, and my plastic Superman chest plate and jump on top of the couch, climbing the pillows to carefully stand on the armrest of the couch, I would look down to the ground, and—in playful imagination—do my best attempt to fly!

As I bolstered up the courage to jump, I would leap as far as I could with some blind faith that I would be able to fly, and that my cape would carry me away. As I jumped with all my might, thinking *is this the moment I will fly?* I would look down and begin to realize the ground was getting closer and closer. And then, crash, I would hit the floor . . .

Unlike the real Superman, my enemies weren't Lex Luthor or General Zod, mine was gravity!

Gravity, the invisible force that influences our every step, every failed picture hanging, and every child's dream to fly. Gravity has a universal effect on everyone, it continuously pulls things down towards the center of the earth, it's invisible yet extremely powerful. And, unless you're an astrophysicist, I don't really think we give much thought to how much gravity affects our lives—it's something that we have just come to accept as a part of life.

Gravity doesn't seem like a complicated thought, there is a force at the center of the earth that draws things with mass towards it. But my oversimplification of gravity is an injustice to scientists around the world.

My point is:

Just because we know that gravity exists doesn't mean we have the full understanding of how it works; as a matter of fact, the nuances of gravity are quite debated amongst scientists today.

I believe we face a similar struggle with our understanding of sin.

Sin is a topic that we are familiar enough with that we feel like we have a grasp on it. Yet it is one of the more controversial topics in all of Christian doctrine. In my opinion, it is one of the most misunderstood doctrines in all of the Bible. Oftentimes sin is viewed as a list of things you can't do because they upset God.

But what are those things? And why do they grieve God?

Why would God care if I get drunk?

Or lie?

Cheat?

Steal?

Eat too much?

Sleep with my girlfriend or cheat on my wife?

Marry someone of the same sex?

Change my gender?

Or that I am a jealous person?

Is that all sin is? A list of things I can't do?

UNDERSTANDING SIN

Theologian Cornelius Plantinga defines sin as the "culpable vandalism of shalom."[64]

Doesn't help much does it?

In other words, sin is the opposite of how God created the world in Genesis 1 and 2.

As mentioned before, the story of Adam and Eve describes how humans and the world got to its present state. Adam's name represents humanity, and Eve's name represents life. Their story is the affirmation of our story, that something isn't right.

The first two chapters of Genesis describe a world without pain, chaos, and division. There was unity between humanity and God—creation and peace amongst one another.

Chapter 3 of Genesis describes how things went terribly wrong with humanity, the world, and our ability to relate to God.

- Before the fall, Adam and Eve lived in a good relationship with animals; after the fall, we see the first animal sacrifice.
- Before the fall, Adam and Eve never experienced shame; after the fall, they hid in shame.
- Before the fall, Adam and Eve were one, so much so that they even shared the same name (Adamah); after the fall, there was enmity between Adam and Eve.
- Before the fall, Adam and Eve's creativity and imagination were blessed; after the fall, they maintained their intellectual capacity, but didn't have the moral capacity to go along with it.
- Before the fall, Adam and Eve were close to God; after the fall, they were exiled from God's presence.

The beautiful world that God created has become infected with a contagious disease known as sin. After the fall of the first humans, God cursed two things. It wasn't the humans! (Even though it can feel that way at times.)

It was the *ground*[65] and the *serpent*[66].

Now, this is really important to grasp because Jesus's future claims of "being born again" can only truly make sense if we realize what the author of Genesis is saying.

To *Adam* he said, "Because you . . . ate fruit from the tree . . . Cursed is the *ground* because of you."[67]

The Hebrew word for "ground" is *Adamah*.

The Hebrew word for "Adam" is *Adam*. (Not too creative, huh?)

Adam was created from the dirt, which as you know comes from the ground. But what else came from the ground? The trees, the plants, and the fruit—all of which were supposed to bless humanity.

The earth, before the fall, was a place of blessing, abundance, and beauty. After the fall, the ground, which is a synonym for earth, springs forth the curse of sin instead of the inheritance of blessing. So, all of humanity (Adam) and all of life (Eve) are now birthed under this curse that is called sin.

The consequences are devastating.

Our ability to relate to God is tarnished. Life went from being eternal to temporal (which is why Paul calls the wages of sin "death.")

The death, tragedy, turmoil, and pain of the world is a result of sin that has been birthed into every aspect of the world. That desire in your heart to live forever is not by accident! God has placed eternity into the hearts of humanity.[68]

So, what is sin?

Sin is the process of *dehumanization*.

Poverty is sin!

Homelessness is sin!

Fatherlessness is sin!

Motherlessness is sin!

Cancer is sin!

Body deformity is sin!

Global warming is sin!

Death is sin!

Addiction is sin!

Mental health pandemic is sin!

Loneliness is sin!

War is sin!

Oppression is sin!

Exploiting others for self-gain is sin!

And the list goes on and on!

That doesn't mean that if you have cancer or struggle with mental health, you are a sinner; it just confirms to your heart that this is not how God created the world. You have been infected with the cancerous cell called sin.

Another way to think about it is: Sin is the opposite of how God created the world.

There wasn't poverty, cancer, oppression, homelessness, fatherlessness, loneliness, or the endemic of mental health in the original Genesis story. Just like there wasn't drunkenness, gluttony, lawlessness, sexual immorality, homosexuality, jealousy, lying, or cheating in the garden.

Cornelius Plantinga says, "The story of the fall tells us that sin corrupts. It puts asunder what God had joined together and joins together what God had put asunder. Like some devastating twister, corruption both explodes and implodes creation, pushing it back toward the 'formless void' from which it came."[69]

In other words, sin isn't about a list of behaviors one can't do, as we can see from the list above, some of the issues of sin are beyond your control.

Sin is about the dehumanization and the disordering of the good things God gave to humanity.

HOW SIN WORKS

Sin operates in a similar way to gravity.

- Like gravity, sin is a constant force in the earth.
- Like gravity, sin has a universal effect on earth and humanity; it doesn't discriminate.
- Like gravity, sin pulls us down and drags us downward spiritually, leaving us enslaved, broken, and fragmented.
- Like gravity, sin is an invisible, yet powerful force.
- Like gravity, you can't overcome sin by human willpower. Only the Holy Spirit can overcome sin.

So, to get this straight, sin is something you can't see; it's powerful, it's constant, and you can't overcome it by yourself . . .

Great . . .

So, what hope do we have?

Jesus!

Jesus didn't see Rome, Greece, Trump, Kamala, police, or government as the main oppressor in society, He saw sin as the true enslaver of the world. This is what led so many people to be confused about who Jesus was.

He was far less concerned about "Making Israel Great Again" or giving you the autonomy to "live your best life." Jesus's concern was about "Making You Holy Again."

For Jesus, sin was the thing to overcome.

Jesus describes sin as a force that lives within you, outside of you, and acts as both active and passive energy in the world.[70] The biblical authors often used the term "leaven" to describe the damaging effects of sin, because it spreads and influences the entire environment in which it is placed.[71]

The Bible describes sin working in four different ways on the earth.

1. Inheritance:

    After the fall, sin spread to every natural-born human. That means we are all born under the curse of sin. This is the reason why Jesus claimed, if you want to live a life where that curse no longer affects you then you need to be born in the spirit.[72] Our physical birth is still born under the curse of sin, but our spiritual birth is one that is birthed in the perfection of Jesus, which is why Jesus is described as our new inheritance.[73]

2. Corruption:

    Sin didn't just affect humanity, but it has corrupted the entire earth. "The earth was corrupt in God's sight, and the earth was filled with violence."[74] Injustice, terror, natural disasters, and oppression happen because sin has spread and grown into every crevice of the earth.

This is why Jesus is so focused on His people administering love, integrity, and justice on this earth.

3. Pervasiveness:

"The Lord saw how great the wickedness of the human race had become on the earth, and that every inclination of the thoughts of the human heart was only evil all the time."[75] Unless our hearts and minds become renewed, our natural inclination as humans is sin.

Paul makes the point for us to be renewed in our mind so that we can know God's will for our lives and the life of the world.[76]

4. Contagious:

You thought Covid was contagious? Sin is the deadly virus that affects humans, nations, and the natural world.

Sin is the invisible shadow that hovers over the earth divorcing God's intention from His creation.

The pain that you see in this world, even though oftentimes caused by people, is driven by the invisible force that is known as sin. Leaving us cracked, fragmented, and broken. Sin is the reason why so many of us have lost hope, become cynical, and have accepted the world on its terms instead of God's terms.

Recently, I was talking to someone who just lost a loved one to a drunk driver. In her anger and frustration, she ranted about how sick and tired she has become with humans, "We are just terrible! Why doesn't God just erase us and start all over?!"

This is a question I have heard more than once and will continue to hear in the future. Though Jesus weeps at the world and the things we do, He still views the redemptive potential differently than we do.

Where we toss out the broken, Jesus sees the broken as opportunities for renewal.

TOSSING OUT THE BROKEN

The West isn't a culture that values things that are broken.

We would hardly view something that is cracked or broken as "beautiful." I mean if we did, Botox wouldn't be a cultural trend. In our culture, we do all we can to hide, fix, and even lie to present ourselves as more *put together* than we really are.

I think this is why so many of us have a hard time relating to God because we believe that He shares our same disdain for things that are broken or imperfect. When a culture has the abundance to just toss out the broken, it removes the beauty, loyalty, and commitment from the things we possess. We can just get a new one.

Imagine if God viewed us that way?

"I'm just going to toss out Dakota and find someone who fits my needs better than him, he's too broken."

I'd be crushed.

Though there is an abundance of people, there is only one Dakota Hauck, and there is only one of you. Though broken we are, Jesus doesn't view us as beyond repair.

The philosophy of kintsugi is the same. The breaking and scarring is what is beautiful about the piece. Nothing is ever beyond repair. In kintsugi, the pain, wounding, and scarring are all indicators that you are alive.

A scar will not form on something that is dead.

American psychiatrist Elisabeth Kübler-Ross says, "The most beautiful people we have known are those who have known defeat, known suffering, known struggle, known loss, and have found their way out of the depths. These persons have an appreciation, a sensitivity, and an understanding of life that fills them with compassion, gentleness, and a deep loving concern. Beautiful people do not just happen."[77]

When something breaks a kintsugi artist doesn't view it as a tragedy—but an opportunity.

God loves this world! And all the people inside of it. It's His love for people that moved Him to enter into the human story. God isn't like us in the sense that He is going to toss us aside because we are broken. We are the ones who ushered in the pain, chaos, and wounding we see in the world, not God. Yet He doesn't do away with us!

He does away with sin!

Jesus saw the implications sin was having on His children, and instead of passively standing by, He enters into the human story and takes on sin head-to-head and, "For our sake he became sin who knew no sin, so that in him we might become the righteousness of God."[78]

Much of Jesus's life and teaching were attempting to get His disciples to see how He had come to give us a different perspective on life, pain, suffering, brokenness, and wounding. The Kingdom of God and the way that it ruled would be vastly different from the kingdoms of the world.

AN UNEXPECTED KINGDOM

Jesus came teaching and preaching the Kingdom of God. He even said out of all things to seek in the world, the Kingdom of God should be first.[79]

If that's the one thing we should seek, then maybe we should pay attention to how Jesus describes His Kingdom.

The Kingdom of God was the fundamental theme of all of His teachings, messages, and actions. Often times when we think of the Kingdom, we sometimes think of it as "heaven" or as something that is away, distant, or "out there." But that's not how Jesus described it. He said that the Kingdom of God was in the midst of the people He encountered.[80]

Something that was near and close.

So, what does this mean?

The most compelling thing about Jesus for the people in His context wasn't His teachings or His signs and wonders.

Blasphemous I know . . .

It was His *authority*.

Jesus was a great teacher, but Israel had also listened to other great teachers. Jesus performed amazing signs and wonders, but Israel had also seen miracles from other people before Jesus, they just accused His miracles to be demonic and not from God.[81] Israel even had other people claim to be the Messiah before Jesus.

But the authority which He possessed was bar none. They hadn't seen anything like His authority before; it was from an unknown world.

The word authority is quite fascinating because when you break the word down; it contains the word "author." Simply put, to have authority means that you have the ability to narrate the story around you.

Jesus's coming to earth was a rewriting of the story.

But what story?

The story of humanity and life: Renewing the effects of Adam and Eve, who were both made in the image of God and both initiated sin in the world. (That is why Jesus is called the Second Adam and the one who creates a new life.)

Jesus's ministry was about restoring the image of God, or in other words, healing people.

That is why Jesus drove demons out of people,

Healed the sick,

Helped the lame walk,

Healed the lepers,

Helped the blind see,

Fed the hungry,

Raised people from the dead.

The way Jesus got to people's hearts was by healing the person. In other words, the healings of Jesus almost always led to spiritual renewal in the heart of the person that He healed.

If sin is the process of *dehumanization*, then Jesus's ministry was about *rehumanization*.

This is why Jesus's favorite term to describe Himself was "Son of Man." In its simplest meaning, Jesus is identifying Himself with us in our human experience. Jesus came to earth to show us what it means to be fully alive—to be fully human. The way He did this was by realigning how His followers saw, interpreted, and viewed the world. That is why I want to focus on one particular healing over the rest: the healing of blindness.

For this, we will focus on the gospel of Mark. Blindness is often used as a metaphor for spiritual ignorance, unfaithfulness, or lack of understanding in the Gospels.

Mark 8:22-10:52 starts and ends with the healings of the blind. The term "on the way" is also a repeated expression, used five times in this section.[82] "On the way" has deep theological implications. The early followers of Jesus weren't called "Christians," they were called *people of the Way*.

This section of Scripture is about defining what it means to be a part of God's Kingdom.

Mark 8:22-10:52 describes Jesus predicting His death three times. After each prediction, a failure of a disciple is highlighted to contrast their inability to see Jesus for who He is.

The first failure: Peter claims Jesus to be the Messiah, and Jesus affirms him in front of his peers. What a moment if you're Peter. The long-awaited Messiah just affirmed you! But this was short-lived. After Peter's correct answer, Jesus responds that His mission as Messiah is to die.

Jesus looks at Peter and tells him he has in mind the things of this world, not of God—just what any disciple of Jesus wants to hear . . .

The second failure: Jesus just got done delivering a young boy from a demon possession. As they are walking away, Jesus starts teaching them—it is here He predicts His death a second time. This time His death is given more detail as He tells them that after three days He will resurrect.[83]

But the disciples failed to understand because they were talking about who the greatest of them was. This is important to grasp because what they were arguing over was position in their imagined kingdom.

In other words, who was going to be Jesus's vice president, secretary of state, and attorney general.

The last failure: Jesus and the disciples are on their way to Jerusalem, and in the plainest words He can find, Jesus tells His disciples what is about to happen to Him when they arrive in Jerusalem. He will be taken, beaten, tortured, and killed.

But He will rise again . . .

After Jesus is done talking, James and John approach Jesus and say, "We want you to do for us whatever we ask."

Jesus tenderly looks at them, "What do you want me to do for you?"

The brothers ask for positions of power during Jesus's inauguration as King.

Jesus, in His frustration, looks at His disciples and makes the point that followership is more important than leadership. Jesus continues to walk to Jerusalem, saddened by the disciple's failure to understand, probably thinking to Himself, *How do they still not get it?*

As He is walking, out of nowhere comes a scream from a blind man on the side of the road, "Jesus!!! Son of David, have mercy on me!!"

The text says many rebuked him.[84] I'm just guessing, but I bet his disciples saw that Jesus wasn't in the best mood . . . thinking to themselves, *Sorry dude, today's not a good day.*

But Bartimaeus (the blind man) shouted all the more!

Jesus called Bartimaeus and uses him to make His point to his disciples. With the disciples watching, Jesus asks Bartimaeus the same question He asks James and John, "What do you want me to do for you?" Bartimaeus was blind! As if Jesus didn't know, Bartimaeus would have needed a guide to bring him close. But, there was something more to Jesus's question. This wasn't just a physical invitation, but a spiritual one. Bartimaeus doesn't ask for a position of power, honor, or status. Instead, he responds, "Teacher . . . *I want to see.*"

Bartimaeus answers correctly, he gives the response that the disciples should have given. Those who were closest to Jesus in proximity failed to recognize Jesus for who He truly was and what His Kingdom offered.

The one who lacked and suffered was the one who answered Jesus correctly.

And the text says, "'Go,' said Jesus, 'your faith has healed you.' Immediately he received his sight and followed Jesus 'on the way.'"[85]

Bartimaeus became a disciple.

The Greek word for "faith" is *pistis*—oftentimes we think of it as some internal feeling or emotion towards God. But that's not quite what it means. *Pistis* is more so defined as "commitment, loyalty, or trust."

Bartimaeus trusted that Jesus was the only one who could meet his physical and spiritual needs. Whereas the disciples trusted Jesus physically, but not spiritually.

- They trusted that Jesus would defeat Rome.
- They trusted Jesus could raise the dead.
- They trusted in Jesus's power.
- They were spiritually blind to the reality of His Kingdom.

Jesus didn't come to make their lives easy, comfortable, or privileged. He came to give them the ability to overcome the dark age in which they lived, a time of darkness, pain, oppression, despair, and hopelessness. Jesus promised the disciples that they wouldn't be saved from the trouble of the world, but they would be a beacon of light and hope in the midst of a troubling world.

I often wonder about the Pharisees.

They were experts in the law, some of the smartest people you would find in all of Israel. It's not like they were apathetic; they were beyond zealous! Yet, they missed the Messiah. But they too, like the disciples, had a flawed perspective.

Jesus was often questioned by them because of whom He had fellowship with: sinners, tax collectors (enemies of the Jews), and prostitutes. The Pharisees' reasoning was if you hung around a sinner, you would be contaminated by sin. That's how sin works, and that's what the Law of Moses claimed. But Jesus said that His Kingdom operates differently.

> "It is not the healthy who need a doctor, but the sick. I have not come to call the righteous, but sinners."[86]

Jesus's declaration is that sin isn't contagious, His holiness is.

It was Jesus's holiness that would call those people out of a life of sin and into a new life.

The implication of Jesus's truth is important for us.

The Pharisees missed their Messiah out of their failure to recognize the brokenness in their life. Jesus's Kingdom can help you overcome the problem in our world and our lives by recognizing our need for His reign in our life. In other words, our recognition of our brokenness is the vessel that brings healing into our lives, and ultimately the world. Like Bartimaeus, we need to shout, "I want to see!"

The unexpected Kingdom that invaded the world is about the process of rehumanization. It's putting back together what was deformed in the fall. What was formed in creation has been deformed by sin and must be reformed in Christ. That includes the world, our lives, our pain, and our worldview.

But who is to blame for the pain and chaos in the world?

Sin is obviously the issue, but is there an evil mastermind behind sin?

Or is sin just a form of uncontrolled energy that causes havoc on earth?

We will talk about that next.

7

HOPE YOU GUESS MY NAME

What do *Star Wars*, *The Lord of the Rings*, *The Dark Knight*, and *Gladiator* have in common?

Well, other than being some of my favorite movies, they are stories of good versus evil, darkness versus light, and right versus wrong. The story lines of each of these movies focus on how evil has come in and distorted people's lives, causing pain, harm, and wounds to innocent people.

World order is on the line.

In each movie, a hero arises who must overcome tremendous obstacles and sacrifice his life for the sake of the greater good. But before the hero can save humanity, he is faced with an overwhelming obstacle, one filled with pain, setback, and often betrayal.

Frodo deals with the temptation of possessing the ring.

Maximus Decimus Meridius is betrayed by his own nation and sold into slavery.

Luke Skywalker struggles with his destiny to kill his own father.

And Batman struggles with sacrificing his moral principles for the greater good of Gotham.

Our world, our lives, and our stories are no different.

Except, for us, our battle isn't against Darth Vader, the Joker, Commodus, or Mordor. Our battle is against . . . ready?

The Devil and his demons.

Now, perhaps you're thinking, "*The Devil? Demons? Really? I'm a little too old for fairy tales.*" I get it. Modern sensibilities maintain that the Devil and his demons are passé, mythical, the stuff of superstition and legend. And yet, the truth of the matter is that Jesus Himself believed in the Devil's existence, and the belief in the existence of the Devil plays a huge role in our story.

Why do we have such a hard time in our modern culture believing in the Devil's existence and influence in our world? Even though we don't *believe in him* anymore per se, we still know that *this world isn't how it's supposed to be*, yet we pin the pain and destruction we see on the wrong things.

Jon Tyson puts it this way, "If your story doesn't have a Satan in it, you will turn inward and begin to hate yourself. Why? Because Satan waged war on God, and when God expelled him from heaven, Satan waged war on those closest to God . . . If your story doesn't have demons in it, you will then demonize the people around you."[87]

We see this in our culture today. How many of us feel like the world will be a better place if it wasn't for "them," them being democrats, republicans, Trump, Biden, capitalists, socialists, Marxists, military regimes, terrorists, big pharma, powermongers, etc. Scripture tells us that we are in a war.[88] Life is a battle for peace, beauty, goodness, and truth; the problem is we are waging war on people instead of the Devil.

Yet, there are others who are living as if we aren't in a war. We tend to live our lives in pursuit of peace and in avoidance of any forms of conflict. No matter how much we try to run, hostility, conflict, and chaos seem to be hiding behind every door

Former heavyweight champion Mike Tyson said, "The worst thing you can do is be in a fight and not realize it."[89]

You are in a fight.

You may not be fighting the Devil, but he is sure fighting with you.

Now I understand depending on your church background, it can seem at times that pastors or church leaders talk about the Devil in ways that seem borderline obsessive. I have been a part of the charismatic stream of Christianity most of my Christian life, and I know people who blame the stubbing of their toe on the Devil.

But just because people may take it too far doesn't mean that the Devil doesn't exist at all.

In our culture we struggle with what C.S. Lewis called "Chronological Snobbery."[90] This is the belief that we, in the modern age, are smarter than people who came before us and therefore, more modern ideas of good and evil are better or truer than beliefs of the past.

To build on what we discussed earlier, with culture's eradication of the transcendent we have also eradicated the belief of the Devil, making it nearly impossible to diagnose the problems we see in the world. If there is no Devil, then people are the problem, and if people are the problem, how do we eradicate evil from our world without eradicating people from the world?

Maybe Verbal Kint, from the movie *The Usual Suspects,* had it correct when he said, "The greatest trick the Devil ever pulled was convincing the world he didn't exist."[91]

If we want to understand the world around us, then we need to have a clear and holistic picture of who the Devil is. As John Mark Comer suggests: "Could it be our souls are at war with another world?"[92]

If so, then we ought to know our enemy. So, who is this guy? What does the Bible say about the Devil?

ALLOW ME TO INTRODUCE MYSELF

First things first: Jesus believed in the Devil. Not only did He believe in the Devil, Jesus was tempted by the Devil,[93] conversed with the Devil,[94] and wrestled with the Devil in prayer.[95] For Jesus, the Devil wasn't some Ancient Near Eastern mythical creature with a pitchfork, horns, and a tail. He was a real person. We ought to take Jesus's acknowledgment of the Devil's existence seriously.

However, just like anything humans are involved in, our view of the Devil has gone a little sideways. There are a lot of theories about his origins; some claim him to be the "angel of worship," others just view him as a created being who rebelled against God.

The Bible isn't extremely clear on the origins or the description of the Devil. Also, in scripture we find that oftentimes the Devil has more than one name. His most common name other than the Devil is Satan.

Satan in Hebrew is more of a *title* than a *name*. It literally means: *the adversary or the accuser*. In the Old Testament, the term "Satan" is only used twice, once in the story of Job, and the other to describe how King David was tempted into taking a country-wide census.

In the New Testament, the picture of Satan becomes a lot clearer.

The Greek word that Jesus uses to describe the Devil is "*diabolos*" which has the same meaning as "Satan" (to slander, accuse, adversary).

Again, the word is more a *title* than a proper *name*.

Biblical scholars disagree as to why a title is used instead of a name.

Not to nerd out too much, but I think we can glean some clarity from *Star Wars*. Darth Vader, literally "Dark Father," is *not a name* but is more so a *title*. His real name is Anakin Skywalker, but Darth Vader is a title that describes his role or identity in the story. As the *Star Wars* trilogy continues, we are introduced to more "Darths" (Darth Sidious, Maul, etc.).

The point is, I don't really think it matters if "Satan" is more of a title than a name because again, Jesus believed the Devil was real. For Jesus, the Devil wasn't a mythical creature that one can just defer blame to for the world's evil. He was the person behind the evil and wickedness that we see in the world.

Jesus and the rest of scripture make some interesting claims about the Devil and his role in the world:

1. Jesus gives an eyewitness testimony to the Devil's falling from heaven.[96]

    We're not entirely sure what this all means, but according to scholars and the long-standing tradition of the church, there was a time in history when the Devil had access to heaven. Then something went down—something big enough to get him kicked out. And Jesus witnessed the event.[97]

2. Jesus acknowledges his power and authority by calling him the "prince of this world."

   The Greek word for "prince" is "*archon*" which had political meaning in Jesus's time. It often described the highest-ranking Roman official in a city or region.[98] By Jesus calling the Devil "*archon*," he is acknowledging the Devil's authority and influence in the world.

3. Jesus calls him the "Father of lies" (meaning the origin of lies), the tempter, the evil one, accuser of the brethren, the dragon, and the prince of the world.[99]

4. In the book of Job, he serves on God's council. When the Devil questions God's policies, it in some way implies that those who served on God's council had some say in how God ruled over the world.

5. One pastor says, "His [the Devil's] original role seems to have been the spiritual formation of human beings through testing. Think of how a teacher tests children to bring them to maturity. But he began to drift from his charter and used his skill set to tempt human beings into spiritual deformation."[100]

   When we think about it, this explains why it's sometimes hard to distinguish temptation from testing in our lives. Scripture affirms that God doesn't tempt, He tests—but Satan tempts us and tests us.[101]

One more thing before we move on; we talked about who the Devil is, but we haven't talked about who he *isn't*.

He isn't divine, he's a created being. If we are honest, we often have this idea that it's Jesus vs. the Devil, but that is simply not true. In fact, that's borderline idolatry. A more equal pairing might be the Devil vs. Michael the Archangel, because like Michael, the Devil was created by God.

Again, we may not know everything that we desire to know about him, but we know enough to know he is created, he is a liar, and he wages war on everything that is beautiful, good, and true.

This leads us to ask a fundamental question: What is the Devil's role in the world and our story?

Since he isn't divine, how much impact can he really have on the world?

Let's look at what some of my favorite theologians have to say about him.

PLEASED TO MEET YOU

In 1968, The Rolling Stones released a song that stirred controversy: "Sympathy For The Devil." The Stones wrote this song from the perspective of Lucifer, a name often attributed to the Devil before he rebelled against God.[102] The intention behind the song was to acknowledge the evil and chaos in the world and to hold up a mirror to their audience's hearts in posing the question, "What role do you play in the evil that we see in the world?"

Are humans the problem?

or

Can we really just blame the Devil for everything?

The Stones paint this picture of who is really the force at work behind history's greatest tragedies—the rise and fall of empires, the bloodshed of revolutions, even the execution of Jesus on a Roman cross.

They make the point that Evil isn't random; it's orchestrated.

Not exclusively from some distant force "out there," but the problem lives in us. It moves through human hands, human choices. The lyric asks, *Who pulled the trigger? Who carried it out?* The answer? *You and me.* (my paraphrase)

And perhaps most unsettling is the idea that evil doesn't just operate through the obviously corrupt, but through those meant to bring hope and healing. The ones called to protect, serve, and lead can become instruments of harm instead. That's the deception—that even saints can become sinners, that justice can turn to injustice, that light can cast a shadow.

It's a haunting thought.

But it rings true. We know the problem with the world isn't just exclusively Satan, it would be easier if it was. But the problem is the root of sin that has embedded and implanted itself in our heart, giving Satan room to operate within us.

Who would have thought the Stones had such great theology!?

When interviewed about why they wrote this song, band member Keith Richards's response was quite remarkable: "You want to think the world is perfect . . . [but] you can't hide. You might as well accept the fact that evil is there and deal with it any way you can. 'Sympathy For The Devil' is a song that says, *Don't forget him. If you confront him, then he's out of a job.*"[103]

For them, the way you overcome the evil in the world is to acknowledge the invisible, transcendent realities that are behind the evil that humans do.

We can't allow the Rolling Stones to have a better theology of the world, God, and Satan than the church. Time to brush up on what Scripture has to say.

So, what does the Bible say about the role of Satan in the world?

1. He brings chaos into the world.[104]

    We live in chaotic times. It seems like the world and the people that we come across are always on edge. Between school shootings; political polarization; nations invading nations; hate crimes at soccer games; and plenty of other forms of devastation, pain, and division, people are going mad.

2. He deceives people.[105]

    Have you wondered why truth is so hard, complicated, and controversial in our day? One of the quickest ways to start an argument in our world is to claim that you have the answers to the truth. People will hate you. When we live in a world of deception, truth then becomes the enemy.

3. He brings confusion.[106]

    We now live in a world where what was unthought of 20 years ago is now normal. Who would have thought that defining "a woman" would be so controversial 20 years ago? David Wells says, "Worldliness is what any particular culture does to make sin seem normal and righteousness seem strange."[107]

4. He influences governments and worldly powers.[108]

   I hate to break it to you, but there is no perfect system. No matter how good, pure, equal, and intentional we try to be in creating structures, somewhere down the line, they fail. When we have broken people leading broken structures, these systems will always lead to broken lives for some.

5. He wages war on God's people.[109]

   The hardship that Christians face isn't by accident. The hostility that we face from culture isn't by accident. Jesus Himself said that the Devil has the authoritative voice in culture. He uses his authority to wage war on the church.

6. He is a murderer.[110]

   Jesus calls the Devil a murderer, and this gives us great insight into the character of the Devil. There is a difference between killing and murder. The Greek word for "murder" is "*Phoneuō*" and it implies the intentional, premeditated killing with malice, whereas the word for "kill" is "*Apokteinō*" which is a more general term used to describe accidental or justified killings that lack evil intent. Jesus describes the Devil as someone who is *intentionally* going around to end life and cause harm to people.

Simply put, the Devil's role in the world is to steal, kill, and destroy.[111] He roams around this earth looking for people, goodness, truth, and beauty to devour.[112] Oftentimes, when facing challenges and hardship, people will sometimes say, "Don't take it personally." What they mean by this is that hardships happen to everyone, and pain doesn't discriminate. Well, that is a lie because the attacks from the Devil are as personal as it gets because of whose image you are made in. There is an intentional and well-thought-out plan that is working against you.

When we have an understanding that the evil we see and face every day isn't an accident but is instead an intentional declaration of war against God and His people, we will truly be able to love those who cause us the most harm.

Our war isn't one fueled by hatred, resentment, or bitterness. The arms we bear are those of enemy-love, grace, and mercy.

I am not naïve to the fact that at times our war seems confusing, foggy, and misguided.

But, the confusion that we see and feel is the nature of the Devil's game. His goal is to bring confusion, to make truth seem like a lie, to make what is good deemed as evil, and what is beautiful portrayed as ugly. Or as the Stones would say, that's just the nature of his game.

THE DEVIL MADE ME DO IT

When I was kid, I was…quite cheeky.

I was the kind of kid who, when my parents would say, "Don't touch the outlet," I would lock eyes with them, and subtly move my finger towards the outlet without breaking eye contact.

Throughout my childhood, I would tend to not be the most obedient child, and when I was caught for breaking rules, I would cry and say, "The Devil made me do it!"

Yes, I was *that* kid.

My poor parents.

The temptation that we face when we have a theology of "the Devil is just there to blame everything on" is that we rid ourselves of personal responsibility in how we cause pain to others and the world. The Bible is clear: though there is demonic temptation that occurs, there is also free will in our decision-making. Avoiding responsibility and blaming the Devil for our mistakes is part of the reason why so many people have been hurt by people in the church.

I have had the privilege of talking to some of the more popular "deconstructionists" on social media. One of the reasons I reached out to them is because I wanted to know their story and what led them to deconstruct? What led them to adopt more secular narratives as truth all while claiming to still be a follower of Jesus?

One of the common reasons as to why they and the people they know have deconstructed is because of bad theology that has led to hurt and abuse in the lives of people. In one friend's exact words, they left the churches of their upbringing due to "inconsistent, hypocritical, and judgmental living from people in the church." I believe that our failure to be accountable for our sin and how our sin has affected other people is one of the principal and most grievous reasons people are leaving and expressing animosity against the church. We often hide our sin out of shame and worry about how others may perceive us.

But Jesus's death and resurrection dealt with the shame of sin. Satan would love for us to believe otherwise, and he's capitalizing on the power of shame, even in the spaces where true freedom should be our bread and butter. What the world is craving is transparency about our lack and weaknesses. We have no reason to be ashamed of our weaknesses and the moments in which we mess up. In fact, our vulnerability about our weaknesses is what helps us to overcome them.[113]

Just think about how much you appreciate when people are honest and transparent with you about mistakes they have made. There is something inviting about that. Sadly, Christians have been deemed as angry guards instead of joyful guides, policing dogma instead of proclaiming the great gift which is perfectly hidden and revealed at the heart of all creation from the beginning of time.[114] We are going to mess up at times; we are going to hurt people at times, but the way that we can bring healing into the world is by saying, "*I am sorry. I was wrong.*"

I don't care who you are—admitting fault without the list of excuses behind it is hard. Why? Because there is a legitimate reason why we do the things we do! And we want people to understand our motivations.

And yet every time we fail to take accountability for our role in the pain that we cause, we build strongholds in our life that keep us enslaved to the lies of the Devil.

Think of it this way: if being honest and transparent breaks barriers, then that must mean pride and unwillingness to ask for forgiveness builds barriers.

BUILDING STRONGHOLDS

In 2017, an online game called Fortnite went viral.

In Fortnite's first year, the game saw more than 200 million people register.

The most popular game mode in Fortnite is called "Battle Royale." This is where 100 people are launched into the world and you must gather weapons and resources to survive. Now, I must admit, I only played Fortnite once, so I am a true novice of the game and its strategies.

With that being said, one of the key aspects of the game is to build and create your own safety structures. This is important because it gives tactical advantages, protects you from others, and gives you space for you to heal and recover if you have been wounded.

The Bible calls these kinds of places "strongholds."

In the Old Testament, a stronghold was a physical fortress or fortified place. Often, strongholds were referred to as secure mountain locations, caves, or fortified cities where people could seek refuge from enemies. God is often used metaphorically as a stronghold; the Psalmist writes, "The Lord is the stronghold of my life . . ."[115]

As you can see in the Old Testament, a stronghold isn't something to be feared or avoided. It's a place of refuge—offering safety to the vulnerable and healing to the wounded.

However, in the New Testament, strongholds possess a different meaning.

The New Testament authors used strongholds as a metaphor for sin and bondage. They often described how sin masquerades itself as a way to bring healing, protection, and wholeness to your life, but often it leads to obstacles for spiritual formation and intimacy with God.[116]

Strongholds in the New Testament were often referred to as false beliefs, negative thought patterns, or sinful habits that people run to for comfort and healing when wounded, that end up hindering their formation.

In both Testaments, a stronghold is this place of refuge—somewhere to run when life feels like too much, when the weight of the world presses in. It's meant to be a safe space, a shelter, even a place of healing. But here's the thing—our modern-day strongholds are built by our disordered desires. Instead of turning to God for peace, I reach for a drink, a pill—something to take the edge off. Instead of looking to God to fill that ache of loneliness, I give myself away to whoever will have me, hoping they'll see me, love me, make me feel whole.

Again, strongholds are things that we run to for safety.

They are made to bring comfort into our lives, keep people out, and to find some sort of healing.

The more we run to our strongholds, the denser and more difficult they become to tear down.

Why does this matter?

Because the Devil loves to strike when we are alone, comfortable, or wounded. His goal is to get you isolated from your community. Jesus refers to the Devil as a lion who seeks people to destroy and kill.[117] Have you ever watched the Discovery Channel? When lions go after schools of zebras, they attempt to get one to separate itself from the rest. Whenever I'm watching, I always scream at the zebras, "Stay together, stay together, stay together!!!"

But they never listen to me!

The one in the back thinks they are Usain Bolt and decides to go a different route, and more often than not, they become the five-course meal on the menu that night.

This is the same with the Devil.

He attacks us, ultimately bringing hurt and wounding to us, yet letting us live, so that we take our hurt and pain and shower it on other people around us. As the saying goes, *hurt people hurt people.* All we are doing is continually fortifying the strongholds of our lives, laying down deeper foundations and reinforcing them with unshakable certainty.

Where does the cycle stop?

It stops when we humble ourselves and go to the person we hurt and say, "*I'm sorry, I was wrong.*" Acknowledgment of our sin brings healing not just to others but ourselves.

In our culture,

We have disguised being a jerk and hurtful as "authentic" expression.

We have disguised quitting on our commitments as a means of "self-actualization."

We have disguised abuse of our bodies as a declaration of "true freedom."

We have disguised our undirected anger and anxiety as "social justice."

And we have disguised enforcing dogmas and shaming sinners as a means of "defending God."

When we partner with the Devil in pride, what we are doing is building strongholds that only isolate ourselves further from God and others. When we isolate ourselves further and further, we become more out of tune with reality. This is where confusion, anger, pain, and feelings of being "misunderstood" come into play.

This is why, when you take an honest look at the world around us, it seems like everyone is buried in their own strongholds and doesn't have time to actually sit and reflect on what is wrong with our world.

Examples of potential strongholds are:

- Doom scrolling on social media after a long day
- Diving into work to avoid the realities of life
- Using boundaries as an excuse to not participate in community
- Uncontrollable eating habits
- Uncommitted nonmarital sex
- Relying on alcohol to take off the edge
- Diving into endless hours of video games
- Binge-watching Netflix
- The gym
- Smoking marijuana or using other drugs
- Pornography
- Lying to make yourself look better

The list goes on and on.

Now, not everything on this list is bad. Going to the gym every day is a good habit to have, but when it becomes *the* thing you bury yourself in when life gets hard, painful, or discouraging, then it is no longer a helpful guide for a healthy life. It becomes an idol. It becomes a stronghold.

It is the Devil's goal to eclipse your relationship with God.

Therefore, we need to learn how to resist the Devil and tear down our strongholds.

RESISTING THE DEVIL

In April of this past year, there was a solar eclipse in the United States.

I was sitting in my office at work, and I could see and hear everyone running down the halls rushing outside to see the solar eclipse. One of my friends came sprinting into my office wearing these funny glasses, and out of breath she shouted, "Let's go! The solar eclipse is happening now!"

She gave me a pair of the dorky glasses, and I looked up. Sure enough, there it was, the moon covering the sun. It was quite a weird thing to comprehend because you could still tell it was daytime outside, yet there was a presence of darkness that is hard to articulate.

It's like looking through a window that has a limo tint. You can tell it's light outside, yet there is a dark purple hue that covers the radiance of the sun.

This is how the Devil attempts to operate in our lives.

He wants to act like the moon does in an eclipse, separate us just enough from God that we know He is still there, yet distort the radiance of our relationship with Him.

In the gospel of Luke, Jesus makes this point to Peter.

> "Simon, Simon, Satan has asked to sift all of you as wheat. But I have prayed for you, Simon, that your faith may not fail. And when you have turned back, strengthen your brothers"[118]

There are a few things to take note of.

1. The Devil asks God if he can "sift" the disciples but more specifically, Peter. We see a similar request from the Devil in Job 1. Sifting was a metaphor. When you sift wheat, you shake the wheat up and down to separate the hardened shell of the wheat.

   The Devil's request was to shake the faith of the disciples, to break the commitment and loyalty of the disciples towards Jesus.

2. Jesus intercedes for Peter and the disciples.

   This is important to understand because what we tend to believe is that Jesus's prayer failed because shortly after this, the disciples bail on Jesus and Peter rejects Jesus three times. But that's not the case.

Jesus's prayer for Peter wasn't that he wouldn't sin; *it was that his faith wouldn't fail.* Remember, faith means "commitment or loyalty." Jesus's prayer was that even in moments of utter failure, Peter would remain committed to Him.

3. The word "fail" is "*ekleipo*" in Greek, which is where we get the English word "eclipse."

   Failure in faith is about allowing things to get between you and God. When we think of things getting between us and God, we typically think of gross sin—like stealing, adultery, fornication, drunkenness, jealousy, etc

   But good things can also come between you and God. Watching TV isn't a sin, but as I know all too well, it can definitely be something that gets between me and God.

   The worst part about an eclipsed relationship with God is it still gives us the impression that we are close to Him, in the same way that in a solar eclipse we can tell it's light outside. The problem is it's a *reduced* light. The intimacy and radiance of the sun's light hitting earth is covered. This is what the Devil wants to do with us.

The way we resist the Devil is by guarding our relationship with Jesus more than we guard ourselves. We aren't capable of bringing healing to our world when we ourselves are divorced from Him. But by prioritizing Him, we can resist the works of the Devil and bring light and healing into our world.

The warning for us is that if we allow the Devil to eclipse our relationship with God long enough, we will begin to get comfortable in that stronghold and settle with this new reality. The Devil's plan isn't to destroy you by mere death; he wants to distort your view of who God is, because if he can do that, he will distort how you view yourself.

If God isn't good.

If He isn't just.

If He isn't worthy.

If He isn't holy.

If He isn't true.

Then what does that say about our lives? We become lost wandering around the wilderness looking for any sense of meaning we can cling to. I guess the saying is true, "What we think about God is the most important thing about us."[119]

Just like our view of Satan can get distorted, we've also built false ideas—false paradigms—about how God responds to Satan's destruction in our world. We've crafted all sorts of theories, worldviews, and theologies to make sense of the chaos, each one shaping the way we see His rule and reign. But if what we think about God is the most important thing about us—then maybe it's time to pause. To pay attention. To ask: *How does God say He reigns in the world?*

Because what if we've been getting it wrong? What if His rule looks different—better—than we ever imagined?

Let's dive in.

8

GOD'S IDEA OR IDEAS AS GOD

Dentists have a bad rap.

If you're a dentist and reading this book, I just want to apologize for the negative talk that surrounds your job. The reason I don't have an issue with dentists is because oral hygiene is important to me. I brush my teeth, I floss, and I schedule regular teeth cleanings with the dentist.

Recently I was at the dentist for my regular scheduled cleaning, and while I was sitting in the waiting room, a mom and teenage son were fighting about why he had to see the dentist. You could tell that the mom was getting a little embarrassed about the public argument, and doing my best not to look over there, I heard the mom say, "If you just took care of your teeth, you wouldn't have to come to the dentist!" As she says this, I glance over, we lock eyes with one another, and she says to me, "He's the one with cavities and I'm the bad guy?"

I gave a little grin and just uttered, "Teenagers . . ."

Finally, my name was called, and I was in and out in 20 minutes.

It got me thinking. The dentist office has a bad rap of being a painful and unpleasant place, but what I realized is that it's only painful and unpleasant based on how well (or not so well) we take care of our teeth.

Nevertheless, even if you do take care of your teeth, comfortable or cozy wouldn't be the words I'd use to describe my experience at the dentist's office.

That's why it is universally held that going to the dentist . . . well, frankly, sucks.

Theologian A.W. Tozer says, "What comes into our minds when we think about God is the most important thing about us."[120]

I believe this to be true.

How we view God will dictate how we view His engagement in the world's affairs. And humans are all over the board with their perception of God. Some people believe that a fly won't land on your food unless God orchestrates it, others view God as a distant dictator who just demands allegiance, and others just believe God is a force of energy that can be manipulated into giving humans their desires.

No matter where we land on our view of God, understanding how God engages with the world is crucial to how we live and participate in the world.

If God is solely "in control," then it creates apathy and disengagement for us.

If God is the distant dictator, then we live at the mercy of his wrath and judgement.

If God has already determined or predestined everything then we just need to sit back, grab some popcorn, and enjoy the show.

You see my point.

What we believe about God and how He engages with our world determines how we view life, pain, circumstance, and our destiny.

This is something that people have been wrestling with for centuries. There is even a whole section in the Bible dedicated to the questions, "How does God engage with our world? And how do we live in light of that engagement?"

Hello, Wisdom Literature (Job, Proverbs, Ecclesiastes, Song of Songs).

The first book on that list is where we will camp for this chapter. We will look at the book of Job and see how pain influences our view of God and how He engages in our world like nothing else, while examining some of the dominant worldviews in our culture.

RETRIBUTION PRINCIPLE: GETTING WHAT YOU DESERVE

Retribution sounds like a heavy word

However, the idea of retribution is an unfamiliar theology that many of us possess, and we don't even realize it.

Simply put, the idea of retribution is that if you do good and don't sin, then God will bless you. But if you do sin or if you don't do what is good, then God will curse you or judgment will fall on you.

Many people have been hurt by this theology.

Recently, at the end of church, a woman came up to me sobbing. She admitted that she was having an affair behind her husband's back. That week, her teenage son was out driving and got into a pretty bad car accident leaving him in a coma. Overwhelmed with shame, eyes full of tears, she said, "I know God is punishing me for my sins, but can you pray that my son will live? I promise I will tell my husband, but I just want my son to be okay." For this woman, God isn't a loving Father, but an angry God who casts His wrath on the wicked.

This is where I want to look at the story of Job.

Oftentimes when we think of the book of Job, we think it's God's explanation for human suffering, but it's not.

The story of Job is more so concerned with how to think about God in the midst of suffering. In other words, it's *not why* bad things happen, but *how* you should respond *when* bad things happen.

At the start of this story, Job has it all!

He's got the money, the house, his kids all go to Ivy League schools on scholarship, his businesses are all Fortune 500 companies, he drives the Benz . . . Job has so much that he makes Elon Musk look poor. It's important to note that in the opening verses of Job, both God and Satan acknowledge that Job is innocent and blameless.[121]

Satan comes and has concerns with God's policies, aka how God runs the world.

Get in line, dude.

Satan asks, "Does Job really love you or is he only obedient so that you will bless him?" (I mean, fair question.) Satan says, "Will Job still love you if everything is stripped away?"

Both Job and Satan's worldviews are both challenged. Job believes that good people shouldn't suffer when they have done nothing wrong (our perspective), and Satan argues that just because you do good doesn't mean you should be blessed.

I personally don't know anyone who would disagree with Job's thoughts. Oftentimes our biggest struggle when it comes to our belief in God is the existence of innocent sufferers.

In our secular culture, this worldview hasn't ceased to exist. We have just removed God from the equation.

Nowadays, we just call this karma.

KARMA: WHAT GOES AROUND, COMES AROUND

Karma is generally the same idea as the one Job was banking on, that if you do good, then good will come back to you. What you give is what you receive.

At times this can sound biblical, another version of "Give and it will be given to you,"[122] or bless and you will be blessed, help others and you will be helped.[123] A lot of times this idea of retribution or karma has been used in prosperity gospel theology.

And this idea is not limited to religious worldviews. Think about the modern expression, "You had it coming." In other words, you received something based on the actions that you gave. As for how one gets "karma" on your side? Well, you need to right the wrongs you made. Or in biblical parlance, you need some good old repentance.

This is the framework and worldview of Job's friends.

Job went through more pain than anyone could imagine. He lost his kids, his business, and his health. Only two things were spared: his life and his wife. In Job's darkest moments, his three closest friends come to his side.

The problem, however, is that his friends already assume that he is guilty because of their worldview and view of God. They didn't need any more evidence; the circumstances surrounding Job allowed them to determine his guilt.

In their best attempts to be good friends, they encouraged Job to repent for any wrongdoing so that God would bless him again. They weren't concerned with Job's righteousness or even his innocence; all they cared about was Job's status and wealth.[124] The righteousness was merely a way to get back to success and peace.

In much the same way, karma is not concerned about doing the right thing or becoming the right person. Karma's ethos is self-serving; it couldn't care less about the benefits of other people. At the heart of belief in karma is one's desire to twist and manipulate God or the universe in one's favor.

Whether you want to call this the retribution principle or karma is your choice. Nevertheless, a lot of Christians are caught up in this worldview. And if what we think about God is the most important thing about us, what does this theology of God's ruling the world say about Him?

> God is distant.
>
> He can be broken down to a principle.
>
> He isn't involved in human affairs because He made a machine to run the world.
>
> And He can't be trusted.

This leaves us with so many unanswered questions!

What do I do with my pain? Is it enough to know that if I'm a good person the universe will somehow reward me for being good? *How* good do I need to be for this formula to work? If for some reason I am facing pain is it because of some unconscious sin or mistake I made?

But what about those who sin or hurt other people? Why do I see the person who hurt me prospering and living a good life? How is that fair? Why does So-and-So get away with everything?

And what about the person who crashed into the son of the mother I prayed for? What happens to him?

Can karma really satisfy the answers of what's wrong with the world?

I don't think so.

PREDESTINATION: KICK BACK AND RELAX, IT'S ALL INEVITABLE

After Job's friends come to him and tell him to repent for what he did so that God can bless him, Job responds and declares his innocence. Job didn't care about the stuff, Job cared about his integrity! He was innocent.

Out of nowhere comes this random bloke named Elihu.

Instead of making the same claims of retribution that Job's friends made, he offers an alternate explanation for Job's suffering. Elihu claims that Job's innocent suffering was a part of God's will and plan for Job's life. Elihu comes to God's defense and says one thing's for sure: God is *just*. So, if you're suffering, it's probably God saving you from making a mistake in the future. God's judgment, according to Elihu, is an act of love to prevent us from doing something stupid.

Do you know of someone who in their purest heart attempts to help in a situation, but in their attempt does nothing but makes it worse?

Hello, my name is Elihu.

In our attempts to console and be there for people in the midst of their pain, we have given cheap and hurtful answers like,

"If it weren't part of God's will, then it wouldn't have happened."

or

"God already knew that was going to happen."

or a personal favorite,

"God gives His toughest battles to His strongest soldiers." (cue sarcasm)

These words don't really help when you're in the middle of a hard season. Instead, we are left to wonder: If God already knew, why didn't He stop or at least warn us about the suffering to come.

The challenge with the predestined worldview is that it paralyzes the mission of the church.

Let me explain.

I spoke earlier that Jesus didn't come to earth to just give us a pathway to heaven. He came to show us what it meant to be human. Jesus was the most alive person who ever lived.

The gospel writers show stories of Jesus weeping. Weeping over the world, the city He loved, friends He lost, and people who rejected Him. Jesus was the answer that the world needed. Jesus's life and ministry were about ushering in a new reality, not accepting the world on its terms, but partnering with the Father and influencing the world to come to His terms.

The ministry of Jesus echoes the blessing and call that was given in Genesis 1 & 2. We are blessed to be children of God who are now commissioned to usher in the realities of our Father's Kingdom on this earth.

The predestined worldview, however, just *accepts* the world on its terms. It says, "God's got it."

If we accept the world on its terms and just allow God to handle it, then where is His justice? How do we trust God? Is He really good? Or is He truly the distant dictator?

THE PROBLEM OF JUSTICE

The term "justice'" has been a trend in pop culture as of late.

Everyone seems to be a "justice warrior." Whether fighting issues of race; gender; sexuality; women's rights; or ethical coffee, clothes, and jewelry, everyone seems to have a fight.

Justice isn't a worldly concept; it's a biblical concept.

God sent the prophets of old to rebuke and call the nation of Israel to administer justice with honor and integrity. Being a just nation was God's heart for Israel.

> "This is what the LORD Almighty said: 'Administer true justice; show mercy and compassion to one another.'"[125]

God sets up justice as a core tenet of his people, and yet one of the main questions in the book of Job is: *Is God just?*

Job's two main concerns are His innocence and lack of justice from God. Job reasons that innocent people shouldn't suffer. And if he had the power, he would know how to administer justice better than God! Sound familiar? Since this is a matter of injustice, Job argues that God owes him an answer! This is the basis of Job's question. *Why am I suffering?* he laments. *I haven't done anything wrong!*[126]

There are three components we need to hold to be true if we want to understand Job.

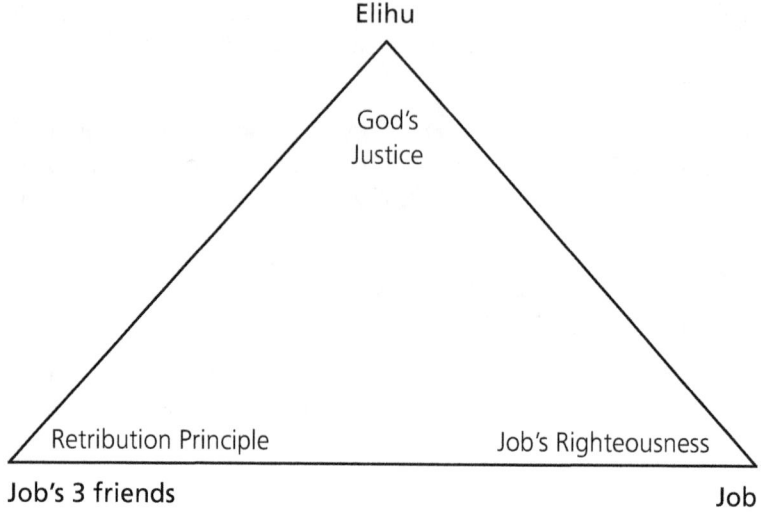

Only one of the corners can be true.

1. **Job**: If Job is truly righteous, then God would have to be unjust. And if God is unjust, then the retribution principle—the belief that God rewards good behavior and punishes evil—falls apart. In the Ancient Near East, people saw this principle as the foundation of how God governed the world. But if God is unjust, then His principle must be as well, because we know Job is a righteous sufferer.

2. **Retribution Principle:** If the retribution principle were true, it would imply that God is unjust because Job would have suffered despite being innocent. It would also mean that Job was not truly righteous, since under this principle, only the guilty experience hardship. However, the text clearly states that Job had not sinned,[127] proving that the retribution principle is false.

3. **God's Justice**: If God is just, then the retribution principle can't be true because Job has clearly suffered. But that still leaves us with the question of Job's innocent suffering . . .

Let's see how this plays out.

GOD'S IDEA OR IDEAS AS GOD

God does, in fact, respond to Job.

God's first response to Job is, "Where were you when I laid the foundations of the earth?"[128]

The question is, can Job do the job that God does?

This isn't some sarcastic response from God. Genuinely, before you criticize someone, you should probably know the ins and outs of their job. God's response argues that the retribution principle is too simple of an explanation to a complicated world.

I always love watching people criticize quarterbacks in the NFL. I think to myself, these are the best 32 men in the world who can play that position. If it was that easy, we wouldn't be sitting on a couch eating buffalo dip criticizing them.

God's response to Job is not offered in the way Job imagined. God immediately brings Job onto a level playing field. Philip Yancey writes, "God took Job on a verbal tour of all the wonders of nature."[129]

Perhaps the reason God showed Job the ins and outs of creation is that He is trying to get Job to understand that He doesn't rule the world based on His justice, but His wisdom.[130]

The Hebrew word for wisdom is "*chokhmah*," which means "the skill at living."

Basically, God is saying it takes wisdom to run the world, not a rigid principle.

Let's look back at the chart to see what remains. The question of God's justice is removed because He changes the venue of "is God just?" to "is God wise?" because He rules the world based on His wisdom not His justice. The retribution principle is eliminated because we know from the text Job really is an innocent sufferer.

So, what's left? Job's righteousness.

What we see from God's response is that Job isn't blessed purely because he is righteous, he is blessed because God loves blessing people. The blessing God gave to Job is part of the Genesis narrative,[131] God blesses humanity before they do anything for Him. Jesus himself affirms that God causes the rain (blessing) to fall on wicked and the just.[132] People are blessed because humans are made in His image, before they *do* anything for God. That's just the kind of God the world has, a God who blesses people without having to earn it.

But where does that leave us with the idea of God's justice?

Is God unjust? Does He just tolerate evil? He may not be a distant dictator, but He still seems distant!

God gives Job a response about His justice as well.[133]

God responds to this question by asking Job another question: "Is it your wisdom that made_____?"[134] (referring to creation).

God's argument is that the world was created through His wisdom, and He maintains the world everyday through His wisdom. Job is satisfied with the response that God gives, but God furthers and underscores His point.

He uses two fictional animals to make his argument: the Behemoth and Leviathan.

For us that's like a grizzly bear and great white shark.

The point is, even though the great white shark and grizzly bear can cause tremendous chaos and damage in people's lives, that does not mean that they are necessarily evil. God might use the natural world as a means for justice, but it doesn't mean the natural world is inherently evil.

Take, for example, Hurricane Milton. Rain combined with wind can cause horrendous damage to people's lives. But does that mean that rain and wind in themselves are bad?

No.

By the way, in no way am I saying Hurricane Milton was God's judgment on people

Because we don't see things from God's perspective, we can't understand how He runs the world. We lack the perspective to question, and we lack the ability to comprehend all the details of running the world.

All we know is that since God created the world through wisdom, we have enough information to know that He is wise, and if we believe that God is wise, then there is good reason to believe that He is just.

But more importantly,

If we focus on *justice*, then we demand an explanation of cause, which gazes at the past. Whereas a focus on wisdom needs only to understand that God in His wisdom has a purpose, as it fixes our gaze on the future.

We can't judge God by His actions. It is impossible to know what God is doing when He is doing it. All we can do is trust His heart.

We see this so clearly in the person of Jesus.

What kind of God would send His Son to earth to die the most painful and excruciating death known to man?

A kind and loving God.

If the Father wouldn't have done this, then we would still be stuck in the bondage of sin. We would still be oppressed by our own disordered desires. But the Father sent His Son to embrace pain and death so that we would experience life on the other side of death.

Nobody knew or could understand the life and ministry of Jesus until after His death. The disciples themselves likely asked a lot of Job-esque questions in the hours after the crucifixion.

Why did this happen?

Where is God now?

What happened to the Kingdom of Heaven on earth and all the promises that now feel empty?

We can't know all the answers to the complexities of the world, but what we can know is that we can trust Jesus.

So, how do we administer justice here on earth?

> "He has shown you, O mortal, what is good. And what does the LORD require of you? To act justly and to love mercy and to walk humbly with your God."[135]

Jesus has shown us what justice looks like: The giving of your life as a source of nourishment, safety, empathy, compassion, and mercy for others.

Henri Nouwen writes, "Real martyrdom means a witness that starts with the willingness to cry with those who cry, laugh with those who laugh, and to make one's own painful and joyful experiences available as sources of clarification and understanding. Who can save a child from a burning house without taking the risk of being burnt by the flames? Who can listen to a story of loneliness and despair without taking the risk of experiencing similar pains in their own heart . . . in short, 'who can take away suffering without entering into it?'"[136]

Biblical justice is to enter into the story of the pain of others, taking it on yourself as if the injustice happened to you, and responding with an intentional act of grace towards the enemy who harmed you.

My hope is that we would view justice through the lens of the cross and not the cross through the lens of secular justice.

Secular justice is rooted in guilt and shame.

Biblical justice is rooted in enemy love.

FREE WILL

Okay so let's recap.

The retribution principle is where you either get rewarded or punished based on your sin or righteousness. If you sin, you get punished, if you are righteous, you get rewarded.

Karma is just like the retribution principle minus the God factor. The universe does the blessing and the punishing.

Predestination is the belief that everything is God's will, all the way from stubbing your toe on the concrete to people getting cancer.

So where does this leave us? With a guy named Nehemiah.

The context of the book of Nehemiah is quite remarkable.

During Israel's exile, Babylon took all of the smart and talented Israelites, and those belonging to the royal family, and forced them to work in the government. It's here you get people like Daniel, Hananiah, Mishael, and Azariah, or better known as Meshach, Shadrach, and Abednego.

When the Persians came and conquered the Babylonian empire, they did the same. The Israelites who were working for the Babylonians now worked for the Persians. This is where Nehemiah comes on the scene. Nehemiah worked for the government, he had the government car, pension, and health insurance.

Life was good.

The Persians allowed the Israelites to go back to their homeland, but some of the Israelites stayed behind because they had built new lives in the land of their exile.

One day, Nehemiah and some friends are having a little fellowship, enjoying some flat whites and croissants. Nehemiah's catching up with his boys and says, "Hanani, how are the wife and kids doing? What does it feel like to be back home in Jerusalem? What's the weather like?"

Hanani responds, "Yeah mate, not good! We are in trouble! There are looters everywhere and our ADT security system is down!"[137]

The walls of Jerusalem were destroyed during the exile, and when they returned, all sense of security was lost. Walls in the Ancient Near East played a major role in the safety and security of a city.

This is Nehemiah's response:[138]

> When I heard these things, I sat down and wept. For some days I mourned and fasted and prayed before the God of heaven. Then I said:
>
> "Lord, the God of heaven, the great and awesome God, who keeps his covenant of love with those who love him and keep his commandments . . . I confess the sins we Israelites, including myself and my father's family, have committed against you. We have acted very wickedly toward you. We have not obeyed the commands, decrees and laws . . ."

This is remarkable! Nehemiah assumed responsibility for his people, his city, and nation.

Nehemiah wasn't even born when Israel was taken into exile. The sins and idolatry that Israel fell into were not his sins. He could have easily deferred blame or accused God of unjust punishment. Instead, he confessed the sins of Israel as if they were his very own.

He assumed responsibility over the situation, and in turn, God assumed responsibility over him.

The beautiful yet challenging aspect of free will is that it exposes our motives like nothing else. Nehemiah could have responded to Hanani with, "Ehh, I can't be bothered with it, not my problem anymore, I don't want to lose my pension."

We often forget that we have the authority to go and make a difference in our world.

Oftentimes when I teach in the book of Genesis, I'm asked two questions:

1. Why would God make a tree of Good and Evil?

2. Why did He create the serpent?

I respond with the fact that we assume God made a perfect world.

When we read Genesis, we assume that the world is perfect, but nowhere does it say that the world is perfect. It says that Creation was "very good," but nowhere does it say that it's perfect.

God's commission to humanity was to participate in *making* a very good world, *perfect*.

This is where free will comes into play.

C.S. Lewis writes that ". . . free will, though it makes evil possible, is also the only thing that makes possible any love or goodness or joy worth having."[139]

The decision to choose for ourselves is one of the most loving gifts God could have given humanity.

Following Jesus is a choice.

We have the choice to opt in to His vision of the good life—and, by extension, our role in the renewal of all things is also a choice. Because every *yes* to Jesus comes with a *no* to something else.

Our choices are never defined by their *yes*; they are always defined by their *no's*.

Think about wedding vows. The weight of "I do" isn't just in the commitment to love one person, but in the decision to forsake all others. Your marriage isn't built on a single *yes*, but on a lifetime of *no's*.

And that's where it gets real.

Because we all have our "others" that need to be forsaken.

The things that are hard to let go of. For some, it's the fear of losing control—of surrendering autonomy and dying to self. For others, it's the cultural trifecta of sex, success, and self-indulgence.

For others it's addiction to the hustle, the dopamine hits, the curated digital identity. Whatever it is, we all have that one thing. The thing that stands between us and a life fully alive in Jesus.

Just ask the rich young ruler. His thing was money.[140] And when Jesus asked him to let it go, he couldn't.

Not because he was a bad person, but because his wealth had become his security, his identity, his god.

And that's the question we all have to answer: What's the one thing keeping us from stepping deeper into life with Jesus?

What blows my mind the most about this story is that Jesus invites the rich young ruler to become his disciple. But the invitation comes with a choice: Keep nothing for yourself. Get rid of your wealth.[141] Perhaps the rich young ruler's response to Jesus would have been "yes" if his "no" wouldn't have been so costly.

The rich young ruler declines Jesus's invitation and walks away saddened.

The sobering reality for us in all of this is that Jesus doesn't pursue or chase after the rich young ruler even though we see that Jesus loved him. That's an important note to make, as the Gospels don't always make intentional observations of Jesus's love for people. So, there must have been something different about this guy.[142]

Yet, Jesus doesn't pursue.

Jesus doesn't compromise and say, "Okay, you know what? That was a test. Just give away 25% and call it good."

In the ultimate display of honoring our choice, Jesus allowed someone he cared about to walk away from him.

Our decisions have tremendous ramifications on the world, and that power is part of the blessing God gave us. As humans we have the ability to create the type of world in which we want to live.

Our observations of the world's brokenness compel us to see that we have the ability to bring change to it. We need to be like Nehemiah and accept the realities of the past while also releasing prophetic imagination back into our world.

The retribution principle gives too much power to humans and limits God. It places us in the driver seat and God in the back. The world's redemption is contingent on our obedience to God.

Karma's problem is that it makes us God, and we manipulate the world into our favor.

Predestination's problem is it makes us spiritually apathetic. We just sit on the couch with our popcorn saying, "God's got it."

Free will, however, honors the Genesis 1 mandate of blessing and commission. We act on behalf of God in bringing perfection to the world, as we ourselves are in the process of being perfected.

Jesus did the hard work of "overcoming the world" so that we can be redemptive participants in the world here and now.[143] He is looking for people to assume responsibility over the world.

Rabbi Jonathan Sacks asks us to consider the questions God might pose to us: "What have you done with the gift I gave you, of life? How have you used your time? Have you lived for yourself alone or have you lived also for others? Is your primary question, What can the world give me? or is it, What can I give to the world? Have you sought blessing, or have you been a blessing?"[144]

I believe that if we assume responsibility for the past, God will assume responsibility over us for our future.

But hey, it's your choice . . . sorry for the pun.

A NEW PERSPECTIVE

We started out this chapter with the questions, "How does God engage with our world? And how do we live in light of that?"

I doubt that this chapter has answered all of your questions regarding how God operates in the world, but maybe that's the point. Maybe our job as created beings isn't about figuring out how God operates in the world but about finding God in the pain and suffering in the world.

Let's turn our attention back to Job.

After God's explanation about His wisdom and how He operates the world, Job is blown away, not by God's response, but by God himself. Job's perspective is illuminated and his response to God is beautiful:

> "You asked, 'Who is this that questions my wisdom with such ignorance?' It is I—and I was talking about things I knew nothing about."[145]

God doesn't reveal His explanation of pain and suffering. Instead, He reveals Himself, and that is what makes Job content. What satisfies Job in the end is not that he understands suffering better, but that he understands God better.

In Job's prosperity, he thought he knew God.

Job now realizes that what he knows about God is far more personal and intimate than what he experienced in the past. It's crazy that once Job had this moment with God, his prayer to be delivered from his suffering ceases, likely because he learns how to rest in God while being in pain.

One last thing:

Remember, Job is considered righteous by God, even after he questions, doubts, and challenges God.

But what about Job's friends?

God has a different message for them:

> He said to Eliphaz the Temanite: "I am angry with you and your two friends, for you have not spoken accurately about me, as my servant Job has. So, take seven bulls and seven rams and go to my servant Job and offer a burnt offering for yourselves. My servant Job will pray for you, and I will accept his prayer on your behalf. I will not treat you as you deserve, for you have not spoken accurately about me, as my servant Job has."[146]

Wow!

Even though his friends in their purest attempts were trying to defend God, they failed to represent God correctly. Whereas Job, though full of hurt, pain, doubt, and concern, is deemed righteous because he ran to God in the midst of his pain.

Maybe our questions, doubts, and pain are conduits that lead to the presence of God?

Jesus affirms that there will be innocent suffering on earth, but He also affirms that painful moments are opportunities for God to be seen by the world.

In John 9, Jesus's disciples ask Him if a man that they saw was born blind because of *his sins or the sins of his parents* (Retribution Principle).[147]

Jesus says neither, that this man was born blind because of the brokenness of the world. But, He assures them, the man will see again because Jesus Himself was sent to restore what was lost in the Garden.

Look at how Jesus heals the man: Jesus bends down, puts His hands in the dirt, spits in the mud, and forms new eyes for the man to have. Jesus doesn't just heal the old pair of eyes; He gives him a new set.

This is what Jesus wants to do for you.

Like Job who received a new perspective of the world,

And like the man who received new eyes,

Jesus wants us to view the world how He does.

Not one that is dark or evil, though the world contains both.

He wants us to see the world as weeping artists, as kintsugi artists who have the heart to heal, mend, and care for the broken fragments of the world and make them whole and new.

Jesus's voice is calling His church through the pain and suffering of the world, "Where are you?"

The world needs you! Creation is waiting for the children of God to take the blessing of Genesis and pour it out on the wounded and brokenhearted. Don't flee from the world; run to it!

> "For all creation is waiting eagerly for that future day when God will reveal who his children really are. Against its will, all creation was subjected to God's curse. But with eager hope, the creation looks forward to the day when it will join God's children in glorious freedom from death and decay."[148]

PART THREE:
OUR WOUNDED LIVES

"Without you, what am I to myself but a guide to my own self-destruction."

— *St. Augustine*

"In those days there was no king in Israel. Everyone did what was right in his own eyes."

— *Judges 21:25 (ESV)*

9
SELF-MADE

We just got done with another vicious election season.

And, depending on who you voted for you may be feeling extremely hopeful for the future or full of anxiety and fear—which is normal.

One of the interesting political analyses I love to look at is the "first 100 days." It's more so known as the President's first work evaluation. This is the time where the president gets to double down on the previous administration's policies or completely eradicate them.

To give an example, in 2016 President Donald Trump signed 55 executive orders in his first 100 days, eliminating and ending policies that President Barack Obama had signed into order during his time as president.[149] Also, in 2020 President Joe Biden signed 24 executive orders overturning or eliminating policies from President Trump.[150]

Whether you agree or disagree with their decisions isn't the point.

The point is, when presidents issue executive orders, it is about eliminating a certain policy and replacing it with another.

The same goes for us.

In the previous section we spoke about how culture has eradicated God from the center of society. By doing this, the stories which humanity has believed about themselves and the world around them have dramatically shifted.

In a pre-Modern world, belief in God, the Devil, and sin weren't such abstract ideas. But as culture developed and gained more knowledge, ideas about sin and the Devil became known as more of a fairytale than a present reality.

So, this leaves us the question: If culture has signed an executive order eradicating God, the Devil, and sin out of the center of society, who then is to replace them? The answer is:

The Self, humans, and . . . humans.

THE HORIZONTAL SELF

We are living in an experiment.

Never in the history of humanity has there ever been a time where people have attempted to live in a culture where God or "the gods" weren't at the center of society. Even kings were subjected to the gods. For example, in Book I of Herodotus's Histories, we find an account of King Croesus of Lydia consulting oracles (the mediators of the gods) before going to war with Persia.[151]

Pastor Mark Sayers calls this the "Vertical Self."[152]

Meaning, that any sense of identity, purpose, or explanation of the world's problems couldn't be explained without reference to the transcendent. Also, humans looked upward to measure their behavior against a "greater moral good."

But times have changed, without newfound knowledge of reality and our lasting concerns over innocent suffering, we now live in a time called the "Horizontal Self."

Sayers defines it like this, "Secular culture drenched in a worldview of suspicion, the individual cannot look higher than the self with any degree of certainty. Thus, religion, spirituality, tradition, and culture cannot tell a wider story that offers the individual a sense of place and meaning. The secular individual can only look sideways—hence the term horizontal self."[153]

Before we move forward, I think it's important to define some words. When we think of the world "secular," we typically think of "non-religious." You know, you have "secular music," Taylor Swift, Drake, U2, The Rolling Stones. Then you have "worship music," Maverick City, Bethel, and the Helsers, but that's not quite what secular means in our world.

Secularism isn't just the air we breathe; it's the soil we're planted in. It shapes the way we see, think, and move through the world—often without us even realizing it.

Simply put, secularism isn't the eradication of religion, it means religion has no sacred position in your life.

In other words, one can still possess a worldview or belief in God. However, when it comes to having sex with your boyfriend or girlfriend, compared to the biblical vision of sexuality—you choose to have sex with your boyfriend or girlfriend.

Jesus and His ethic that is revealed in scripture doesn't have as much authority as fulfilling your desires and living a life with as much pleasure as possible.

Mark Sayers puts it this way, "One can have an evangelical Christian worldview, a secular sex life, an economic rationalist approach to money, a conservative vote, and a liberal approach to humor."[154]

In other words, "you do you!" and no one has the right to tell you otherwise. Life is like a buffet of options and opinions that you can choose from to build your life however you see fit.

That means humanity has become the measure of all things and the very thing that society now builds its life around. We, unlike those in the story of the Tower of Babel, have become the gods of our society. The difference though is that we aren't trying to make our way to heaven, it's that we are making our own personal heaven through our life and experiences, here and now.

SELF-DEIFICATION

Tim Keller once said, "Secularism is the biggest threat Christianity has ever faced."[155]

I believe that he is right. If I take a look at my own life, I am guilty of putting my own needs, desires, and wants ahead of God's plan countless times. In moments of my life, I have claimed to be a follower of Jesus all while making plans to participate in hookup culture. I have ignored opportunities to apologize to people all because I wanted to be in the right. We have all done this in some way or form.

This is why secularism is such a threat, because it gives us the illusion that we can have both Jesus and our own way.

But what we don't realize is that Jesus can't work with a divided heart. We have already seen an example of this with the rich young ruler; Jesus wants us in our entirety. This is how secularism gets away with deceiving us, it acts like an eclipse giving us the illusion that Jesus is closer to us than He really is. In reality, we have subtly moved Him to the side and now rule our own world.

We rule our own world based on how we *feel*.

Theologian Carl Trueman calls this, "*Aesthetic Emotion.*"[156] Our feelings are the true authority of our life. Since we no longer find ourselves a part of a greater story, the purpose and meaning of life has also shifted. Our life's purpose is now about filling ourselves with as much happiness, comfort, and freedom as possible.

And the barometer to determine if you're successfully living the good life is determined based on how happy and free you *feel*.

This is why the doctrines of secularism says:

> Sin is when you're unhappy,
>
> Hell is when your desires are restrained,
>
> The Devil is anyone who doesn't approve of the life that you choose to live,
>
> Salvation is freedom from anyone or anything that restricts you from living your best life,
>
> And the virtues to pursue are happiness, comfort, freedom, and exercising your rights.

This is why Canadian Philosopher Charles Taylor calls our modern age "the Age of Authenticity."[157]

He explains modern man's goal in life as this, "That each one of us has his or her our own way of realizing our own humanity, and that it's important to find and live out one's own as against surrendering to conformity with a model imposed on us from outside by society, previous generation, religious or political authority."[158]

Pastor Jon Tyson furthers the point, "If all there is a 70–80-year run (life), your goal is to get through life with as much meaning as you can derive, with as much pain as you can avoid, and people are constantly fine-tuning spirituality, philosophies, preferences of life for people to get through."[159]

Part of being the god of our own lives means that we must determine what is good versus evil, right from wrong, truth from lies, happiness versus pain, the role of pain in one's life, and what is good for healing and what causes more harm.

You are responsible for your reality is the mantra for Self-Deification.

In some ways we have become like Job in our accusations against God that, "I can run my world better than You."

These ideas seem liberating at first, but what we fail to realize is that the world is full of people who possess the same perspective that they are god. The problem when everyone plays the role of god is that everyone does what is right in their own eyes and doesn't realize how their new cosmos hurts the lives of those around them.

EVERYBODY DID WHAT WAS RIGHT IN THEIR OWN EYES

One of the most depressing books in all the Bible is the book of Judges.

The book of Judges describes a chaotic and complicated time in Israel's history. Joshua (the leader who followed after Moses) had just died, and Israel was lacking a true spiritual leader.

Before Joshua's death, he renewed the covenant with Israel which said if Israel were to obey the commands that were listed in their law, then they would be a blessed nation and be a blessing to the world and nations around them.

A repeated theme in the book of Judges is, "In those days there was no king in Israel. Everyone did what is right in his own eyes."[160]

The book has a circular/ repetitive theme to it.

1. The people of Israel do what they want and fall into sin and idolatry.
2. God allows the effects of sin to take place, and Israel is conquered by their enemies.
3. The people cry out to God for help.
4. God raises up a Judge to deliver Israel from their pain.
5. There would be a slight period of peace.
6. The cycle would repeat after the Judge's death.

Starting from the opening chapters, the book of Judges describes the ongoing and growing corruption of Israel's judges and the intensification of sin in the lives of the people of Israel.

In other words, it goes from: good, not too bad, not good, absolutely terrible, to what the heck!!

Israel had a command to push the Canaanites out of the land because God didn't want Israel to fall into the idolatry and evil practices of the Canaanites. (The Canaanites were sacrificing their children and doing all kinds of detestable things.)

God called Israel to be a "Holy" people and nation.

Israel failed to push the Canaanites out and just decided to live with the Canaanites. Israel began to adopt the same religious and cultural practices of the Canaanites.

This begins the pattern of sin, oppression, repentance, deliverance, and peace.

With each chapter, the character of each judge worsens and worsens.

Gideon, once a shy and insecure man, becomes boastful, proud, and a murderer who sets up Israel with an idol leading them into more sin. Jephthah treats the God of Israel like the gods of Canaan and sacrifices his own daughter to "earn favor" with God in his next battle. Samson, though full of talent, potential, and God's spirit, uses his gifts for himself and lives a life of hedonistic pleasure and narcissistic power.

However, the real tragedy in the book of judges isn't in the leaders of Israel (we all know about bad leadership), but the people of Israel.

Bad leadership isn't an excuse for moral decline.

Chapters 17-21 recount two horrifying stories about the people of Israel. This section highlights the recurring phrase, "In those days there was no king in Israel. Everyone did what was right in their own eyes,"[161] which underscores the chaos and lawlessness of the time, while also painting a picture for us in our modern culture.

In the first story, a man named Micah steals silver from his mother, but Micah ends up returning the silver he stole, and his mom ends up making a household god for his family to worship.

He creates a new religion for himself and his family. This is no different from secularism. In secularism, the individual possesses the power to create the cosmos of their own life. Truth becomes unknown and subjective... echoes of the secular phrase "that's your truth" are ringing in my head.

In the latter half of chapter 17 and the whole of chapter 18, something really interesting happens. Micah sees a young man who is wandering. This young man is from the tribe of Levi (who was considered the priestly family—only those from Levi could be a priest in Israel).

Because the wandering man was a Levite, Micah appointed him to be priest of his "new religion" instead of his son.[162] This is a subtle attempt of partial obedience to Yahweh (Israel's God).

You may be asking, how is this partial obedience?

Because only Levites could be priests, and Micah's son was not a Levite, therefore he couldn't be a priest. But since Micah found a Levite, he empowered him to be the priest of his new religion, mixing some ethics of Judaism (only Levites could be priests) with his new created religion (Secularism).

Secularism believes in religious pluralism.

Derek Rishmawy puts it like this, ". . .There are no more singular monolithic obvious takes on the world, belief has become less of an 'on' and 'off' switch and more of a series of dials you can set in various degrees; post secular humanist, romantic libertarian, ecofeminism and on and on. . ."[163]

The *second* horrendous story starts in chapter 19.

In chapter 19, a Levite and his concubine are walking together. As they enter the town called Gibeah, two wicked men demand to rape the Levite. The Levite, who is afraid for his life, decides to offer up his concubine instead.

The two men then perform detestable acts on the woman, leaving her for dead. The next morning the Levite sees that his concubine is dead and decides to cut her into twelve pieces and sends a single piece to each of the twelve tribes of Israel.

This was an outcry of injustice; almost like a "look how far we have fallen" moment.

The tribes then team up together and go to the tribe of Benjamin (that is where the crime occurred), and the tribes demand the two men who raped the woman to be handed over. But the tribe of Benjamin refuses to hand them over. This starts a civil war amongst the Israelites leading to hundreds of thousands of people dying. The book of Judges closes with the phrase that matches our current cultural state, "In those days, Israel had no king, and everyone did what was right in their own eyes."

The irony is:

We have become like the people in the book of Judges who "do what is right in our own eyes." And we are even caught up in the same repetitive cycle of pain, shame, and unhappiness that they were.

1. Sin: A life that is unhappy.

2. Oppression: Shame from previous attempt of happiness. The oppressor is whatever trend or choice that led to pain.

3. Repentance: Turn from the lifestyle and curate a new one.

4. Deliverance: Emancipation of your old self, and reconstruct identity based on the new you, either adding or removing from previous self—pluralism, deconstruction, or total annihilation.

5. Peace: Excitement on the new self-help journey. Finding new friends, community, and career to support the new you.

6. Repeat Cycle.

The more this cycle repeats in our life, the more fragmented we become, and the more secularism digs its roots into our heart, worldview, and thinking. We become further and further removed from the idea that God can help. Where the people of Israel cried out to God for help, we cry out to ourselves.

Even though belief in God is still possible, we don't believe He can rescue us, and the desire to put ourselves back together leads us to a life that is filled with more and more pain and fragmentation. Ultimately filling our lives with hopelessness, cynicism, and despair.

IS THIS ALL THERE IS?

The lasting question secularism asks us is: *Is this this all there is?*

Secularism says yes.

Before the modern age, the organizing principle of people's lives wasn't the desire to be happy, comfortable, or peaceful. Not saying that people didn't desire those things, they did, it's just that those things weren't the driving force of people's lives.

Written in our constitution is, "We hold these truths to be self-evident, that all men are created equal, that they are endowed by their Creator with certain unalienable Rights, that among these are *Life, Liberty, and the pursuit of Happiness.*"[164]

Our Founding Fathers believed that God gave certain rights to all of humanity: the right to have life, liberty, and to pursue what makes them happy.

Our modern culture shouts, "Amen!"

What most people don't know is that the phrase "life, liberty, and the pursuit of happiness" was originally written by John Locke as "life, liberty, and property." Locke's intention was that people had the rights to life, freedom, and the ability to own land which the government didn't control.

After the phrase was written, Thomas Jefferson exchanged the "property" aspect of the phrase for "pursuit of happiness."

In our modern world, we view this phrase as a declaration of individual freedom to pursue whatever we deem that will make us happy. For some, this is about pursuing a career to provide for a better life, for others it's the right to own property, for others it's to start their own business.

The point is: You're free to do what you want without interference from the government.

But Thomas Jefferson had something else in mind when he added "pursuit of happiness" to the Declaration of Independence.

Thomas said this about the pursuit of happiness, "health, learning, and virtue will ensure your happiness; they will give you a quiet conscience, private esteem, and public honor."[165] He believed that dedicating your life to the service of others was the most important thing one could do to have life fulfilled.[166] Lastly, Thomas believed that pursuing a vocation that ushered in tranquility and meaning was the way to pursue a career, not pursuing wealth, power, or greed. "It is neither wealth nor splendor, but tranquility and occupation which give happiness."[167]

Though he wasn't a Christian, he still held firm to the fact that our lives matter, and we need to live our lives in a way that leaves a lasting impact on the next generation.

Comparing the secular belief to Thomas Jefferson's intent is quite clear; he believed our lives served a greater purpose beyond ourselves; whereas, secularism leaves us stuck on the *here and now*. Meaning there is nothing beyond the *here and now*.

Have you ever wondered: *Why on earth am I here? What is my purpose in life?*

We feel these things because even though we believe in God, we have subtly taken ownership of meaning, purpose, and every other existential answer that we used to receive from God. But because our needs and desires have shifted from an eternal perspective into an immanent perspective, we have looked to the physical world for answers of meaning, purpose, and happiness that have left us feeling void.

Charles Taylor describes secularism's impact on culture as, "The utter emptiness of the ordinary."[168]

He goes on to say, "It is as though living in a world free of transcendence, enchantment, and an organization around divine action has given us a freedom that leaves us with a discomfort we can't pinpoint, a dull boredom we can't shake."[169]

Recently, I was talking to someone from church. He is a police officer, and I vicariously get my police fix in by listening to his stories. Anyway, after church he comes up to me and tells me he just made the SWAT team. An incredible honor, and extremely hard to do. As we were talking, he began describing the process to me and how hard it was to make it on the team, and how he is finally able to live his childhood dream.

Curious to know what that felt like I asked him, "How does it feel to have finally made it?"

He quickly responded, "Good!"

But as he continued to think about my question, his smile and excitement started to vanish, and what he said changed my life forever. "Actually, I thought it would feel better than it does. I don't know what to pursue next . . ."

Wow.

How many of you have experienced or know someone who has spent their entire life in pursuit of a dream, and as soon as they get it, they are left feeling empty or lost?

Or how many of you have told yourself, "If I could just have that thing then I'd be happy?"

Or thought,

"If I can just be friends with 'so and so' then I will know I have made it."

Or believed,

"If I could just have 'X' amount of followers on IG then I'll be happy."

Or, "After I buy this house then I can finally rest."

This is the immanent frame.

All sense of meaning is lost, and worrying about living a life that is unfulfilled becomes the driving force of one's life. The problem with this is that when pain and hardship come our way, believing that we are just victims of circumstance means there is no grander meaning to our pain and suffering. So, pain becomes the enemy of our life, and happiness is the friend that we cling to, and the goal of our life is to fill our lives with as much happiness and pleasure as possible and avoid pain at any cost.

COMPARING TATTOOS

If you don't know what I look like, you might be surprised at how many tattoos I have, especially as a pastor.

At the last church I worked at, I was known as the "tatted pastor." Now, that doesn't mean other pastors didn't have tattoos, that just means I had an abundance, or as Christians say, "My cup was overflowing!"

One of my favorite verses to jokingly misinterpret in the Bible is Revelation 19:16, "On his robe and on his thigh, he has this name written: King of Kings and Lord of Lords."

Jesus is tatted!!!!

Funny enough, I have tattoos on my thighs as well.

No, it's not King of Kings or Lord of Lords—that would be blasphemous! What's tattooed on my thigh is *far more blasphemous* than claiming to be the Messiah.

What's written on my thigh is…"Self-Made."

Yes, you read that right, on my legs is my claim to self-existence, value, worth, and complete independence from God.

After I was fired from the LAPD I went through an identity crisis.

I lost all sense of who I was.

Twenty-one years I planned for this dream to have it vanish in a matter of minutes. Life doesn't stop though; life doesn't care if you just lost your dream. The world continues to spin, the bank still wants your car payment, the rent needs to be paid, and your wife still needs love and support.

I bounced around from job to job—from construction, to warehouse worker, sushi chef, private security, and Uber driver.

With each job I began to feel like I was losing more and more of myself. I began to get embarrassed to show my face at family parties out of shame of having to answer, "How's work?" I would tell fictitious stories about me reapplying to the police department claiming that "God's in control" while simultaneously doubting the very words as they came out of my mouth.

I would show up to church, put my hands up during worship, and pray, hoping that God would somehow part the Red Sea of shame and guilt.

Every time I attempted to draw closer to God, the more overwhelmed I became by the shadows of my own life. Jesus wanted to bring me through the valley of shadow and death in my own life, but the thought of more pain was more than I thought I could bear.

Enough was enough.

I was done with God.

There were too many unanswered prayers, too many moments of pain. I thought Jesus had failed to rescue me in moments I needed Him the most.

I decided to take control of my life. I joined a gym, hired a personal trainer, and was ready to live on my terms. My personal trainer looked like a Viking! He was big, shoulders the size of bowling balls, he was tattooed from head to toe, he just looked like someone who demanded respect.

He was loved by his peers, people looked up to him, and I wanted that. At that point, my whole life was wrapped up in my body and how I looked. I curated an image that I believed society desired and embraced.

I began to get tattoos and, in an attempt to expedite my ideal body type, I began to take steroids. I also began the journey of becoming a personal trainer. I took classes online, apprenticed under a nutrition coach, and moved towards having my own business.

It felt great, with each new tattoo and lost percent of body fat, I began to gain the attention, acceptance, and love I desired all along.

As I was launching my personal training business, I decided to contract with a gym called Self-Made Training Facility. They looked like they had it all put together. The trainers were jacked and all drove nice cars; that's what I wanted for my life.

My journey as a trainer started off great. I made more money than I could have imagined, and my business was thriving! I bought a nice Jaguar and lived in a beautiful apartment in Orange County, California—I was officially Self-Made.

I finally found my piece of happiness here on earth. But most importantly "I did it my way," as Frank Sinatra would say. I didn't need religion, Jesus, my parents, my pastor, or the Christian morals that people demanded that I should live by.

One Friday stands out more than most. I had just come from the bank, where I'd deposited a solid sum of money earned through grit, persistence, sacrifice, not a single prayer to God. As I walked out, anger swelled quietly in my chest. But behind that anger, a storm of old memories stirred: the sleepless nights, the unanswered prayers, the shallow and empty words from friends and family that said I needed to "surrender to God."

I found myself thinking back to my church days, back when my pastor would talk about escaping to the mountains behind his house. He said he'd go there to pray, to be alone with God. He spoke of it like holy ground—where silence wasn't empty, but full of something sacred. A place where God felt close.

That thought lit a fire in me. Anger gave way to something darker—grief, resentment, rage. I was angry. Not just frustrated, but deep-in-the-bones angry. Angry at life, at pain, at the silence I thought was God ignoring me. And in that moment, I made a decision that felt long overdue: I was going to find Him. And I was going to say everything I'd swallowed over the years.

I got in my car and drove—out of the city, past the noise, toward those same mountains my pastor used to climb. I parked at the base and hiked until I found a quiet, hidden place. Just me, the wind, and the endless sky above. My heart was pounding—not from the climb, but from the sheer audacity of what I was about to do.

I had come to let Jesus have it. Years of unanswered prayers, pain with no explanation, and silence that echoed too loud for too long—I brought it all with me. With hatred in my heart, tears flowing down my cheeks, hot and relentless, carving silent trails through the dust of everything I'd endured I climbed to a secluded spot.

My chest felt like it might burst, my heart was pounding like war drums, each beat louder than the last. I stood there, shaking, not from weakness but from everything I had carried to get here. And in that moment—raw, defiant, and trembling—I looked up, eyes burning, and with all the strength I had left I yelled to the heavens, "*I made it. I f****** made it without You.*" Not out of pride, but out of my anger and pain. Out of survival. Out of the aching silence that followed every prayer that went unanswered.

After this moment, the following week, I got the infamous tattoos "Self" tattooed on my left thigh and "Made" tattooed on my right thigh. Now, I must add, these aren't cute little dainty tattoos; they literally take up my entire thigh—pretty much from hip to knee.

This is what secularism does: it removes God from our hearts, desires, purpose, and meaning. All that is left is for us to redefine those things for ourselves, and anyone who steps in the way needs to be cut out from your life.

You redefine what is good, true, and beautiful for yourself.

Secularism has made us become a culture of redefinition.

10

A REDEFINING CULTURE

Do words really have power?

Sometimes when I am lost in my thoughts or spacing out, I go on these random rabbit trails of thoughts. One of my recent rabbit trails was how do we create words? I mean, who decided that the word "time" would mean "the indefinite continued progress of existence and events in the past, present, and future regarded as a whole."[170] I am sure there is an explanation out there somewhere, but it's something I like to get lost in.

But do words matter? Does their meaning actually matter? And can the definition of a word actually change?

The answer is yes, yes, and yes!

The meaning of words changes all the time. For example, the word "awful" used to mean something that was "full of awe or inspiring wonder." And now we use it to describe something that is very bad or unpleasant.

The word "gay" used to mean something "lighthearted or joyful," and now it's used to describe someone's sexual orientation.

And my favorite example:

"Literally" used to mean "a literal matter of fact," but today it's more so used as a means for emphasis such as, "I literally died of laughter!" (Queue the valley girl voice!)

So, we can see the definition of words can change depending on how a culture uses them.

But does it matter that cultures can change the meaning and definitions of words? Do words actually matter?

Recently I happened to stumble across a German Dictionary, random I know, and as I was skimming through the dictionary I started to notice "NS" by certain words. What intrigued me was the fact that there was no consistent reason as to why "NS" was by certain words.

I pulled out the source of all knowledge—Google—and went on a deep dive into the reasoning for "NS."

What I found was quite fascinating: the "NS" stands for *Nationalsozialismus*: This refers to Nazism, the ideology associated with the National Socialist German Workers' Party. What the Third Reich would do was manipulate language and the meaning of words in the dictionary for ideological indoctrination, social engineering, and identity formation.[171]

I was so fascinated with how Nazis influenced millions of people into believing a twisted ideology that I bought a book on the matter: *Language of the Third Reich: LTI: Lingua Tertii Imperii* by Victor Klemperer.

Victor Klemperer was Professor of French Literature at Dresden University. He was Jewish and during the war, he was removed from the university because he was Jewish. The only reason he survived WWII is because he was married to an Aryan woman.

In his book, he describes how the most subtle, yet influential way the Third Reich gained influence was by redefining words, not creating new ones. "The Third Reich coined only a very small number of the words in its language, perhaps–indeed probably–none at all . . . But it changes the value of words and the frequency of their occurrence."[172]

So, the answer to my question becomes quite clear: yes, words have power and yes, their definitions play a significant role in how we see and view the world.

As we spoke about before, God has been removed from the center of society and has been replaced with "the Self" or the individual. But something interesting has happened as well when we replaced God in the center of culture, there has been a rise of the need to redefine words, meaning, movies, pain, happiness, etc. all for the purpose of placing the individual at the center of society.

I guess Winston Churchill was correct when he said, "The empires of the future are the empires of the mind."[173]

In our modern world, we have become a redefining culture.

REWRITING THE SCRIPT

Have you noticed how Disney and Hollywood are remaking old movies from the past?

Have you ever wondered why they are doing this?

I mean, have we as people run out of good ideas, creative plots, or ways to recapture the human experience?

I don't think so.

It's an attempt to rewrite the script.

For example, the movie *Snow White*. The first movie came out in 1938, and the basis of the movie is how love conquers all things. Snow White's jealous stepmother attempts to kill her on several occasions and eventually, the evil queen poisons the apple, putting Snow White in a deep sleep. She ultimately is rescued by the prince and defeats the queen.

In the remake, actor Rachel Zegler, who plays Snow White, said how the remake of *Snow White* has a modern edge to it. "It's no longer 1937, and we wrote a Snow White where she won't be saved by the prince, and isn't dreaming about true love, she's dreaming about becoming the leader she knows she can be."[174]

Snow White is just one example of many.

Movies of the past aren't the only thing that are being redefined.

Words are being redefined.

Words like gender, marriage, racism, truth, goodness, health, hate, and sexuality are all being redefined by culture.

Now, please hear me out, I'm not taking a shot at culture or even attempting to make insensitive political statements towards a group of people. My point in using these examples is to show how we have gone from a culture where people generally agreed on what these words meant to a culture where the definition of these words became more fluid. The reason for that is because of the rise of the individual.

It's about taking the power back.

Psychologists have mentioned that the "un-doing" or the "rewriting" of the past is a way to promote self-enhancement. What this does is create the illusion of improvement.[175] The past, particularly in the West, was a time where God, family, and state were considered pillars of a society. God, family, and state all served as boundary markers for individuals.

People believed that they would have to give an account for their life to God. They also lived their life based on what would give their family name the most honor and would do all they could to avoid bringing shame to the family. And the state wasn't something that enabled you, but the state was something that you contributed to for the betterment of all. As the famous John F. Kennedy quote goes, "Ask not what your country can do for you but what you can do for your country."[176]

Now, God, family, and state are all things which the individual needs to be emancipated from, and the best way to do that is to rewrite the script, retell the stories in the past that used to shape us—take a page out of the Third Reich's playbook.

Hungarian professor and sociologist Frank Furedi gives four ways on how modern culture is attempting to erase the past in order to elevate the individual:[177]

1. Reshaping Values: Explain how the values of the past are restrictive and oppressive.

2. Altering Language: Redefine words.

3. Promoting Identity Politics: Forget policy, focus on identity, one's personhood.

4. Cultural Power Consolidation: Have elites affirm the message. (Hollywood, Disneyland, influencers, etc.)

I think if we take a closer look at culture, we can see how all of these things are shaping all of our lives, for example:

1. Reshaping Values:

    Jesus's vision for sex is a monogamous marital relationship that contains two people with opposite gender. Culture believes that Jesus's vision for sexuality is the most oppressive thing one can do with their body.

2. Altering Language: "Hate" used to mean emotional disdain for another person. Now, it means someone who disagrees with your moral choice.

3. Promoting Identity Politics: One of the greater topics in the 2024 election was LGBTQIA+ rights

4. Cultural Power Consolidation: In the 2024 election, both Trump and Harris sought endorsements from celebrities and influencers over their political peers. Some people even say Joe Rogan's endorsement of Trump is what pushed him over the top.

What does this mean for us?

It means we are being formed and shaped into something that we don't even know or realize. We as humans tend to give ourselves too much credit, thinking that we are more autonomous than we really are. In reality, we are very sheepish. Humans cannot find themselves without some sort of guidance or steering. The secular narrative of individualism is a lie because humans are not made or even designed to live autonomous lives. We always find ourselves as individuals when we find ourselves a part of something beyond ourselves.

What we don't realize is that the rewriting of culture's story is the rewriting of our story.

REWRITING OUR STORY

In 2014 my grandpa and I bought tickets to watch the Los Angeles Kings play the Chicago Blackhawks in the western conference hockey finals.

It was game six, the Kings were up three games to two, and if they won, they were going to the Stanley Cup Playoffs. I had always loved going to games early, that's just how my dad raised us. So I told my grandpa I wanted to be at the game an hour early to watch the warm-ups and soak up the ambiance.

We lived about an hour away from the stadium and as we were about to leave his house I asked him if he wanted me to set the navigation. He looked at me and said, "I know those streets like the back of my hand."

"Okay," I thought. I mean after all he did grow up near downtown, so I trusted him.

As we got closer to the stadium, traffic started to build up—typical LA.

My grandpa, however, decided to "take a back way."

Now, I don't claim to have grown up in LA, but I am decently familiar with the streets, so when he decided to get off the freeway four exits away from our destination, I had some questions.

"Are you sure you know where you're going?" I asked.

"D, I grew up here, I could drive here in my sleep," he responded.

"Okay."

As we were driving through downtown, my grandpa made a left turn on a street he swears he knew, and before you knew it, we were driving the wrong way on a one-way road…

"Pops! This is a one way!" I said.

"Oh, that never used to be a one way," he nervously replied.

Before you knew it, we made two more wrong turns, got somewhat lost, and I finally asked, "Do you want me to put in the address?" He finally conceded and told me to put in the address to Staples Center, we ended up missing the warmups…

Road maps are a lot like our worldview. What we believe about our road maps will either lead us to our destination or it will leave us wandering around downtown LA like the Israelites in the wilderness. Much like our worldview, it will either lead us to the life we desire, or it won't.

Before the modern age, God used to be the one guiding us along, step by step, leading us to our destination. If my grandpa and I didn't have an iPhone, we would have probably been lost and missed the entirety of the game. But my phone was able to get us on the right path to our desired destination. But in a redefining culture, we are left to guide ourselves to the destination we desire. Not only that, we are left to guide ourselves when we also experience loss, pain, and confusion.

This is what we face today in our culture.

We are left to write our own story and determine what is good, true, and beautiful for ourselves; we are left to determine what happiness, freedom, and comfort is for ourselves. Does secularism's unleashing of traditional beliefs actually deliver on its promises for a better, freer life for everyone?

I don't think so.

Because what happens when what makes me happy is your oppressor?

What happens when my truth violates your truth?

or

What I deem as good is your evil?

You get the point.

But even worse than all of these philosophical questions, what happens when we experience pain? We are then left to make meaning of our pain and brokenness. Are we able to attach meaning to our pain that will transform it into our blessing?

Am I even capable of making undesirable circumstances something good?

I think these are questions that we all need to be asking ourselves because the quality of creation will always match and reflect its creator. If we are broken and fragmented people, we will only create things that are broken and fragmented.

I think this is what we are seeing with people in our day, a bunch of innocent sufferers who are living at the expense of themselves because they have bought into a narrative of false freedom that has only deepened enslavement to their wounds.

You, me, or others don't have the ability, capacity, or moral understanding to rewrite a story that brings flourishing, healing, and blessing to everyone.

I don't say this to mock anyone I genuinely applaud culture's attempt to create a more equitable, fair, and just world. I admire people for becoming more empathetic and understanding of people's wounds and traumas. It's just that the foundations these are built on are broken themselves.

We need something and someone who isn't diagnosed with our condition of sin to come and give us an alternate story to live by, one that truly can enable us to live in a world where pain, truth, goodness, and beauty radiate from our lives.

COMPARING STORIES

Jesus came to give us a different road map.

He could have come as a general, a janitor, a chef, or a professional athlete. Instead, He came as a teacher. Someone to awaken our subconscious to a different reality and show us a different way of living.

Jesus understood that something needed to be awakened and redirected in the human heart.

Swiss psychiatrist Carl Jung says, "Until we make the subconscious conscious, it will direct your life, and you will call it fate."[178]

Meaning, when we remain unaware of the things that are shaping our lives, we will attribute the outcomes as "fate" or as we say, "it was or wasn't meant to be."

In a lot of ways, it leaves us with the "this is just how things are" or the "that's just life" view of reality or society.

We have come to accept things in our culture that grieve the Father's heart as normal, for example, death, divorce, and pain.

Those are not things you will find in the Genesis story. We were made to live forever; eternity is placed in our hearts![179] Divorce has become so normalized people aren't even surprised when it happens anymore, and pain, though we all experience it, God never intended it.

We have become too familiar with the stories and narratives of our culture, and Jesus has come to awaken our subconscious to a different reality.

In the Sermon on the Mount, Jesus compared and contrasted teachings: "You have heard it said, but I say to you."

Why did He do this? He wanted to show people how what they believe is contrary to how He believes, because ultimately what you *believe* affects how you will live.

We need to do this same thing with the stories of our culture.

The main characters of the secular story are human rights, individualism, and the sovereignty of the self. When we take a look at what culture says and teaches, a lot of it sounds good and appealing.

For example:

Love is love, is the cultural affirmation of love, but what kind of love?

You need to be true to yourself. Authenticity is good—but at what cost?

Pain is the enemy. Yeah, nobody likes pain, but should it be avoided at all costs?

You do you. Thank God we live in a free country where I have the right to live how I want; can freedom live up to its promises?

We need to become cultural practitioners and learn how to biopsy the culture's beliefs and compare them side by side to Jesus's teachings because both can't be true. The way of Jesus and the way of culture are diametrically opposed to one another.

Secularism leaves you with two options: either leave Jesus's teachings behind or shape His teachings to match your reality.

Take a look:

> You have heard it said . . . *You need to be true to yourself,*
> But I say to you . . . *Be true to the one who made you.*[180]

We have already seen culture can't define truth, it doesn't allow us to! So how can we be true to ourselves? Being true to Jesus is about giving ourselves to the one who is true, and He can create a true reality in and through our lives.

> You have heard it said . . . *You do you,*
> But I say to you . . . *Count others above yourself.*[181]

Culture says no one has the right to dictate for you how to live. You are the king and queen of your world. The way of Jesus says you really find your life when you give it for the sake of other people. When you assume responsibility for the world and those around you, you birth life into the world.

> You have heard it said . . . *My body, my choice,*
> But I say to you . . . *This is my body, broken for you.*[182]

Culture says dispose of anything that may be inconvenient for you. The way of Jesus says you are never an inconvenience, I love you, and I am willing to have my body broken so that you can find life.

> You have heard it said . . . *You only live once,*
> But I say to you . . . *Live in light of your future glory.*[183]

Culture says you are the most important thing, and the only way to find life and happiness is to fill your life with as much pleasure as possible. The way of Jesus says this life is just a foreshadowing of your real life. Don't settle for the things of this world, live for a life that will last forever.

> You have heard it said . . . *Become the best version of yourself,*
> But I say to you . . . *I am faithful to complete my work in you.*[184]

Culture says, you are responsible for determining what is good, true, and beautiful—you need to create your own sacred cosmos. The way of Jesus says He will be the one who does the work in you; all you need to do is stay in and trust His faithfulness and commitment to you.

> You have heard it said . . . *Pain is your enemy,*
> But I say to you . . . *You are perfected in pain.*[185]

Culture says if it hurts, it's not good and should be avoided. The way of Jesus says pain, though uncomfortable, is the very thing that will bring healing to you and the world around you.

As you can see, the way of Jesus and the way of culture are so vastly different! This isn't a declaration to stay away from culture, it's actually the opposite. We are to be a beacon of hope in our culture and show how a life with Jesus is more lasting and satisfying.

The disordered desires of culture are leading to disordered lives, and what we believe will lead us to a satisfied life. And this will draw others to Jesus.

11

DISORDERED LOVES, DISORDERED LIVES

We just know something isn't right with ourselves and the world.

Like a meal that's missing an ingredient or like the weird noise a car makes after hitting something, we have an inner voice that is telling us that we aren't who we are meant to be. I think that is why we as humans have this natural desire to transcend expectation, crave the attention to be known, and enjoy a good compliment!

We live in this world with the desire to be seen, valued, and appreciated for who we are. Yet in moments of pain, inadequacy, or insecurity, we lash out. We become defensive, hurt, and isolated beings. We look to consume instead of contribute, and we begin to doubt instead of love.

There is a void in our heart that can't seem to be satisfied no matter how much we try to fill it.

Pastor Jon Tyson says that we all have "glory deficits."[186] Jon coined this term to describe how we all have this sense of inadequacy, and we are overwhelmed with the existential dread of being insignificant, stemming from a disconnection between our potential as people and our current reality which is affected by sin.

In other words, no matter how much we try and try to fill our hearts with things, we are always left feeling empty and unsatisfied.

But this hasn't always been the case. This desire that we face on the daily is a consequence of the fall and sin entering into the human story.

In his book *Reordered Love, Reordered Lives,* David Naugle talks about how God didn't create humanity with these deficits in our heart. Naugle shows how, in Genesis, God created a beautiful world and garden and charges Adam to sustain and cultivate the garden, giving Adam work and a vocation. Adam was allowed to enjoy the world which God created. He could eat from the garden for his pleasure and delight.

Despite all the abundance in Adam's life, the only thing that wasn't good was that man was alone. So, God made Eve out of Adam, displaying a beautiful poetic notion of intimacy and oneness. Adam and Eve were one, even in name, and enjoyed selfless sacrificial love, unhindered communication, and full acceptance of one another. Genesis says that both were naked and not ashamed.[187]

David Naugle makes the point that Genesis highlights six components humans need to live a life that is fulfilled.[188]

1. Spiritual - Made to enjoy union with God. Our identity is formed in Him.

2. Vocation - God gave Adam a vocation. We were made to have fulfilling work.

3. Social - We were made for human companionship, community, marriage, all steeped in love.

4. Nutrition - Food and drink are a generous gift. God gave an abundance to enjoy.

5. Sabbath - We were made to rest and enjoy our world, work, and lives.

6. Habitat - God gave us a world of beauty to enjoy. We are called to take pleasure in our world and delight in what God created for us.

This is why we are driven to find purpose, meaning, and intimacy with one another.

However, when the fall happened, all six of the components became distorted, and the start of our glory deficits were birthed. In order to heal our deficits, Jesus came to offer salvation for the world.

Dutch theologian Herman Bavinck puts it this way, "The essence of the Christian religion consists in the reality that the creation of the Father, ruined by sin, is restored in the death of the Son of God and recreated by the grace of the Holy Spirit into a Kingdom of God."[189]

This is why Jesus is oftentimes referred to as the "Second Adam."[190] What was good, created by God, was deformed by Adam, and now has been reformed again in Jesus. But the only way to have our glory deficits healed is to come to Jesus and allow Him to heal those deficits.

This is why what we believe about the world, creation, pain, and the fragmentation of our lives is so important.

If you believe in the God of the Bible, your view of happiness is found in a loving God as creator and redeemer of the broken world.

If you believe in some other god, then your happiness is tied to your ability to "be good" and to properly worship your deity.

Pantheism, the way to be happy is to live in harmony and peace with the "Universe."

Pluralism/ Polytheism / Coexist, the way to be happy is karma.

Naturalism, the way to be happy is by exalting yourself above all and enjoying the world and adapting with the changes.

Materialism, the way to be happy is to find as much pleasure by consuming as much as you can.

Secularism, the way to be happy is "you do you!"

Paganism, the way to be happy is by worshiping the gods of self: the environment, social issues, technology, money, career, body, etc.

The glory deficits that we feel have to be filled with something, and we attempt to fill them with whatever we can.

DISORDERED DESIRES

Like everyone, I have a broken and painful story.

I've experienced abandonment from a parent, sexual abuse, emotional abuse, and come from a broken family. The way that I attempted to fill my glory deficit was by relationships. I would often look for affirmation from girls and fill the void with the feeling of being wanted.

I remember one time during a breakup my ex shouted, "I can't be the thing that fixes you."

And she was right, but what I have come to realize is that she was a disordered love.

A disordered love is the misplacing of order in which something should be loved. For me it was relationships, for you it could be work, school, family, money, or even food. In the church we often think of disordered loves as things that are bad or sinful.

And I don't agree with that.

God created this earth and the things in it for us to enjoy and to satisfy.

Work is satisfying.

Sex is satisfying.

Friendship is satisfying.

A ribeye steak paired with a nice Zinfandel is satisfying.

The problem is that those things can only bring a certain level of satisfaction in our lives. When we expect sex, work, food, or money to be the ultimate source of satisfaction in our lives, we do all we can to have as much of them as possible.

The more we possess those things we attempt to fill our deficits with, the less satisfying they actually become. The glory deficits in our hearts need to get filled with something. We tend to fill those voids with things that can't love us back.

St. Augustine calls this the "scale of value." "There is a scale of value stretching from earthly to heavenly realities, from the visible to the invisible; and the inequality between these goods makes possible the existence of them all." [191]

David Naugle describes it further, "God is one thing, angels are another, as are people, terriers, red oaks, squash, rocks, and dirt. Each item fits in God's overall scheme of creation. The nature of things in the hierarchy is unchangeable, and so is the kind of satisfaction it can provide when we are related to it through love." [192]

When we expect things that can't love us back to fill the wound, pain, and deficits in our heart, it only leads us to deeper pain, disillusionment, and dissatisfaction. This reality of worsening pain and dissatisfaction creates a domino effect that leads to further fragmentation.

THE DOMINO EFFECT

The Bible refers to misplaced hierarchy as idolatry.

What the Bible teaches about idolatry is that, even though there is no such thing as "other gods," humans make gods out of the gifts that God has given through creation.[193]

Even though human beings create these gods, idolatry still makes physical demands.

In his letter to the Galatians, Paul says, "The acts of the flesh are obvious: sexual immorality, impurity and debauchery; idolatry and witchcraft; hatred, discord, jealousy, fits of rage, selfish ambition, dissensions, factions and envy; drunkenness, orgies, and the like."[194]

Notice what Paul is saying.

First, he lists three general words for sexual sin (physical sin).

Then he lists two types of pagan idolatry (spiritual sin).

Finally, he moves from spiritual sin back to physical sin.

Paul's point is that idolatry will lead you into greater sin, even though idols aren't real, they will still make physical demands on your life.

Psalms 115 says, "Those who make them will be like them, and so will all who trust in them."[195]

When our desires become disordered, it will lead to disordered lives. The tricky part is even things that are good can become harmful for us. Let's look at the six components from Genesis that we spoke about earlier through the lens of disordered love.

1. Vocation: Work can either be a great joy or burden.

    Having a sense of vocation was supposed to bless and enhance our lives. Instead, work has become something we are enslaved to. In the US, 52% of people struggle from burnout.[196] We choose careers based on income, status, and power instead of regenerative work that can bring healing and redemption to the world around us. We've become unhappy with work and made the goal of one's life to reach retirement with enough money to finally live out their dreams.

2. Social: Sex, what a gift!

    A physical act that creates union, intimacy, and oneness like nothing else. Sex is something that is pleasurable and satisfying. It has the power to procreate, build up, and restore love. The irony about sex is that it often leads to heartbreak, disconnectedness, and hatred. Of women, 54% reported that they regretted their first time having sex.[197]

3. Nutrition: Food is a great thing!

    But when food is used to numb the pain, silence the anxiety, or create comfort it gives birth to an unhealthy lifestyle that can lead to a shortened life. The irony is that food is supposed to prolong life, yet in America, food is often the comforting killer.

4. Sabbath: We don't sabbath, instead we vacation.

    In our attempt to escape our exhaustion from work, we fly 15 hours to Europe, charge everything on our credit cards, fight with our spouses and loved ones nonstop because we're burnt out from work and jet lag, all so we can take a photo on the marble streets of Santorini, so that we can post it on Instagram to make our coworkers and family jealous.

5. Habitat: Creation, what beauty!

    We use creation for our own gain and benefits instead of caring and stewarding the world around us. We've lost all sense of wonder—we are more fascinated with TikTok than Yosemite. We have made ghettos out of a glorious world.

6. Spiritual: God is a way to manipulate the universe in our favor.

    Jesus isn't Lord, but He is someone who can bless me and help me become my most "authentic self." Our prayers are self-centered, mostly aimed at the items in which we want most. We have taken Jesus's invitation of prayer and flipped it in a way that is self-serving.

Lord's Prayer	Our Prayer
Our Father in heaven,	Deliver me from the evil one
Hallowed be Your name,	Lead me not into temptation
Your Kingdom come,	Forgive those who sinned against me,
Your will be done,	Forgive me,
On earth as it is in heaven.	Give us today our daily bread
Give us today our daily bread.	Your will be done on earth as in heaven
And forgive us our debts,	Your Kingdom come
As we also have forgiven our debtors.	Hallowed be Your name
And lead us not into temptation,	Our Father in heaven
But deliver us from the evil one.	In Jesus's name.

We wonder why our prayers go unanswered.

None of this is meant to sound harsh. If I am being honest, I am mostly writing this about myself. It is so easy for us to get consumed with what our culture's vision is for happiness, goodness, and truth. But I think if we are honest, we can see why the secular beliefs aren't living up to their promises. When our scales of value are off, we live lives that are unbalanced, ultimately causing more harm to ourselves than good.

We need to shift our love and desire back to its original design so that we can love and enjoy the things of life in a way that doesn't cause more harm or pain to our lives.

LOVING THE GIFT, NOT THE GIVER

The book of Romans is a theological feast!

I will not dive into all the ins and outs of the book. We will focus on the first chapter. Chapter 1 in the book of Romans gives us an insight into the struggles of humanity.

"They exchanged the truth about God for a lie and worshiped and served created things rather than the Creator—who is forever praised. Amen."[198]

Humans have the tendency to worship the gift and not the giver of the gift. Paul doesn't argue by saying created things are bad. Paul is saying that the failure to acknowledge God as the creator of created things is what is ultimately the issue.

One doesn't look at the Sistine Chapel and think to themselves: *Wow, look at how that painting created itself!*

No, the painting points to the artist behind the painting.

We behold the beauty of the Sistine Chapel and the mastery of Michelangelo.

This is the point that Paul makes; looking at creation, the sheer enjoyment of things created should point to the fact that there is a loving and intentional heart behind all of creation. Creation itself points to the existence of God![199]

Paul continues by saying, if you want to see and know the power of God, look at creation! There should be no reason for your doubt, unbelief, or idolatry. Creation should lead you into worship of God, not the worship of created things.

Because human beings failed to give thanks and acknowledge God as the great giver of gifts, Romans says that, "God gave them over to their sinful desires."[200]

The important thing to notice here is that God isn't punishing humanity. He is simply allowing nature to take its course. Disordered love will lead to disordered lives.

An improper view of yourself, sex, work, money, food, working out, etc., will always lead to a life that is disordered. It will lead you to a road of destruction. Why? Just as we are created beings, the things which we give ourselves to outside of God alone are created things as well and therefore aren't suitable to build your life on.

If you build your life on these things, the foundation of your life will come crashing down when rain and storms come.

There was a colleague of mine named Katie (not her real name,) who was a personal trainer at the gym I worked at. Katie was beautiful—she caught the eye of every guy who walked in the gym.

At the time, she was casually dating my best friend.

She was a really sweet girl. Her dad was a former US Olympic soccer player, she grew up in the church, was very generous with her wealth, and was intentional with everyone she spoke with. Just a stand-up person. She was also a hopeless romantic. She always talked about how she wanted to be swept off her feet.

However, she really struggled in her relationship with her dad. He had a lot of money and would give her money every month, but that is all he would give her. He never took the time to be intentional with her. So, often, she sought affirmation and attention from guys.

Katie and I would talk whenever she would come over to the house about our life, hopes, and dreams. Listening to her, I could just hear how she longed to be loved. Eventually Katie and my friend stopped seeing each other, and I started to notice a trend in Katie's life. Katie would find a guy that she liked, fall head over heels, post about him on Instagram about how he is the LOML (love of my life), they would move in together, and after a year they would break up.

Katie would then begin her "self-help journey."

Read the books about personal development.

Rededicate herself to the church and make a vow of celibacy.

She would focus on the gym and get back into phenomenal shape.

Post inspirational quotes in her bikini on her IG story.

Get a new tattoo with her favorite Bible verse.

Get her lips filled, Botox, or some other kind of cosmetic work done.

And right about summertime, a 6'4" tattooed monster with a beard would catch her eye, and she would fall in love.

I knew Katie for about four years, and this same circle of events happened to her over and over and over again; it was almost seasonal.

Now, I don't say this to make light of Katie. I actually deeply care about her.

All Katie wanted was to be loved. The wounds and pain from her childhood pursued things like men, working out, and sex to fill the void. In her pursuit to get pursued, she built her life on temporal and broken foundations that ultimately led to a repetitive crash.

I am positive that Katie didn't mean or want to repeat the same cycle again and again, but this is what sin does to us.

Naugle puts it this way, "Sin within leads us to decisions and actions repeated so often that after a while we can't resist them anymore. We still believe that these things hold the key to a better life, where in the form of alcohol, psychoactive drugs, work, food, pornography, sex, people, shopping, gambling, television, movies, music, sports, the internet, you name it. When we recognize the destructive consequences of these uncontrollable behaviors, we resolve to do something about it, but typically with little self-improvement."[201]

This is where the cycle of sin and pain multiply in your life. This leads to the corroding of your heart and life.

DESIRE, CURIOSITY, WONDER, AND THANKFULNESS

C.S. Lewis once wrote, "It would seem that Our Lord finds our desires not too strong, but too weak. We are half-hearted creatures, fooling about with drink and sex and ambition when infinite joy is offered us, like an ignorant child who wants to go on making mud pies in a slum because he cannot imagine what is meant by the offer of a holiday at the sea. We are far too easily pleased."[202]

I would tend to agree with C.S. Lewis. Ashley's desires for love, acceptance, and being wanted weren't so out of control that she gave into every and any man who gave her eyes.

It's that her desires weren't strong enough.

Desire in Latin derives from the verb "*desiderare*," which means "to long for" or "to wish for." However, *desiderare's* prefix *de-* meaning "from" or "the," combined with *sidus* translates to "star" or "heavenly body." The phrase *desidere* literally means "from the stars" or "the heavenly body" showing an original connection to the transcendent.

All of our desires are signposts, billboards, flashing arrow signs that point to something beyond themselves.

Bruce Marshall wrote, "The young man who rings the bell at the brothel is unconsciously looking for God."[203]

We need to reassess our priorities and values. C.S. Lewis called these "First & Second things."[204]

His argument was that "You can't get second things by putting them first; you can get second things only by putting first things first."

In other words, having your desires in proper alignment will give you the freedom to enjoy your desires in a much richer and fruitful way.

> Misplaced desires = crooked and pain-filled life
>
> Directed desires = satisfying life

Work becomes life-giving to you and others when directed towards God.

Sex becomes different, amazing, and safe when confined in God's design.

Food creates unforgettable moments when consumed with self-control.

Sabbath becomes a day to celebrate when you don't try and out-provide God.

Habitat is enjoyed when embraced with thanksgiving.

Spiritual life is blessed when He is the organizing principle of your life.

Sounds amazing right? But I would also say that in order for our desire to grow, we also need to grow in curiosity of who God is!

Go back to the moment when you first fell in love with someone. Your curiosity about that person is off the charts. You wonder what makes them laugh, what their favorite food is, what their favorite genre of music is, or what movies they like. You're on a journey of searching and curiosity.

We don't view God this way.

He's just up there and we're down here. We don't view God as the Lover of Lovers; we view him as the Dictator of Dictators.

We must obey or else . . .

Our desires are off because we haven't grown in curiosity about Him.

Marriage counselors often share how a lack of curiosity in one another is one of the reasons marriages lose their spark and why affairs occur.

The Bible shows that God is a jealous lover!

Disordered desire in the Bible is pictured as spiritual adultery. God is jealous for us, not in some insecure way, but He's looking to woo us. Yet we fail to recognize it because we are consumed with other things![205]

The book of Ezekiel talks about how God wants to be generous to His bride (His people), but His bride is consumed with disordered desire towards others.

We are often so curious about things that don't lead to life—drugs, being drunk, that one night stand, or driving that one car.

Imagine what our life would look like if we grew in curiosity about the Creator of the world. Would our desires change? Would our interests change? Would pain and suffering affect us differently?

Moses is a great example of someone who continued to grow in curiosity after every encounter with God.

Moses had an amazing relationship with God; they spoke to one another like one spoke to a friend.[206] But that wasn't good enough for Moses—he wasn't content with what he knew about God—he knew there was more.

God and Moses are having a conversation about whether or not God is going to go with Israel into the promised land. They had just fallen into idolatry and God had enough.

Moses pleads with God, *Your presence is the only thing that separates us from the other nations, we need you to come with us.*

God honors Moses and begins to affirm Moses's faithfulness towards him.

Moses, caught up in the moment, asks God if he could see His face.

Most of us would be content just to have the conversations with God that Moses had. We wish Jesus would speak to us as immediately and clearly as He did with Moses. Yet Moses wasn't content; he wanted to see God face-to-face.

In my own life, I had come to realize that the reason why my curiosity wouldn't grow towards God was because I had no idea who God actually was in the first place. I knew He "loved" me intellectually, but I never experienced His love because I never gave myself to Him. Once I gave my whole self to Him—my pain, my wounds, my insecurities, my sin, my strengths, gifts, talents, and desires—my curiosity for who He is began to grow. Our curiosity needs to be like Moses, because it's the curiosity that leads to wonder.

To be lost in wonder means to be completely captivated, mesmerized, or awestruck by something to the point where you become unaware of your surroundings or lose track of time. It describes a state of intense fascination or amazement that fully engrosses your attention and senses.

King David puts it this way, "One thing I ask from the Lord, this only do I seek: that I may dwell in the house of the Lord all the days of my life, to gaze on the beauty of the Lord and to seek Him in His temple."[207]

King David wrote this during wartime.[208]

Nothing else mattered to King David other than gazing on the beauty of God.

Even though people were trying to kill him and enemies were coming for his throne, nation, and people.

Picture that for a second.

I mean really, take a moment to put yourself in David's situation. When your life is in shambles, when your life feels threatened, do You really stop in the middle of your storm and say, "Jesus, show me your beauty!"

Nooooo!

I'm usually say something like, "Jesus, save me! I need your help!"

The last thing I care about is His beauty. I'm more like, "Give me the quiver and sword and I will help You destroy my problem!"

That's probably why David is considered a man after God's own heart and I'm not . . .

David understood that whether he won or lost, his life was found in God. David wasn't captivated by fear or anxiety because he had already been captivated by God!

Being lost in God's wonder is what enables us to give thanks for everything.

As I mentioned before, St. Ignatius believed that the root of all sin could be traced back to a lack of gratitude.

When you assume that life, happiness, and the fulfillment of your desires is a right and not a gift, you will travel down a path of disillusionment, discontentment, and deconstruction.

Thanksgiving keeps us on the correct path.

I think it's quite ironic that we celebrate Thanksgiving and prepare for Black Friday on the same day. One moment you're holding hands, going around the table declaring in front of your family what you're grateful for, then after dinner your bumping elbows with your neighbor in line so you can get to the Black Friday sales before him.

Oh, the irony!

We are disillusioned with what our hearts are really yearning for, so we buy things we don't need, with money we don't have, to please people we don't know.

But practicing thanksgiving (not the holiday) reorders your desire and in turn reorders your life.

Thanksgiving will help you:

- Enjoy your run-down car more
- From going into extreme debt over an unrenovated house
- Stop from having an affair
- Erase competition between your peers
- Enjoy your job, family, and tax bracket

Thanksgiving, ultimately, removes the bombardment of worries and allows you to enjoy God for who He is.

Your desires matter!

They matter to you, and they matter to God! Therefore, they need to be checked as much as you check your social media.

Because if you don't, you just might lose yourself.

12

LOST IN A MASQUERADE

In the Gospel of Mark there is a story of a man who lived in a cave and was demon possessed.[209] This man doesn't have a name, all that is known of him is that he had super strength, he would cry out day and night, and he would cut himself with stones.

Obviously, this guy had caused some sort of trouble with people, because the gospel mentions that he had previously been bound with chains, which he ripped off himself, and that no one was strong enough to subdue him anymore.

Not a guy you would hope to run into as you were walking the roads from town to town.

Sure enough, Jesus does.

As Jesus and His disciples approach, the man starts to run towards Jesus. Now if I'm a disciple I'm thinking to myself, "Grab a rock, cause a diversion, ruuun!"

But in clasic Jesus fashion, He decides to ask the guy what his name was . . . typical Jesus, able to see the person at their core beyond the surface or scary exterior.

The man replies that his name is Legion, "For we are many."[210]

The name gives us insight to what's going on with the man. In Roman military terms a "legion" normally consisted of 5,000 soldiers. What is being conveyed is that the man is possessed by 5,000 demons.

No, that is not a typo . . .

This man was filled with 5,000 different persons and personalities.

Imagine what it must have been like to be in his head.

Each voice was telling him a different story about who he was and what to do with his life.

Jesus sees the man and drives the demons out of him and brings healing to his mind and body. The gospel records that when Jesus first met the man, he was naked, out of his mind, and bleeding. After Jesus heals the man, it says that he is clothed, sitting calmly, and in his right mind.

I think many of us are the same as this man, not in the sense that we are possessed, but that we have 5,000 different masks that we wear in an attempt to cultivate this ideal version of ourselves.

This leaves us like the man in the cave, lost and out of our mind, not knowing who we actually are. With each new mask that we put on, we simultaneously cut off a piece of ourselves, leaving us more unrecognizable than we were before.

More often than I would like, people have come into my office after hitting rock bottom and say, "I just don't know how I got here." In those conversations, I try to bring up life-altering moments from their story and ask them to reflect on how they responded to those moments. More often than not, in attempts to deal with the pain and uncertainty of those moments, people hide and try to cover up their pain with a mask that disguises itself as healing.

Compile enough of those moments together and we slowly become like the man in the cave who possesses 5,000 masks—5,000 disguise mechanisms that ultimately lead to complete and utter deformity of who we were meant to be.

5,000 YOUS

After high school, I went to visit a friend who went to a university not too far from where I lived. Her college was having a masquerade ball, and she invited me to go with her.

A masquerade is an event where everyone dresses in their best. Men wear a tux, and women wear some elegant dress and before you enter the ballroom there are a plethora of masks you can choose from.

Typically, everything from the nose up to the forehead is covered, revealing just enough of your face to still recognize who you are.

Each mask had a different mechanism for how to wear it. Some masks came with a stick to hold so that you could reveal yourself as much as you pleased, and others came with ribbons to tie it on.

Typically, in large groups of people I remain to myself—large crowds freak me out. However, when I put on my mask, I noticed something different about myself: I became more outgoing, cheeky, and relaxed.

The mask brought some sort of safety and comfort where I felt I could be at ease.

There was this sense that I could be whoever I wanted without anybody really knowing me or "seeing" me. The insecurities of "being liked" or "accepted" were gone. I didn't have to worry about being hurt; I could just have fun without any fear.

This is how many of us live.

This is why social media is so addictive for us. We get to create a world and false reality of who we want people to see us as without the risk of being truly seen and hurt. We cultivate different identities, personalities, and different stories to live by with the almighty "post" button, creating our own sacred cosmos.

With each new trend, we begin to change and grasp at different masks and present ourselves in ways that we deem will be accepted and affirmed by society. Mark Sayer describes it like this, "Our identities today are constantly being remade. As soon as one public persona is mastered, it becomes out of date . . . the reconstruction of our identities is normal. Whole industries are built around offering people various ways to reinvent themselves. Reinvention isn't just encouraged in our culture; it is demanded."[211]

We do this subconsciously without even realizing that we do it. But as time continues to move forward, what we fail to realize is that with each new identity that we curate, we subtly begin to lose ourselves.

Or in other words, we become lost in a masquerade.

A little experiment to prove my point: go and look back at your high school photos and see the various identities you portrayed yourself as.

For me, my freshman year I portrayed myself as "skater Dakota." I had the Linkin Park beanie, tight pants, long hair, and rebellious attitude. Sophomore through senior year, I realized I was good at sports, so I tossed out the tight pants, beanie, and Linkin Park and exchanged them for shorts, a baseball hat, and rap music.

Now, as you're looking back on these photos, think about your friend groups. Did you maintain your same friend group? Or did your friends change when your style and interests changed?

For me it was the latter.

After you're done looking at your high school photos, do the same for each year until your present date. On a piece of paper, write down each identity that you held.

I think you will be surprised.

Now I don't bring any of this up as an indictment against anyone. As we grow up, we are on a journey of self-discovery, figuring out our likes, dislikes, growing into our personality, and whatnot.

But the question I often reflect on is: Do we change as we age, or do we change as a result of our circumstances?

During a time of silence and solitude I was reflecting on my life and how much I have changed as a person. I wanted to trace my likes, dislikes, and my attitude towards people and the world throughout my life.

All throughout my childhood, I remember my dad telling me how social I was. He always used to say, "You could walk in a room full of strangers and talk to people as if they were your best friend." It's always strange when he says that because today, I hate new places. I am scared of large crowds and getting to know new people; I absolutely hate the "first day of school" feeling.

When I meet new people, I am often very talkative, so people find it strange when I tell them I am an "introvert." The reality is, the past Dakota that my dad speaks about is someone I don't know. Again, I get it, people change. It's clear I'm not the same person I was when I was as a child or a teenager. But the question remains, did I change this drastically because of my age, or was something else going on?

During my time of reflection, I thought back on my dad's comments to me and to moments as a kid. My dad was right: I love people, I am fascinated by people, I love hosting people, hanging out with people, making people feel seen and honored, and just all around being with people.

Yet, I also realized that when I hang around people, the idea of it always seems better than the reality of it.

So, what was going on? Why was there this divide?

What I came to realize is that the pain of my life had formed me more than I realized. Over time I had become scarred and hardened. In attempts to cover my shame, pain, and wounds I would mask them up, presenting myself as a whole and put-together person who is charismatic and outgoing. Yet internally, I would feel social fatigue. But what I discovered was the reason I continually get tired from hanging out with people *isn't* because I'm an introvert. The social exhaustion comes from holding up the mask. Holding up your masquerades long enough will wear you out.

Truth of the matter is that I'm not an introvert, I'm a wounded extrovert who just wants to be loved for who I am, yet I don't even know who I am, so I put on a mask in an attempt to find myself and be loved and welcomed by my peers. I am socially exhausted because I don't have the stamina to maintain the façade and hold up the mask.

As time continued on, I began to examine how I act, think, and feel when I am around people. What I noticed about myself was that I acted differently when I was out in public than I did when I was at home with my wife and kids.

One evening Brenda, Kennedi, and I were having a dance party in the living room to one of Kennedi's favorite songs. Kennedi was doing her thing, Bren was jiving along, and so was I. For the record, I can't dance to save my life; it's as if the rhythm gene skipped me. Nonetheless, I didn't care, I was having the time of my life, not caring what anyone thought, I was just enjoying dancing with my daughter.

Out of nowhere it hit me. I would never dance like this in public or in front of anyone who wasn't my wife or kids. I had a glimpse of freedom, a moment where I was metaphorically "naked and unashamed" about who I was. Then I thought to myself, "Why can't I be like this in front of anyone?" All of a sudden, a dark shadow of shame filled my gut, and I began asking myself, "Who am I? Who am I really?"

I am one way in front of my wife, kids, and parents. Yet I am someone completely different in front of my friends, peers, and co-workers.

Reflecting on this brought feelings of shame and losing myself. As I went to bring these emotions to Jesus I felt a sense of hopelessness. *Would I ever find who I really am?*

LOST BEYOND REPAIR

The longer I walk with Jesus the more I am convinced that the Devil's tactic isn't so much an attempt to convince you that God doesn't love you, it's more so about trying to convince you that you are beyond repair.

I truly believe that most—not all—but most Christians know that God loves them. But I am more sure about the fact that most Christians believe that their current insecurities, shame, and cycles of sin will always be a part of their life.

The reason this tactic is so effective is because it turns our gaze from Jesus being our source of identity to ourselves. If we are beyond repair, then the temptation for us becomes one of hiding and running from God, shielding ourselves with the masks of our day.

The lies of shame and the idea that we are beyond repair are exposed all throughout scripture.

Adam and Eve hid from God because of their shame.[212] When they became aware of their nakedness and their separation of oneness, Adam and Eve took leaves to cover themselves and hid themselves from one another.

Can you see the similarities between Adam and Eve and ourselves?

We, like them, use masks to hide our wounds, pain, nakedness, and shame. We believe the lies that if people were to really see who we are they will either reject us or wound us.

Or, how many of us are like the man in the cave who was possessed?

We mask ourselves because we feel like we are isolated in this world. Even though deep down we crave the intimacy that Adam and

Eve had with one another, our masks isolate us and hinder us from making real genuine connections with other people. This leads us on a path of self-destruction like the man in the cave, hurting ourselves with disordered desires in order to silence the pain. When our pain becomes the loudest voice in our mind, it is nearly impossible to discern between God's voice, our pain's voice, and our own voice.

Many of us live our lives with what I call *functional oppression*.

Functional oppression is the internal battles that we have grown accustomed to; the negative thoughts about ourselves, addictions, pain, and trauma that affect how we see God, ourselves, and the world. Just like a functioning alcoholic can get drunk and properly work, drive, and communicate, those who face functional oppression live every day with their soul removed from society, are numb to the pain, and have no idea who they truly are.

We truly become lost; lost in our faith, in our identity, and lost in reality. Life becomes this unsolvable, unrelenting force of pain that never ceases to relinquish its grasp on us. There is something about the force of pain that leaves us with two solutions: either give up or give in.

Giving up is the sense of hopelessness that many feel that leads to self-harm, shame, or even worse, the taking of one's life.

Giving in is the sense of adopting the world's vision of curating identity, meaning, and happiness.

Is there a way out of this functional oppression that many of us feel?

Yes!

NAZARETH OF THE WEST

The United States is the Nazareth of the West. Not because Jesus is from here or because His family or desired model of church lives here, but because we are too familiar with Him. We hear of how He does miracles, helps people overcome trial and turmoil, and how some find themselves in Him and without any real devotion or desire to follow Him, we feel this entitlement that He owes us something because "we are a Christian culture."

When Jesus first came out of the wilderness, the gospel of Luke records how Jesus went to His hometown to publicly declare His mission. He proclaimed His mission as such:

> "The Spirit of the Lord is on me,
> because he has anointed me
> to proclaim good news to the poor.
> He has sent me to proclaim freedom for the prisoners
> and recovery of sight for the blind,
> to set the oppressed free,
> to proclaim the year of the Lord's favor."[213]

This is quite remarkable, so let's unpack this.

- He came to proclaim good news to the poor. Meaning, that he came to share about an alternate way of living life. "Good News" in Greek is *euangelizomai* which carried political and messianic implications that life would be different under His rulership.

- He came to proclaim freedom for those who were imprisoned to themselves. Meaning, to declare innocence and freedom of those who were once guilty.

- He came to recover the sight of the blind. Meaning, to give humanity a fresh perspective and a new outlook on life that won't lead people down the path of imprisonment or bondage.

- He came to set the oppressed free. Meaning, the oppression of sin, self-hatred, and our disordered desires are no longer the defining force in our life. But not only that . . .

- He came to proclaim that the year of the Lord's favor has arrived. The year of the Lord's favor is the year of Jubilee, a reference to the Old Testament. The year of Jubilee was a year of release and restoration, a forgiveness of debt, releasing of slaves, and whatever was lost was now given back.[214]

Jesus has compassion and grace for you and longs for all of us to be restored and healed from our wounds. He wants to restore and give back what was taken from you: the innocence that you once possessed when you first came into the world, the peace you once had before life came in like a hurricane and flipped your world upside down, and hope of renewal.

In the deepest parts of our hearts, we want to believe that these statements by Jesus are true, but I think if we take an honest reflection deep into our heart's, part of us doesn't believe that Jesus will do that for us. Part of what has made us turn our backs to Jesus is that we have grown cynical in His ability to redeem us. We have seen too many unanswered prayers, innocent suffering, experienced too much pain, and seen too much moral failure of those who hold spiritual authority to believe that Jesus is just as active in people's lives today as He was back then. So much so that when we hear about people getting healed, delivered, or redeemed, we become suspicious of their reality and believe their story is one of self-righteousness or their religious mask that they are hiding behind.

We need to learn to believe in Jesus again.

We can't allow our circumstances to outweigh the eternal reality of Jesus's claims. When all we do is treat Jesus as someone who can make our life better, we become like the people of Nazareth who failed to see a miracle from Jesus.

One way to see if you are like the people of Nazareth is to take an audit of your prayer life. How much of your prayer life is about you? Prayer for favor on the new job or favor that you will get the house or that you find a spouse?

I am not knocking these prayers, but the reality is if all we do is treat Jesus as someone to get things from, we lose out on what it really means to be made in the image of God. To take His character and nature and fill the earth with it, by creating a world that is good, true, and beautiful; not escaping the pressure points of pain but walking through pain, allowing it to do its sacred work of refining, forming, and shaping us into something beautiful for the rest of the world to find hope in.

One final thought.

There is a beautiful word in Hebrew—"*Ishon*"— it's an idiom for the saying "apple of one's eye." For us, this phrase is one of affection or desire towards someone. In Hebrew *Ishon* has the same meaning but goes one step deeper. Have you ever been so close to someone's face and looked into their eyes that you begin to see yourself in their eyes?

That's the picture.

God, when His people are struggling and in pain, refers to His people as the "apple of His eye" as a promise and a reminder that He will be faithful to them even in the midst of their pain and suffering. Why? Because when He sees us, He sees Himself in our eyes and our life.[215]

This is what is important.

God isn't the type of god who is distant in our pain, He isn't someone who is unfamiliar with our pain, He is the one who left His throne in heaven to take on our pain for us, so that we can become like Him. God removed the one thing that separated us from Him—sin. Which is why scripture says that when we remove our mask, God becomes the *Ishon* of our lives, we are then able to gaze on His beauty. It is in this gaze that we begin to see ourselves in His eyes, which leads to transformation into His image.[216]

Hwee Hwee Tan has a line, "You are what your mind thinks about, you are what you contemplate."[217]

If we set our gaze—our contemplation—on God, I think we will find that His story is very similar to ours.

13
MORE SIMILAR THAN EXPECTED

Perhaps no other person has been talked about, written on, and discussed more than Jesus of Nazareth. Whether you are atheist or religious, there is something compelling about the person of Jesus.

One of the doctrinal truths that Christians believe is that Jesus is God.

He is both fully human and fully God.

Growing up in Sunday school this is something that we know, but I don't think we realize the full implication of what that means. We have become overly familiar with the story of Jesus.

Depending on which church you grew up in, typically when we think of Jesus, we have been taught how Jesus was sent down to earth to die for our sins so that we can go to heaven.

Rarely do we talk about the humanness of Jesus. How Jesus, who is fully God, didn't just come to die for our sins so that we can go to heaven, but Jesus came to show us what it is to be human. Jesus re-writes the story of what the human experience is to look like on earth.

When you compare other religions' stories of how their gods act with people, there is a stark difference to Christianity. Most other deities are distant and don't want to get near humanity, so humans are given rules, laws, and various methods to make their way up to god. In the Christian story, God leaves His throne and comes down towards humanity. Oftentimes we are taught that salvation is something we possess when we accept Jesus as our Lord and Savior. But scripture actually teaches that salvation is something quite different.

Salvation isn't something, it's someone.

Salvation is a person.[218]

Jesus's ministry on earth was to conquer and defeat the ultimate oppressor in people's life—sin and death. Salvation was accomplished in the life, death, and resurrection of Jesus. Yes, through pain, perhaps the most painful death ever known to man, is the way that salvation was accomplished.

Now, He invites us to partake and share in His life, to live as He did, and to reflect Him to the world. Unfortunately, that also means to embrace a life that is filled with pain.

In this chapter, my hope is to paint Jesus in a different way, one that is relatable and human.

Why?

Because Jesus is deeply human.

He knows loneliness, rejection, isolation, and pain—the very struggles that shape our own stories. He faced the pull of temptation yet remained free of sin.[219] His heart felt distant from God at times, even though He is God. (I know, weird concept to grasp.)

His perfection wasn't the result of moralism or religious routine. It didn't come from chasing happiness or avoiding discomfort. It was forged in suffering, in the fire of pain and loss.

Jesus lived fully alive, embracing life with love, joy, and wonder.

He savored good food and wine.

He laughed with friends.

He got frustrated.

He felt the weight of the world and still leaned into love.

He never numbed Himself to suffering.

He never turned away from the hard, holy work of becoming. And in the same way, our own suffering can shape us, refine us, and transform the world around us.

For Jesus, pain wasn't an obstacle to be avoided; it was a force to be embraced. He knew it had a purpose, even when we don't fully understand how it's shaping us.

The story of Jesus shows us that we can trust Him because He knows what it is to experience what we feel.

LIFE ON EARTH

Jesus is God, which means He created everything, there is nothing outside of Himself that He didn't create.[220]

When He created the world, He made it in such a way that He would partner with humanity to fill the world with His glory. In other words, humanity would have a part in the perfecting of the world.

However, Adam and Eve had their own plans.

This is why God had to come to earth as a human. What was broken through humanity had to be fixed by humanity. In order to restore every aspect of the human story, He had to take on the full experience of humanity—from conception to death.

I'm not going to lie, sometimes that idea trips me up . . . when God was born, He had to wear diapers!

That is a trip!

Yet it had to be done.

We don't know much about Jesus's childhood, teenage years, or early adulthood. The only things we know about Jesus's upbringing is from the Gospel of Luke when he was twelve years old and went into the temple without His parents' permission[221] and the fact that He was a carpenter.[222]

He had four brothers and two sisters,[223] who weren't his full biological siblings. A lot of us know what it's like to grow up in mixed families—it's not always easy. Especially when your brother is God.

I mean, imagine being Jesus's sibling, hearing your mom say to you, "Dakota, why can't you be more like Jesus?" I have a little brother; nothing is more annoying than when your parents remind you how great he is.

Jesus went through puberty; He had to learn what it is like to navigate the changes of His body.

He probably grew up most of His life feeling misunderstood and like an outsider.

Jesus knew what it was like to grow up with a single mom. We don't know exactly when, but we know that Joseph died before Jesus went into His public ministry. Even though Joseph wasn't His biological father, Jesus still knew what it felt like to lose someone whom He loved.

That also means that part of His adult life He had to take on the burden of being the family's provider. His trade as a carpenter had to pay the bills; there were seven other mouths to feed.

Jesus grew up in a time of Roman rule. The Jews were taxed heavily by the Romans, which means Jesus had to balance a budget and be truthful in paying His taxes.

Jesus loved hanging out with the boys!

John 2 talks about Him being invited to a wedding, which shows He obviously had friends that He was close to. A lot of scholars believe that Martha, Mary, and Lazurus were actually some of His closest friends before He started His public ministry.

Jesus knew what it was like to go to church and listen to "out of context" teachings. I feel bad for those poor rabbis who taught in synagogue while Jesus was in the audience.

I can just picture Jesus giving a compassionate chuckle at every verse that was misinterpreted or read out of context.

He knew what it was like to wait patiently for His calling. Can you imagine how hard that must have been for Jesus to look around seeing His friends get married and start families, all while knowing He'd never have that opportunity?

Or what about sitting at a community dinner listening to people complain and critique about how You (or more so God) is slow on keeping His promises of sending the Messiah in the face of Roman persecution.

Why, Adoni, are we still suffering?!! Deliver us from the hand of our oppressors.

I wonder how many times Jesus was tempted to start His ministry early out of compassion for hurting people.

These are often things we don't really think about when we talk about Jesus. Scripture teaches that He had to grow in wisdom and stature. Jesus had to trust the Father's plan and timing in His life.

The majority of Jesus's life was navigating the same day-to-day mundane things you and I deal with. Yet, Jesus did them with a holy intention.

KAVANAH

One of the things that separates humans from other created beings is that we have the ability to attach meaning to all that we do.

Think about it, we attach monetary value to everything! Quite remarkable when you think about it.

The Jewish rabbis call this practice *"Kavanah."* It is about living with a holy intention, attaching meaning to all aspects of life.

We see this over and over again in the life of Jesus.

How much of what Jesus valued in other people was simply overlooked by other people?

Jesus saw people's faith, He noticed those who stood on the outskirts, He was able to discern laziness from worship, He washed the dirty feet of His friends, He prepared meals of fellowship, He blessed a newlywed couple with the best wine they've ever tasted, He created space for little kids to sit on His lap, He napped when he was tired, and He involved himself in the mundane tasks of everyday life (like with the woman at the well).

There was nothing that Jesus did that was selfish in nature. He wasn't frustrated when His quiet times were interrupted, instead He used those interruptions as a means of worship. He wasn't angry when His sleep was disturbed, instead He invited God to be His source of rest.

When His best friend Lazurus died, He didn't rush back to bring him back to life. He sat in the pain and used those three days to allow His heart to break. Jesus attached meaning to everything He did no matter the circumstance.

How much different would the world look if we did everything with a holy intention?

How much more would we see, feel, and heal if we just stopped and attached meaning to all things of our life?

How much more alive would we be?

THE TEMPTATIONS OF JESUS

Jesus was a man of sorrow.

Perhaps nothing paints a clearer picture of His humanity and sorrow than His ministry.

Before Jesus enters into His public ministry He is baptized, aligning Himself with the human experience.[224] Immediately after His baptism, Jesus goes into the wilderness to be tested.

Just like us, Jesus is tempted with the three longings we crave the most:

Identity, status, and power.

During Jesus's baptism, the skies open up, and the voice of the Father says, "This is my Son, whom I love; with him I am well pleased."[225] The very next scene, the first words Satan uses to tempt Jesus are, "If You are the son of God . . ."[226]

The temptation that Satan offered to Jesus was: If You are suffering, that clearly means God doesn't love You, because if God loves You why would He allow You to suffer? And if God doesn't really love You, are you really His son?

Jesus's response is: My Father's love for Me isn't based on My present circumstance, and My love for Him isn't based on My present comfort, but My outright allegiance to Him.

The second temptation is one of status: If You are God's Son, shouldn't You be worshiped for it? Perform this miraculous sign and You will be loved by all.

Jesus's response is: I know the calling that My Dad has given Me, I'd rather be celebrated by My Father even if that means no one else accepts who I am.

The third temptation is one of power: You don't need to go to the cross and endure that painful death to gain power. Take a shortcut to the throne and the road of less pain, all You need to do is acknowledge me as lord and the world is Yours.

Jesus's response is: My power isn't for self-gain, My power is used for the benefit of other people and the way I am inaugurated as King is through the path of pain.

It's quite remarkable to see that Jesus could have taken an easier route to become King of the world. One of the craziest parts of Jesus's temptation is that He doesn't contest that Satan had all the authority, He acknowledged it. Jesus was aware that defeat over darkness could only be won by entering into the pain and death that darkness offers.

Our response to Jesus's resistance to temptation is often, "Well of course He resisted, He is God." Scripture paints a different picture—Jesus was very human in His temptation.

In the Garden of Gethsemane, the night before His crucifixion, Scripture shows how distressed Jesus was. We often have this idea that Jesus wanted to go to the cross, almost as if the idea of the cross didn't faze Him. That night, being faced with the weight of humanity's sin and the anticipation of being separated from His Heavenly Father almost became too much to bear.

The whole context of the situation gives us an insight into Jesus's state of mind that night. The Garden of Gethsemane was located on the Mount of Olives. The name Mount of Olives literally means "oil press"—it perfectly displays how Jesus was feeling in that moment.

As Jesus enters into the Garden, He brings His prayer warriors with Him—Peter, James, and John.

Jesus asks the boys to cover Him in prayer while He goes to the Father in prayer. Apparently, Peter, James, and John had too much to eat for dinner and couldn't stay awake. This had to be the first time they had ever seen Jesus like this. They have seen Jesus walk on water, calm a storm, and bring a dead guy back to life. Not much fazed Jesus, so they probably thought, "Just another day at the office."

Jesus was left to deal with His temptation alone.

Matthew 26:37-38 (ASV) expresses that His soul was "exceedingly sorrowful, even unto death." As He prayed, He experienced such anguish that it manifested physically; Luke 22:44 describes how His sweat became like great drops of blood.

Jesus, overwhelmed and in despair, asks His Father if there is another way to accomplish salvation for humanity. "Is there any other way?" He asks His dad.

Knowing the answer to His own question, He accepts his fate. He leans into one of the most pain-filled and isolated moments of His life and says, not my desire but your desire for my life.[227]

Jesus's prayer isn't for the Father to rid Him of His desire. Instead, Jesus's prayer is for the Father to redirect His desire into alignment with the Father's desire.

Hebrews talk about how the Father answered Jesus's prayer. Hebrews 12:2 says, "For the joy set before him endured the cross, scorning its shame."

This doesn't mean all of a sudden Jesus was stoked to die; it doesn't mean that His death hurt a little less. It means He was able to look past the moment and realize that through His pain others would find healing, through His wounds others would find wholeness, and through the ugliness of His death beauty would be restored to humanity.

The joy which Jesus felt was rooted in His love for you.

Imagine what we can endure if we redirect our desires to match God's desire?

MISREPRESENTED

In the Old Testament, God gave Israel's priests a vital role for His people.

The priests represented God to the people and represented the people to God. In the Old Testament, Jesus referred to the priests as shepherds—a symbol of those who care for every need of the flock and protect the flock from danger. More than that, the people of Israel were chosen and given the task to represent Yahweh to the world. The world would know Yahweh based on the character of His people.

Yikes . . .

Honestly, I still don't fully understand why God would choose this method. He has so much faith in us. As you know, Israel failed to represent God well to the world, and in turn over 20 times in the Old Testament, Yahweh declares that He is bringing judgment on Israel for "His name's sake."[228] This ultimately results in the exile of Israel.

Jesus often responded to people who were struggling in sin with mercy, compassion, and grace. Often, He performed some physical healing that led to their spiritual repentance. You don't really see Jesus upset with those who are "outside the Kingdom."

However, where Jesus gets upset is when those who were tasked to represent Him do so in a deplorable manner.

Let me introduce you to the religious leaders.

Their job was the same as the Old Testament priests; they were to represent God to the people.

How many of us like being misrepresented?

How many of us have been hurt by those misrepresenting Jesus?

How many of us have misrepresented Jesus ourselves? I know I have!

It hurts Jesus to His core when He is misrepresented and others walk away from Him because of something His children did.

Or better yet, those who are supposed to represent you attack you personally because they believe they know you better than yourself!

This is what the Pharisees and religious leaders did to Jesus.

They attacked and killed Jesus all because He didn't fit their Messianic perspective.

Jesus knew church hurt!

He was kicked out of synagogues.

He was called a sinner, a glutton, and a drunkard.

He was even accused by the church of His day to be possessed by a demonic spirit.

Those who were supposed to represent Him best were the very ones who killed Him, in honor of His own name!

Yet Jesus loved His church. His heart broke for the people in His church, and He died just as much for the oppressive religious leaders who misrepresented Him as He did for you and me.

In no way am I excusing the pain that you have felt from people in the church. All I am trying to say is Jesus also understands what it is to experience pain from those who are supposed to spiritually protect you.

USED, MISUNDERSTOOD, REJECTED, AND ABANDONED

A lot like you and me, Jesus understands what it feels like to feel used, misunderstood, rejected and abandoned. Most of Jesus's rejection and abandonment came from those He was closest to.

When Jesus started His public ministry, He went viral!

"Who is this guy?" people asked.

There was something different and compelling about Jesus that people hadn't seen before. Crowds gathered and people came to see Him from all over the surrounding area. Jesus was the "A-list" celebrity of His time.

One day, as Jesus and His followers are sitting down to enjoy a meal, somehow word got out that Jesus was at this house eating with His friends. (Someone probably posted it on their Instagram story.)

All of a sudden, crowds gather and surround the house Jesus is at. His family catches wind of it and attempts to get Jesus to stop His ministry. We don't know what their motivation for it was, all we do know is that they thought Jesus had lost His mind and gone crazy.[229]

Imagine if that was you: Those who are closest to you, who should know you the best, are accusing you of being crazy because people are drawn to God's anointing on your life.

Those who should be in His corner supporting Him are the ones who are ashamed of Him. Imagine if you were someone who was gathered at the house to see Jesus, and all of a sudden you saw His family say to Him, "Stop acting this way, You're bringing shame on us, You're losing your mind!"

What would that make you think about Jesus?

Jesus had to have been one of the most misunderstood people who ever lived.

Jesus is the only person on this earth who has healed people, brought someone back to life, fed thousands out of a lack, and yet, was hated for doing it.

Jesus even acknowledged that people only came to Him to get their needs met.[230]

Think about it this way: the Gospels testify to the fact that on two occasions Jesus fed over 10,000 people even though they were short on food. He miraculously multiplied the loaves and the fish to feed all those people. This wasn't a little snack before dinner kind of feeding, scripture says that people ate until they were full and satisfied!

Oh, and there were leftovers! Abundance!

Isn't that the best feeling? When you eat a meal that's so good and the chef looks at you and says, "There's more if you'd like, help yourself to seconds."

Yes, and amen!

This is what happened.

Jesus also healed hundreds if not thousands of people and performed miracle after miracle. The Gospel of John says that Jesus did so much that, "If every one of them were written down, I suppose that even the whole world would not have room for the books that would be written."[231]

Yet do you know how many people were at His crucifixion?

His mother, a few other women, and John.

That's it . . .

His closest friends bailed on Him, those He healed bailed on him, those He fed bailed on Him, and the one He brought back from the dead bailed on Him.

The remarkable thing about Jesus is He knew this was going to happen. Scripture says that He knew what was in the hearts of people, and yet He still chose to heal and help people.

He knew that people were only there for what He could do for them, yet He helped them anyway. Jesus knew what it was like to be used, and He still poured out His love for them.

This is something I struggle with. When I do something nice for someone and it's not reciprocated or appreciated, there is a temptation in my heart to be like, *okay that's the last time I'm helping you.*

But what we see with Jesus is that He gave himself wholly for people, all the while knowing in His darkest and most vulnerable moment He would be abandoned and left alone. Perhaps one of the saddest and most pain-filled moments in Jesus's life isn't the fact that He was used by people, but rejected and betrayed by His friends. When Jesus chose His twelve disciples, they were your everyday guys. I don't mean that disrespectfully, I mean that truthfully.

Six of them were fishermen.

One was a traitor tax collector.

One was a MIGA (Make Israel Great Again) patriot.

One was good with money.

And the others . . . well, we don't really know.

Oh, and another thing, all twelve of the disciples weren't chosen to continue their education after Torah school. In Jesus's time every male had to join *"Bet-Sepher"* which is where the boys would memorize the entire Torah (first five books of the Bible).

After they completed Torah training, the students would go to a Rabbi of their choosing and ask if they could apprentice under that Rabbi, and if they were good enough, the Rabbi would accept their request.

Jesus's followers were tradesmen and everyday laborers. They weren't "good enough" to be Rabbi's. Yet Jesus's method of discipleship and Rabbinic training was different. He sought them out and invited them to partake in His ministry.

One of the most beautiful things about Jesus is that even though He was their Rabbi, their master, and teacher, He referred to them as His friends. He was doing ministry and life with His best buds!

Jesus treated them as such.

They on the other hand treated Jesus differently. James and John viewed Jesus as a means for self-exaltation. Peter, Judas Iscariot, and Simon the Zealot saw Jesus as a Donald Trump figure who would make Israel great again. The others were torn between the person they saw and their imagined expectation of who the Messiah was.

Jesus wasn't looking to conquer and overthrow people, He was looking for friends; He was looking to overthrow the forces and barriers that hindered people from being friends.

Jesus was violent in the spirit and sweet in the flesh.

His disciples couldn't see that.

Jesus took on the role of a servant to elevate others ahead of Himself, even those who would betray Him.

When Judas came to the realization that Jesus was not going to overthrow the Romans, doubt birthed in his heart, and he was flooded with disappointment. In a moment of unclarity and blindness from his own truth, he betrays his friend Jesus.

For 30 pieces of silver (around $340.00 in today's currency), Judas agreed to set Jesus up to be captured and arrested. That evening Jesus washed the feet of His betrayer, whom He still called *friend*.

Later that evening as Jesus is in the Garden, struggling, Judas executes his plan. As Judas approaches Jesus, he kisses Jesus on the cheek (a sign of reverence and honor). Jesus doesn't pull away, He doesn't call him a fraud or a traitor. Instead, Jesus looks at Judas with a soft and tender look and says, "Do what you came for, friend."[232]

Jesus is a friend to those who hurt Him most.

As Jesus gets arrested, His friends flee in fear, leaving Him all alone.

To put salt in the wound, Peter, the one who professed his unwavering commitment to Jesus in front of all the other disciples, rejects knowing Jesus three times.

What is Jesus's response to His friends who betrayed and rejected Him? What is His response to those who used Him for self-gain? What is His response to His family who declared Him crazy in front of a crowd? What is His response to those who put Him on the cross to experience the most shameful and gruesome death known to man?

"Father, forgive them, for they know not what they do."[233]

Jesus offered them forgiveness without them even asking to be forgiven. The betrayal of His friends and the sin of humanity led Jesus to experience something He never experienced before—separation from His Heavenly Father.

Jesus knows what it feels like to feel abandoned by God.

The paradox of Jesus's abandonment was that He needed to be abandoned by the Father so that we could be brought near.

Isaiah 53:10 says that it *pleased* Him to send Jesus to the cross, not because God is a sadist, but because of what Jesus going to the cross meant for us—oneness with our Heavenly Father.

Jesus was a man who lived a life of incredible pain and sorrow, like you and me. He knows what it's like to have church hurt, familial hurt, people hurt, while also dealing with rejection, loneliness, and abandonment. What we see in the life of Jesus is how the pain of His life led not only to His perfection, but the perfection of the world.

PERFECTED BY PAIN

We tend to misunderstand the term "perfect."

When we think of something as perfect, we think of "absoluteness" or "as good as something can possibly be." With that understanding, it's no wonder why we struggle with verses like, "Be perfect as your father in heaven is perfect."[234]

Our understanding of perfection isn't how the Bible describes perfection. The Greek word used for perfect is "*teleioō*," which suggests a completion or fulfillment of purpose.

Hebrews makes the notion that Jesus was made perfect in His pain.[235]

Wasn't Jesus already perfect?

Yes, He was, but His perfection was something that was learned only through pain and suffering. Hebrews 5 says that, "Son though he was, he learned obedience from what he suffered and, once made perfect, he became the source of eternal salvation for all who obey him."

In other words, Jesus's experiences of pain and suffering were essential for Him to fully embody His calling as Savior. The pain of rejection Jesus felt, the loneliness, the church hurt, being used, people hurt, and all the other forms of pain He experienced were somehow used as a tool that empowered Him to make it to the cross.

Remember, Jesus was human. He asked for a different way to accomplish salvation; He didn't desire the death of the cross. Yet all the moments of pain that He experienced prepared Him for His redemption of the world.

Our pain, suffering, and wounding will not be in vain—our pain is used as a means to bring redemption and healing to this world and to the people around you.

Pain hurts, it's not fun. But it's vital.

You know the saying "no pain, no gain."

What does that mean?

It means without experiencing the ripping and tearing of your muscle, it's impossible for you to grow and get stronger.

The same is true for our spiritual lives. Our becoming like Jesus is attached to a life of pain that we must be willing to embrace.

Pain always births something new.

The question is what is being birthed?

If our pain is rooted in ourselves, then other channels of pain become birthed that lead to our destruction. But if our pain is rooted in Jesus (not that He causes it but uses it), then our pain will birth a transformation.

We become perfect, as our Heavenly Father is perfect.

The death and resurrection of Jesus has given us the power, through His Spirit, to live like He did here and now on this earth. That means to embrace what He embraces, love how He loves, heal like He heals, and become like He is.

I AM AND I AM NOT

The gospel of John sets out to answer the question, "Who is Jesus?"

As we know, Jesus is God.

In the opening chapter, John writes, "In the beginning was the Word, and Word was with God, and the Word was God."[236]

The Greek word for "Word" is "*Logos.*"

The *Logos* for the Greeks was a transcendent force that helped you to understand reason and the plan for your life. In other words, the *Logos* was a means for self-actualization, finding out who you are. The closer you got to the *Logos*, the more you would know yourself.

For most of history, people believed that when you came to know who God was, you became more aware of yourself.

This is John's point.

He continues writing that the *Logos* became human, took on flesh, and lived amongst humans.[237] The true *Logos* is Jesus. Another way put, if you want to find yourself, you have to get close to Jesus. Jesus makes it easy for us in the Gospel of John, He gives us seven "I am" statements so that we know who He is . . . so that we ultimately know who we are.

The *first* "I Am" Jesus discloses is: "I Am the Bread of Life."[238]

Meaning that Jesus is spiritually satisfying. He doesn't only give us life, but He keeps us satisfied even in times of wilderness and hardship. When Jesus makes this statement, it's to the Pharisees who would have been familiar with the Exodus story where God provides bread for Israel in the wilderness, and they were satisfied.

For us, our lives are testaments to this truth. When we are in a "wilderness" season, do our lives show that Jesus is enough?

People watch Christians in hardship to see how we live. We preach about how to handle suffering, pain, and wounding. But when push comes to shove, we look like the world. We question Jesus's goodness and faithfulness towards us.

Jesus says that He is lasting and satisfying even in the wilderness. Our lives need to be a testament to His lasting satisfaction.

Second, "I am the Light of the World."[239]

You want to get out of the wilderness? Jesus is the light that will illuminate the path out of darkness. He is here to guide you in dark times into a life that is full and satisfying.

Jesus calls His followers the salt and light of the world. Our lives are living testimony to the light of Jesus. How we do community, life, and hardship should be attractive. A light draws people in, and our lives are called to draw people to Him.

Third, "I am the Door."[240]

That cry in your heart for eternity isn't in yourself, but it's found in Jesus. The door to Jesus is always open, all you need to do is follow the light to the door. Eternal life, which Jesus describes as a knowing relationship with the Father and Himself, is found in Him.

We need to be like Paul who considered himself a household manager for the Kingdom.[241] Household managers helped guests navigate their way through the home. We are called to help people navigate life and pain, pointing people to the door that leads to life.

Fourth, "I am the Good Shepherd."[242]

Jesus cares for people and is willing to lay His life down for the sake of His flock.

Jesus has given us the same role; the New Testament says that we are a Kingdom of Priests. People who rule the earth and represent God. But our rule isn't one of power, it's one of sacrificial love. Jesus calls us to lay our lives down for others as well.

Fifth, "I am the Resurrection."[243]

When we lay our lives down, Jesus raises our life up!

Jesus has authority over death. His resurrection conquered sin and death. Now He gives access to eternity.

We are called to live in light of that reality. As Jesus-following people, we are called to live out that new reality here and now. Death and pain on earth isn't to be feared, it's our reward and graduation.

Sixth, "I am the Way, the Truth, and the Life."[244]

Jesus is the only way to life and truth.

We have a hard time with this in our pluralistic and inclusive society. We often don't like the idea of exclusivism and tend to believe that Jesus wasn't exclusive, but He makes this claim about Him.

Life and truth can't be found apart from Himself.

Our lives are a testament to this reality. Do we live our lives like there is no other option but Jesus? We are called to forsake all others and cling to Him. When we live lives of sin and partake in idolatry, our claim to belong to Jesus is taken less seriously.

Jesus calls us to complete allegiance to Himself.

Seventh, "I am the Vine."[245]

In the same way the Spirit was with Jesus, the Spirit is with us. Jesus affirmed that He only did what the Father asked and spoke what the Father said to speak. This led Jesus to a fruitful ministry. The same is for us, when we take control of our lives and play the role of God, it leads to disordered lives. But when we live attached to Jesus, our life brings blessing and satisfaction not only to ourselves, but to others.

You want to learn how to manage and navigate pain? Then you must remain attached to the vine. He is faithful to finish the good work that He started in you.

Life may bring bumps and bruises (after all Jesus did say that He rewards those who bear fruit with pruning), but ultimately, it's so you can bear more fruit and bless other people with your life.[246]

In the seven "I Am" statements we find who Jesus says He is, but we also find who we are.

We are people who are called to present Jesus as the ultimate source of satisfaction in this life and that following Him means to serve others, embrace pain, and live with hopeful expectations of the future.

Part of embracing who you are also means to embrace who you aren't.

Next to the seven "I Am" statements, Jesus gives us three "I am not" statements.

First, "I am not alone."[247]

Jesus knew He would face opposition, pain, and struggle in this world. But the truer reality for Jesus was not the circumstances that He faced, but His Father's lasting presence in this life.

In this world you will face trouble, but you are not alone.

Jesus has given you a community of believers who love and care for you. He has given us His Spirit, who He calls the Comforter,[248] to be there for us in our time of deepest need. No matter how isolated, rejected, or wounded you feel, you are not alone.

Second, "I am not of this world."[249]

Jesus knew that His way of living was the antithesis to how the world operated. Yet, He loved the world and was determined to bring healing to the world even though the world would misunderstand and reject Him.

This should bring us comfort.

Our home isn't this world, it's the world to come. But we are called to love this world in the same way that Jesus loved us. Our love for this world will usher in the world to come.

You have been placed here in this world at this moment for a specific reason. God has equipped you with certain gifts and strengths that the world needs.

The world will hurt us, but we don't need to worry because Jesus has already overcome the world.[250]

Third, "I am not seeking the glory for myself."[251]

In the same way Jesus wasn't looking for status, praise, or glory for Himself, we are called to embody that lifestyle. Jesus came to show what the Father looked like. In today's culture everyone has different ideas of who and what God looks like.

But Jesus calls us to live like He did. When the world sees us, they should see Jesus, and when they see Jesus, they should see who God is.

So, who is Jesus?

Jesus is God. He is the loving heart behind creation, who left His throne because He saw His beautiful creation captivated by self-inflicting pain. God became human, lived a life full of sorrow, pain, and suffering so that we would have full access to His joy, wholeness, and satisfaction.

He is the God who died on the cross for you and me, so that we might live in Him.

He is the God who rose from the dead, bearing the same wounds on *His* body as a reminder of how much He loves us.

And He is the God who turns our deepest pain and wounding into sacred and hallowed reminders of His faithfulness towards us.

It is by Jesus's wounds we are healed.

And it is by our wounds the world is healed.

PART FOUR:
SACRED WOUNDS

"Rich wounds, yet visible above,
In beauty glorified;
No angels in the sky
Can fully bear the sight . . ."
— *Matthew Bridges*

"Now Thomas (also known as Didymus), one of the Twelve, was not with the disciples when Jesus came. So the other disciples told him, 'We have seen the Lord!' But he said to them, 'Unless I see the nail marks in his hands and put my finger where the nails were, and put my hand into his side, I will not believe.' A week later his disciples were in the house again, and Thomas was with them. Though the doors were locked, Jesus came and stood among them and said, 'Peace be with you!' Then he said to Thomas, 'Put your finger here; see my hands. Reach out your hand and put it into my side. Stop doubting and believe.' Thomas said to him, 'My Lord and my God!'"
— *John 20:24-28*

14

THE PATH FORWARD: BEAUTY, GOODNESS, & TRUTH

Thus far, we've asked the question: *What is wrong with our world?*—only to find that no one really has a satisfying answer. We've examined the responses through different worldviews and perspectives, yet all roads seem to lead to the same conclusion: something is off, and no one knows quite how to fix it.

In Part Two, we explored how these worldviews shape the way we live. We live in a culture that tells us we are the *captains of our own ships*—that we alone must decide what is good, true, and beautiful.

In Part Three, we discussed how, in our pursuit of self-made freedom, we've somehow become even more enslaved. We try to heal our own wounds, yet in the process, we only inflict more damage—on ourselves, on others, on the world around us.

And so we're left with the question: *Is there another way?*

Yes. There is.

The answer lies on the highways of beauty, goodness, and truth.

Each their own road, leading somewhere beyond themselves—to an unknown destination—yet met with a familiar voice. A voice we somehow recognize, though the face remains a mystery.

For centuries, philosophers have debated what is true, what is good, what is beautiful. Each arriving at their own definitions. But in our modern world, one of these has been quietly forgotten.

With political campaigns raging, social justice movements marching, and activism at an all-time high, our culture is obsessed with the questions *What is true?* and *What is good?*

But beauty?

Somehow, beauty has been left out of the conversation.

What if these three cannot be separated? What if the reason we struggle to define truth or goodness is because we've neglected beauty?

Beauty, goodness, and truth are mirrors—each reflecting and revealing the others. To truly see one, you must see them all. Maybe this is why Jesus's invitation was never just to *believe*, but to *come and see*.[252] For many of us, we've grown up thinking of Jesus's life and ministry as a pathway to salvation. And yes, it is.

But when I read the Gospels, I see something deeper: Jesus revealing the *beauty* of what it means to be human. A beauty that unveils the *goodness* of the Father. A goodness that leads us to believe and trust that Jesus is *true*.

And maybe that's the invitation for us.

Instead of joining the world in fighting over truth and goodness, what if we pursued beauty? What if, by following beauty, we found ourselves led into what is good and true?

That's what Part Four is all about.

In a storytelling move borrowed from George Lucas (not that I'm George Lucas, I'm just stealing his format), we're going to start with the end:

Death.

Why?

Because in the secular story, death is *the end*. The full stop. The final curtain.

But in the biblical story, death is *promotion*. *Inauguration day*. *Graduation day*. Take your pick.

The biblical story tells us that what we do in this life matters. Not in some religious, *earn-your-way-to-heaven* sense, but because we are actually participating in building what is to come.

In this section, we'll follow a similar format to Parts One and Two. We'll see how the biblical story brings healing—not in spite of pain, but *through* it. How God uses the wounds of His people as the very antidote to the brokenness of the world.

From there, we'll move backward—looking at how the life of Jesus ushered healing into the world. How His life became the blueprint. The roadmap. Jesus introduced a kind of stubborn, defiant love that turned the world upside down. A love so powerful, it wooed humanity off its feet.

This love invites us into a life that is lasting and deeply satisfying.

Not a life *without* pain, but a life where pain no longer has the final word.

How is that possible?

Because Jesus is *real*.

Jesus is *near*.

Jesus is *enough*.

And in the final chapter, we'll get practical. How do we live with *Sacred Wounds*? How do we carry pain in a way that no longer defines us, but instead becomes sacred ground—holy space where others can find healing, too?

As you step into this section, turn your attention to Jesus. Ask Him to reveal the wounds in your heart. Name them. Let Him pour the oil of grace over them.

Let the Holy Spirit hover over those places—breathe fresh life into them. And watch as beauty, goodness, and truth begin to emerge, shaping you into the person you were always meant to be.

HOVERING OVER THE CHAOS

The biblical story begins in chaos.

Genesis tells us that in the beginning, the earth was formless. Chaotic. Dark.

And yet, from the first pages of Scripture, we see a God who moves toward the chaos. A God who speaks into the darkness. A God who forms and fills, who hovers over the void and breathes life into what seems like nothing. This is the pattern of the biblical story—God bringing the opposite reality into the lives of His people.

He sent Jesus so that we could be *formed* into His image, escaping the deformity of sin by the power of the Holy Spirit.

He sent His Spirit to bring *order* into our chaotic lives.

He gave us His presence so we could be *light* in a dark world.

Do you see the pattern?

The Holy Spirit.

Genesis says that the Spirit hovered over the waters of the unformed, chaotic, and dark world. And what happens? Life and light begin to break through the void.[253]

Notice—God doesn't *eliminate* the chaos, the darkness, or the formlessness. He doesn't erase them.

Instead, He hovers over them. He subdues them. And from them, He creates something new.

Chaos is conquered by the perfect order of creation's design. Formlessness is conquered as God shapes the earth and breathes humanity into being. Darkness is conquered with the simple, powerful command: *Let there be light.*

These aren't just themes from the opening pages of Genesis. This is the *whole* story.

Romans 12 tells us, "Do not conform to the pattern of this world, but be transformed by the renewing of your mind."[254]

In other words, don't get caught up in the way of the world—chaotic, deformed, dark. Instead, let your mind be reshaped by the sacred story of Jesus. Because when you do, order, formation, and light begin to break into your life.

Growing up, my family had a tradition: movie nights. After dinner, we'd all pile into my dad's 1987 Toyota 4Runner—the top down, the night air rushing in—and head to Cold Stone. (If you've never been to Cold Stone, I highly recommend it. The glory of God is on full display in that place. As King David would say, "You leave with your cup overflowing.")

One by one, we'd customize our ice creams. I always went with mint chip, loaded up with Reese's, Snickers, and brownie bites. (For those wondering, yes, that is still my go-to order.) Then we'd rush home, huddle up, and start the movie.

One night, my dad suggested we watch *Rocky*. One by one, we worked our way through the series (not all in one night, of course). For the record, my favorite is *Rocky III*. My dad argues it's the first one because, as he passionately reminds me, "HE WENT THE DISTANCE!" But for me, *Rocky III* is where it's at. This is the one where Mr. T plays Clubber Lang.

There's a scene before the big fight where an interviewer asks Clubber Lang for his prediction. He looks straight into the camera and says, in his legendary voice:

"Pain."

And if you've seen the movie, you know—Rocky gets *destroyed*. Clubber Lang beats him so bad he loses his championship title. And worse, it sends Rocky into an identity crisis. He starts to doubt himself. Was he ever really a champion? Was it all just a fluke? The defeat is so brutal, so disorienting, that he does what so many of us do when we hit rock bottom.

He quits.

Enter Apollo Creed.

If you don't know, Apollo is the guy Rocky went the distance with in the first movie. The guy who eventually lost to Rocky in the second. A legend. After losing to Rocky, Apollo retired, walked away from boxing. But when he sees Rocky lose to Clubber Lang, he knows what's happening. He recognizes the shame, the despair, the temptation to walk away. So he comes back into Rocky's life and tells him: *Don't quit.*

Because quitting was Apollo's biggest regret.

He tells Rocky something that shifts the entire story: "Losing has its benefits. It forces you to reinvent your game." So Rocky starts training again—but this time, under Apollo's guidance. He has to unlearn his old way of fighting. At first, it fells unnatural. Awkward. Like he's stumbling through a style that doesn't fit.

But then, something clicks.

Slowly, he masters this new way of fighting. Slowly, he becomes a different kind of fighter. Stronger. More precise. More dangerous. And then, the inevitable rematch with Clubber Lang.

Now, I won't spoil the ending for you. But let's just say... there *is* a *Rocky IV*. Life is a lot like Clubber Lang. It brings the pain. But if we allow the Holy Spirit to hover over our pain—if we let Him move over the chaos, the formlessness, the darkness—something begins to happen.

New life.

From the chaos, God creates beauty. From the void, He forms something new. From the darkness, He speaks light.

And yet, if we're honest, we've grown *too* familiar with the chaos. We've adapted to the darkness. We've come to expect the formlessness.

Maybe that's why we struggle to see what is *beautiful, good, and true.*

When all we see is war after war, injustice upon injustice, it forces the question: *Is God really good?* And if we can't answer that, then how can we ever believe He is true? And if God isn't true, then how could He ever be beautiful? But here's the beauty of Jesus: He engraves our pain into His own body. Your life. Your story. Your wounds.

He carries them. Wears them. Marks Himself with them for all eternity.[255] Where we feel ashamed of our pain, Jesus wears it like a badge of honor. And when we draw near to Him, we begin to notice something familiar in Him. The wounds on His body—they contain every emotion of despair we've ever felt. Every lie we've believed.

Every hidden wound we've carried.

And yet, those wounds are *sacred.*

This is why Romans 8:28 is not just a verse we slap on our fridge and hope is true. It's a reality we begin to experience firsthand.

> "And we know that in all things God works for the good of those who love him, who have been called according to his purpose."

What makes God good?

He takes everything that was meant to destroy you—everything that was meant for evil—and turns it into something beautiful. Something good. Something true.

And when you begin to see that, the argument over *truth* loses its power. Because what was meant to break you has now become the very thing that makes you whole.

The battleground for truth is beauty.

And maybe that's the shift we need. Maybe instead of fighting for truth and goodness like the rest of the world, we need to fight for beauty. Because beauty cuts through the noise. Beauty *draws us in*.

Paul knew this when he wrote to the Corinthians. He didn't just argue for truth. He pointed to the sheer beauty of a life transformed by the Spirit.

And maybe that's the invitation for us.

MORE THAN AN EVENT

Besides Genesis 1-3, I believe one of the most important chapters in all of Scripture is 1 Corinthians 15.

Paul's letter to the Corinthian church wasn't just a theological lecture—it was an urgent, heartfelt response to a group of people caught between two worlds.

Like us, they were struggling to follow Jesus in a culture that had its own definitions of truth, goodness, and beauty. They lived in a world shaped by Greek philosophy and pagan religion, a world with its own stories about what it meant to be human, what it meant to be free, what it meant to be alive.

The result? A church full of division. Chaos. Deformation.

If you read through 1 Corinthians, it can feel like Paul is just handing out rules—*this is how Christians live, this is how they don't.* But that's a shallow reading of the text. Because for Paul, it wasn't about behavior modification. It was about reality.

Something had happened that changed everything.

Something that rewrote history, reshaped humanity, and redefined the way we live, think, and love.

The resurrection of Jesus.

For a lot of us, the resurrection is one of those things we know is important. We celebrate it on Easter. We teach about it in church. But if we're honest, we don't really grasp the full weight of what it means for our lives.

We know Jesus's *death* matters. His death covered sin. Took the weight of our iniquity. Paid the debt we owed. That's what theologians call *justification*—we are declared innocent because of His sacrifice.

But what about His *resurrection*?

Paul makes the point that Jesus's resurrection isn't just about *eternal life someday*. It's not just about what happens after we die. The resurrection is about *right now*.[256]

We see this in John 11, after Lazarus dies. Jesus intentionally waits three days before arriving—making sure there is no mistake. Lazarus isn't just sick. He isn't in a coma. He is *dead*.

When Jesus finally arrives, Martha runs out to meet Him. And let's just say, she isn't thrilled.

What took you so long?! Didn't you get our message? Our brother is dead. Why didn't you come sooner?[257]

Jesus looks at her, tenderness in His eyes, and simply says, "Your brother will rise again."

Martha responds the way most of us would: *Yeah, Jesus, I know. I know he will rise again at the end. I know he'll be with You in eternity. But that doesn't help my pain right now.*

And then Jesus drops a reality-altering statement.

"I am the resurrection and the life."[258]

Not *I will bring* resurrection. Not *I will one day* resurrect the dead.

"I am the resurrection."

For Jesus, resurrection isn't just a future event. It's a *present reality* found in a *person*.

Martha and Mary then invite Jesus to *come and see*[259]—but not in the way Jesus invited His disciples.

Their invitation wasn't one of wonder and discovery. It was an invitation into *pain*. Into grief. Into the chaos, darkness, and deformation that death brings.

And Jesus accepts.

Just as the Spirit hovered over the dark, formless void in Genesis, Jesus hovers over their grief. Over their sorrow. Over the death of their brother.

Then, with a word, He calls Lazarus out of the grave.

The resurrection of Lazarus is a glimpse of what Jesus Himself would accomplish. Unfortunately for Laz, he would die again. (Poor guy.)

His resurrection was just a signpost. A glimpse of the greater reality to come.

Jesus's resurrection wasn't just proof of *life after death*. It was an invitation into *a new way of living here and now*.

For Paul, the resurrection wasn't a theological footnote. It was the foundation for everything.

He tells the Corinthians: If Jesus didn't rise from the dead, then honestly? Just go live however you want. None of this matters. But if

He did? Then you've been birthed into an entirely new reality, and it changes everything.[260]

N.T. Wright puts it this way: "People who believe in the resurrection, in God making a whole new world in which everything will be set right at last, are unstoppably motivated to work for that new world in the present."[261]

Paul wasn't interested in religious guilt trips. He wasn't handing out rules to shame people into better behavior.

Paul was talking about identity formation. "This is what some of you were."

He doesn't deny the Corinthian church's sin. He *acknowledges it*. But his argument isn't one of shame or condemnation. His argument is: *This isn't who you are anymore.*

In God's sight, you have already been *washed*. You have already been *sanctified*. You have already been *justified*. Now, live in that reality. Yes, life will bring trials. Pain. Temptation. Wounds. Chaos. But in the reality Jesus ushered in, those things no longer have to define you.

There is a way through pain that *births life*.

That's why Paul doesn't just tell them *what to do*. He tells them *why it matters*.

Because what you do matters.

Not just in some abstract moral sense.

What you do has eternal implications.

Since Jesus overcame death and sin, we now live in a new reality. A reality where, through His Spirit, we get to partner with Him in creating beauty, goodness, and truth in a world that is still formless, chaotic, and dark.

Again, N.T. Wright says it best: "What you do in the Lord is not in vain. You are not oiling the wheels of a machine that's about to roll over a cliff. You are not restoring a great painting that's shortly going to be thrown on the fire. You are not planting roses in a garden that's about to be dug up for a building site. You are–strange though it may seem, almost as hard to believe as the resurrection itself–accomplishing something that will become in due course part of God's new world. Every act of love, gratitude, and kindness; every work of art or music inspired by the love of God and delight in the beauty of his creation; every minute spent teaching a severely handicapped child to read or walk; every act of care and nurture, of comfort and support, for one's fellow human beings and for that matter one's fellow non-human creatures; and of course every prayer, all Spirit-led teaching, every deed that spreads the gospel, builds up the church, embraces and embodies holiness rather than corruption, and make the name of Jesus honored in the world—all of this will find its way, through the resurrecting power of God, into the new creation that God will one day make."[262]

Every act of love.

Every work of art or music.

Every moment of teaching, care, and nurturing.

Every prayer, every conversation, every sacrifice—it *all* carries into eternity.

On my desk, next to a picture of my daughter, I used to keep a white stone.

As a pastor, I often found myself sitting across from people in deep pain—people crushed by the weight of sin, trauma, or loss. And more often than not, my job wasn't to *fix* anything. It was simply to remind them of who they are. The white stone comes out of the book of Revelation:

"To the one who is victorious . . . I will give a white stone with a new name written on it, known only to the one who receives it."[263]

In ancient Rome, victors of athletic competitions were awarded a white stone inscribed with their name. It wasn't just a trophy—it was their *ticket* to a grand celebratory feast. Revelation takes that image and expands it.

The white stone isn't just a symbol of victory over sin and death. It's a symbol of *identity*.

On it, God writes *your real name*. The name He's had for you since before the foundation of the world.

When people would come into my office, I'd hand them the stone and invite them to imagine—what would it feel like to finally have peace? To no longer strive? To no longer feel like you have to prove or perform, but to simply *be* who you were always meant to be?

Scripture tells us that this is already our reality in Jesus.

And nothing—not sin, not trauma, not suffering—can take away what God has already sealed.

The resurrection of Jesus created space for us to live our eternal reality *here and now*.

And the pain we walk through?

It's not just something to endure.

It's the very thing that forms us into the people we were always meant to be.

THE POETIC MEND

To make this even clearer, let's return to an image I introduced earlier in the book—*kintsugi*.

Kintsugi is the Japanese art of taking broken pottery and mending it back together using *urushi* lacquer. Once the shattered pieces are reassembled, the artist traces the fractured lines with gold, highlighting the pottery's brokenness rather than hiding it.

The result? A piece more beautiful *because* of its brokenness.

The philosophy behind kintsugi stands in stark contrast to our modern culture.

We do everything we can to hide our wounds. To mask our pain. To make sure no one sees the cracks in our story.

But in kintsugi, the artist isn't trying to erase the brokenness. He's drawing attention *to* it.

And while the gold may be what catches our eye, what actually holds the pottery together is the *urushi*.

Urushi comes from the Japanese lacquer tree. It's sometimes called *the blood of the tree* because, once the sap is extracted, the tree dies.

Let that sink in.

For the pottery to be restored, something had to bleed.

Something had to be poured out.

Something had to die.

The reason urushi is used in kintsugi isn't just because it's a strong adhesive—it's because it has a unique property. When exposed to moisture, urushi hardens. It *absorbs* the conditions around it and becomes more durable—able to withstand acids, alcohol, and extreme temperatures. For the Japanese, urushi represents *adaptability through adversity*. Strength. Resilience. The ability to endure.

And here's the parallel: For us, urushi represents our pain, our wounds, our tears.

We often think pain weakens us, that it takes something from us we'll never get back. But in the hands of Jesus, our wounds become the very thing that makes us whole.

Pain, when surrendered, becomes the poetic mend that holds us together.

There's a saying: *What doesn't kill you makes you stronger.*

It's cliché. Overused.

But maybe, it's also true.

On April 20, 1999, two high school students, Eric Harris and Dylan Klebold, walked into Columbine High School and carried out one of the deadliest school shootings in American history. Twelve students and one teacher were killed. Many others were injured. The trauma rippled outward—through the school, the city, the country. In the years that followed, something unexpected happened. Instead of being defined by tragedy, the Columbine community, which is known as the "Kintsugi Generation" became known for something else.

Forgiveness.
Reconciliation.
Hope.

The parents of some of the students who were killed became messengers of the gospel. They traveled the country, telling their stories—not to spread bitterness or revenge, but to share the radical love of Jesus.

Their deepest wounds became the very thing God used to bring healing to others.

I should know. Because I am a product of their faithfulness.

My dad didn't grow up a Christian. In fact, he mocked Christianity. Church was never something he considered. But in one of his darkest seasons, he decided to give it a try. That Sunday, there was a guest speaker. One of the fathers who had lost a child in the Columbine shooting.

The message?

Pain.
Loss.
Forgiveness.
Reconciliation.
Love.

My dad had never heard anything like it. He couldn't comprehend a love that would extend forgiveness to someone who caused so much pain. At the end of the service, the speaker invited anyone who wanted to follow Jesus to raise their hand. And my dad describes the next moment like this: "I felt like if I didn't raise my hand, I was going to die. I was overwhelmed by the love of God."

Now, my dad isn't a dramatic man. He's one of the strongest people I know—physically and emotionally. He doesn't exaggerate pain. So when he describes this moment in such stark terms, I can only come to one conclusion:

God took the immensity of my dad's pain and exchanged it for the immensity of His grace.

And from that moment, my dad's life changed.

I grew up watching him sit in his old, brown man-chair, Bible open, praying for my brother and me.

Even when I walked away from Jesus, he never stopped praying.

I wouldn't be where I am today without my dad's prayers.

And my dad wouldn't be where he is today if it weren't for a grieving father who allowed Jesus to touch his deepest wound.

Kintsugi doesn't erase the fractures—it honors them. It transforms what was once shattered into something new. Something stronger. Something whole.

The gospel does the same.

Our pain is not wasted. Our wounds are not useless.

They are the poetic mend that transforms our fragmented lives into *sacred* works of art—stories of resilience and renewal, woven with gold.

THE VOICE WE'VE ALWAYS KNOWN

When people talk about human transformation, they rarely use words like *truth* or *goodness*.

Even though the end result will be true and good, we don't often describe people as being *transformed into truth* or *shaped into goodness*.

Instead, we say they become something *beautiful*.

We talk about human beings as works of art—paintings in progress, sculptures still being chiseled, clay still soft in the hands of the Potter.

But how does this transformation happen?

In our *imminent* world, eternity feels like an eternity away. We are caught in the here and now—our attention spans shrinking, our thoughts consumed by whatever is urgent in the moment.

So how do we live in the tension of *becoming*? How do we hold both suffering and hope? How do we stay anchored in the reality of eternity while living in a world that constantly pulls us into distraction?

This is where *remembrance* comes in.

The practice of remembering is at the heart of what it means to follow Jesus.

The night before His death, Jesus gathered His disciples, took the bread and the cup, and told them: "Do this in remembrance of me."[264]

But what did He mean by *remembrance*? It's not like they were going to forget who He was. He was their Messiah, the one they had left everything to follow.

There had to be something deeper.

In the Old Testament, when Israel was enslaved in Egypt, God gave them a meal—*the Passover*. He commanded them to celebrate it every year as a way of remembering how He had delivered them.

> "This is the day you are to remember . . . from generation to generation, you must celebrate it."[265]

And when God led Israel into the wilderness—their season of spiritual formation—he didn't just ask them to *remember* once. He told them nearly 30 times to *Zakhar*—to *bring to mind* what He had done.

Why?

Because He knows us. He knows how quickly we forget.

And because remembering His faithfulness is the very thing that keeps us from falling into idolatry.[266]

Fast forward to Jesus, and once again, a meal becomes the boundary marker.

"Do this in remembrance of me." Not just a ritual. Not just a tradition. But a practice of *anchoring* ourselves in the reality of His Kingdom.

Because remembering keeps us from being enslaved to the present moment.

It reminds us that pain doesn't mean God is absent. That suffering doesn't mean our story is over. That even when we are wounded, we are part of something much bigger—something eternal. At the table, we remember that Jesus lived a perfect life and still faced judgment, hate, and betrayal. And we remember that, just like His wounds brought life to the world, so can ours.

The second practice is *encouragement*.

Because transformation doesn't happen in isolation. One of the mistakes of Western Christianity is that we've individualized the Bible. When we read verses like, "For I know the plans I have for you, declares the Lord, plans to prosper you and not to harm you . . ." we assume that "you" means *me*.[267]

But God wasn't talking to an individual. He was speaking to a *people*.

Even in the New Testament, Paul's letters weren't written to individuals, but to the *church*.

So when Paul says, "You have been washed, sanctified, and justified," he's speaking to a community.

Of course, this doesn't mean our personal faith isn't important—it absolutely is. But it does mean that we were never meant to follow Jesus alone.

Robert Mulholland says, "Jesus forms himself in us for the sake of others."[268]

Our faith, our formation—it's always about *other people*.

We need each other. We need voices in our lives who remind us of what is true when we're tempted to forget. We need encouragers—people who have more faith in us than we have in ourselves. People who see the glory in us before we even dare to believe it's there.

If you are one of those people, let me just say: *We need you.*

When life hits, we need people who will come alongside the wounded, the brokenhearted, the weary, and remind them that *God is still writing their story*.

That what was meant for evil can be redeemed for good. That pain does not have the final word.

I know reminders don't take away the pain of the moment. But what they do is remind us that pain doesn't have to be the *authoritative* voice in our story.

It is *a* voice, but it is not *the* voice.

While writing this book, my wife gave birth to our son—Josiah David.

Or as we call him, JD.

I've already shared how fatherhood was something I feared—how I worried about failing, about not being the example my children needed. And while much of that fear faded after our daughter, Kennedi, was born, a new fear emerged when we found out we were having a son.

Because this time, I wasn't just raising a child.

I was raising *a mirror*.

A mini me.

Someone who would copy my every move.

Talk about a *fear of the Lord* moment.

Throughout the pregnancy, I found myself doing something I never thought I would. Late at night, while my wife slept, I would lean over, whisper prayers over her belly, prophesy over my son, and play worship music for him. And I noticed something. Every time I spoke, he *moved*.

He recognized my voice.

Then came the moment. The day my son was born. Standing beside my wife, watching her labor in pain, I felt helpless. I held her hand. I prayed. I waited. Contraction after contraction, the anticipation built. And then, with one final push—he was here.

The doctors placed him on my wife's chest, facing me.

Tears welled in my eyes as I looked at him for the first time.

"Hi, son. It's so nice to finally see you."

Immediately, he opened his eyes and locked onto mine.

As if to say: *You're the one. You're the voice I've been hearing all this time.*

And in that moment, I realized—that's how it will be when we see Jesus for the first time.

Our whole lives, we hear His voice. We learn to recognize His whisper in the chaos. He prays for us. He intercedes for us. He sings over us. We are being formed into His image now. But one day, we will step into eternity. And the moment we see Him, face-to-face, we will hear the words:

"Hi, son."

"Hi, daughter."

"It's so nice to finally see you."

And we, lost in wonder, will whisper back: "It's you . . . You're the voice I've been hearing my whole life."

So don't lose hope. Don't let pain be the loudest voice in your story. What we suffer now doesn't even compare to the joy we *will* have in the future—and the joy we *can* have in the present.

Jesus calls us to take our hope of eternity and *hover* over the chaos, the formlessness, the darkness of this world.

To bring healing where there is wounding.

To bring beauty where there is brokenness.

To bring renewal where there is despair.

To participate in the revolutionary, stubborn love of Jesus.

This is the call.

This is the invitation.

And this is the voice we've always known.

15

REVOLUTIONARY STUBBORN LOVE

I firmly believe that there is nothing more annoying than when you are sick and the doctor tells you, "Nope, everything seems fine."

When I was a teenager, I had an abscess in my throat, on my right tonsil specifically. I had a high fever, could barely swallow, and had a headache like I never had before. My parents took me to the doctor and when the doctor checked out my throat he diagnosed me with strep throat. Strep is incurable, you just have to ride it out.

So, he recommended drinking some tea to soothe my throat and to gargle with salt water to keep my mouth clean. At this point I had been sick for about a week, and I knew I didn't have strep; I'd had strep before, and something was different this time.

After a week, my mom took me back to the doctor, but this time, we had a different doctor.

This doctor, after looking at my throat, threw the other doctor under the bus and said, "Oh, you don't have strep!"

I was like, "Yeah! I know!"

She said, "You have mono!"

And like the first doctor she said, "There is no cure, you just need to go home and rest."

Even though I was frustrated, I couldn't argue because I'd never had mono before, so I was unsure of what the symptoms were. I just had to trust the doctor.

Another five days passed, and I am in excruciating pain because at this point, I can't really swallow, and what I come to find out later is that the abscess is pushing up on a major nerve in my throat, so I'm feeling all the pain.

I tell my mom we need to go to the hospital ASAP because I can't take this anymore. She drives me to the hospital, and we explain how two other doctors have diagnosed me with various viral infections and I don't seem to be getting any better and my fever is continuing to rise.

The hospital refers me to an ENT (ear, nose, and throat) specialist.

I must admit, in my frustration, I was quite cynical about the specialist. I just assumed he would misdiagnose me as well. The ENT specialist walks in, asks me to open my mouth, and takes a look at my throat, and within 1.7 seconds he says, "Oh, you don't have a viral infection, you have an abscess."

A bacterial infection!

I must admit, I wasn't sold.

I was like, "I'll believe you when I start to feel better."

He looked at me and said, "You ready to feel better?"

Thinking to myself, "No dude! I want to stay in this misery!" instead, I responded, "Yup!"

He began to explain that I had this bag of pus that built up and became infected, and it hurt because it was pressing on a major nerve in my throat. He explained that they were going to lacerate the abscess and that I would immediately feel better.

While waiting for the procedure to happen, I was frustrated with the other doctors—I mean, they went to med school as well! I was thinking to myself they must have gone to USC! (I'm joking, I only say that because I am a UCLA fan.)

When the doctor and the nurse came back in, they gave me a shot to numb the pain and lacerated the abscess. Immediately, and I mean immediately, I felt relief in my ear, head, and throat!

I have argued throughout this book how the world has misdiagnosed the world's condition and how that misdiagnosis has only led to more and more pain in the lives of people and the world. What we see in the person of Jesus is that He diagnoses the world with a condition called alienation from God through sin.

When Jesus entered into the scene, He declared how humans were made for more than their present reality. He shared how humans are designed for a relationship they haven't been told about, and how there is a beautiful, good, and true identity that humans were made to possess.

And to Jesus's own self disclosure, He claims Himself to be the good doctor who has come to be the medicine for the brokenness of humanity and the world.[269]

The medicine Jesus offered was His love, and no matter how much people tried to resist, rebuke, and deny His love, His love overcame the world, so much so that scholars and theologians make the point that Jesus's death and resurrection ushered in a new age in our world.

An age where evil, pain, and darkness no longer have the final say.

So, what is this love? And how does this love impact our lives?

RUSSIAN DOLLS

Everyone is fighting an unseen battle; everybody you see is carrying an invisible burden. Often, we don't see what is really going on beneath the surface in the hearts of people. We typically make assumptions about people based on how they look, dress, or speak. In our process of making assumptions, we determine if we "like" or "dislike" a person.

As I mentioned, growing up I wanted to be a police officer, and as a police officer, we were trained in how to observe people—assessing based on how they presented themselves and making logical conclusions to determine if they were involved in criminal activity.

I must say this: Contrary to the gospel of Jesus—my eye was trained to see the worst in people.

Part of my walk with Jesus has been retraining my eyes to see people differently. I've learned to be intentional about hearing their stories before making assumptions.

Because like you, I hate to be misunderstood. Oftentimes I am given the compliment of, "You are a lot different than I imagined you to be."

Based on my tattoos and demeanor, people typically associate me with the word "direct." But those who really know me would probably describe me as "soft."

What I have come to realize is that we are all Russian dolls.

Russian dolls are a set of dolls of decreasing size that nest inside one another. Each doll is dressed differently but maintains the same face.

I say this because we are born into this world innocent and pure, knowing of no evil or discord. But somehow with each passing day, week, month, year, and decade you have been formed into the person you are today.

You have a story—there is a reason you are the way that you are. Each milestone and each painful moment is like the decreased size version of your old self that has formed you into something new.

Oftentimes when we are misjudged or mischaracterized, we jump to our defense and say, "If you only knew my story, you wouldn't have judged me that way." Yet when we judge others we call it "discernment."

When was the last time you sat and reflected, *I wonder why Hitler turned out the way he did?* Or *I wonder why Putin turned out the way he did?* We often don't care. But the truth of the matter is if we were to see Hitler or Putin as a two-week-old newborn baby we would probably deem him as "cute."

But over time they turned out to be the people that we know them as today. Scripture however tells us that even Hitler and Putin were deemed worthy enough to die for—the havoc and pain which they have caused in the world isn't who they really are and isn't what Jesus called them to be.

The reason so many people love Jesus is because we feel like He understands us. Even in our mistakes we have this trust that He can see that our desire was pure. We believe that Jesus is able to see past our shame and insecurities, so in some way we allow Him past our walls, but when He sends other people in to see past our shame, we bulldoze them away.

We love the fact that Jesus died for our sins, but we, like Jonah, are quite disappointed when we find out that Jesus also loved and died for our enemies' sins.

Even though we may not say those words out loud, I believe that if we are honest with ourselves that statement wouldn't be entirely untrue.

I know that it seems like I am coming at you with rapid fire, and in some ways maybe I am. But in no way am I trying to shame you—because the interesting thing about pain is that it often speaks the lie of: *You are the only one who understands what you're going through. You are alone in this.*

But more often than not, God puts people in your life who have experienced similar pain in their life so that you both can find healing together. John Ortberg says, "When you notice and care about other people's stories your own story begins to get healed and find meaning."[270]

Sometimes your greatest source of healing comes as your greatest adversary.

ENEMY LOVE

What do you think God's heart is for really bad people?

What's his heart for rapists, child molesters, murderers, Hitler, Putin? Or better yet, what is his heart towards Satan?

Earlier in this book we looked at the book of Job, but we mostly focused on the person of Job and his response to God in the midst of his pain. Although Job is the main subject of the story, there is also a framing story that we should take note of. In chapter one of the book of Job, we are told somehow and in some way, in the heavenly places, God is having a conversation with Satan about Job.

The book of Job doesn't give any background on the relationship between God and Satan; all that we see is that Satan seems to be estranged from God.[271]

What we see next from God is quite tender and merciful. He asks Satan, "Where have you been?"[272]

Sound familiar?

It's similar to the question that God asks Adam after the fall. Adam is hiding from God, full of shame, and tenderly God asks Adam, "Where are you?"

That question is an invitation for Adam to reflect and come out from his shame and enter back into a relationship with God. Interestingly enough, He offers the same invitation to Satan, "Where have you been?"

Could it be that God offers Satan an invitation to come back home?

If we deem church history to be correct and connect Satan in the book of Job with the serpent that is found in Genesis 3, this makes God's invitation to Satan all the more scandalous.

The one who is responsible for the entire mess of the world is welcomed back by God with open arms.

This is a challenging reality for us to swallow (at least for me it is). Does God really love the Devil? Sometimes we are offended by God's love towards our enemies.

We love and cling to the stories of Jesus challenging the status quo of religious fundamentalism. We love to see Jesus eating with sinners, prostitutes, and the outcasts of society, and we often feel this boastful pride when He rebukes the Pharisees and other religious leaders. But what we sometimes fail to acknowledge is that Jesus died just as much for the sins of the religious oppressor as He did for the religiously oppressed.

The revolution of love that Jesus ushered in didn't happen because He loved those who loved Him; it happened because Jesus loved those who hated and harmed Him.

We know this in theory, but it's so hard to live out practically.

One of the greatest examples I can think of when it comes to enemy love comes from this family at our church—the Cruzes. In the middle of the night, the Cruzes phone started to ring. On the other end of the line was the hospital, and they informed the Cruzes that their son, Antonio, had just been shot and had died. Antonio was a good kid, he had good grades, he was a thoughtful, caring older brother, he just happened to be at the wrong place at the wrong time.

As any parents would, they began to question, "Where is God?" As they continued to pray and process their pain and uncertainties, the cops called and mentioned that they had arrested the man who shot and killed their son. This brought a whole new level of pain; they could finally put a face to the person who took their son's life—a lost 18-year-old who just wanted some money. Lost in their unanswerable questions, they turned to God and asked, "How do we move forward?" The Cruzes said God told them that the only way to heal was to forgive and bless the one who took Antonio from them. They called the courthouse and found out when the arraignment for the young man's case was and decided to go. The young man declared himself guilty. The judge asked if there was anything that the Cruz family wanted to say to him before sentencing. Together, they looked at the young man and said, "We forgive you; we don't hold this against you, all that we pray is that you would turn your life over to Jesus."

Wow...

This is the kind of love that brings healing into the lives of people. I remember when I heard their story, I was haunted by their tangible expression of love.

I believe that the main way we can bring healing to the world is if we lay down our rights to be correct, hurt, and unforgiving and offer a grace back to the people who have caused us the most harm.

As a pastor I hear it all the time, people claim to forgive those who have hurt them but "don't want anything to do with them anymore."

Imagine if Jesus said that to you.

"Yeah, Dakota, I forgive you, but I don't want anything to do with you."

What kind of grace is that?

The very thing we love about Jesus is what Jesus calls us to offer other people. Distant forgiveness will not be the testimony that wins people for the gospel—washing the feet of your betrayer, forgiveness without apology, and handing over your life to those who want to end it is the only way healing will mend our fractured world.

What about justice? What about what is right and wrong? Aren't we called to administer justice and call out sin?

Yes, but Jesus will sort all that out. He invites us, His church, to embrace the paradox of His scandalous grace. We are called to love the world and people who have hurt us. If we believe Jesus is who He says He is, then we need to embrace His call to enemy love. Dallas Willard furthers this point; "We don't believe something by merely saying we believe it, or even when we believe that we believe it. We believe something when we act as if it were true."[273]

SCANDALOUS GRACE

One of the hardest felt tensions we feel as Christians is *how to navigate grace and moralism.*

We have seen more fundamental churches overemphasize morality which has led to shame and condemnation in people's lives. On the other end of the spectrum we have seen progressive churches say, "We are covered by God's grace, so we are now free to do whatever we want."

If Jesus's love revolutionized the world, which would He typically lean towards? The answer is neither; we are called to live in this tension.

Jesus teaches that there is a third way—the way of beauty.

John 8:1-11 gives us insight into the way of beauty. The religious leaders caught a woman in the act of adultery. Now, according to the Jewish law, a woman caught in adultery was to be punished by death.[274] The interesting part about this is that the religious leaders didn't care that this woman was caught in adultery. In this period in Israel's history, they didn't have the right to just kill anyone who broke their law. The Israelites were still under the rule of the Romans.

The woman would have known this as well—she wasn't in fear that she was going to lose her life; the worst that would have happened to her is that she would have been publicly shamed. The heart behind the Pharisees' question was to prove that Jesus wasn't the Messiah.

John records that when Jesus is questioned, He begins to write something in the sand with His finger.

Where have we seen this?

Two different places in the Old Testament: First, when God writes the 10 commandments with his finger. Second, when the finger of God appears and writes on the wall in Daniel 5.

All three instances when God's finger is mentioned have to do with the themes of law and judgment.

In Exodus, God writes the law with his finger, showing Israel what it means to live as a holy people.

In Daniel 5, King Belshazzar is being judged by God for defiling the sacred items that belonged in Israel's temple.

In John 8, Jesus is challenged to judge the adulterous woman who is defiled according to the law. It's ironic the one who wrote the law, Jesus, is now being challenged to defend His own law. And what is His response?

"Let anyone who is without sin throw the first stone." This is kind of a rhetorical statement; Jesus would know that no faithful Jew would ever claim to be without sin—only one is sinless, and that is God.

What is the response? One by one people leave, leaving only Jesus, and as we know Jesus doesn't throw the stone at the woman either. He chooses grace.

But what about sin? Does Jesus all of a sudden adopt a more progressive theology?

No, Jesus doesn't tell the woman, "You do you! Go live your life as you see fit. I celebrate your sexual liberation from religious oppression!" He doesn't celebrate her sexual autonomy, instead He says, "Leave your life of sin."[275]

What Jesus seemed to understand is that sin was enough of a consequence—He didn't need to pour salt in the wounds of people. Tim Keller brilliantly says, "If you want God's grace, all you need is need, all you need is nothing."[276]

God's grace is scandalous. There is nothing He wouldn't give to see people healed and restored. In our justice-focused society, we look forward to when people are judged, but Jesus says sin is enough of a consequence. The Gospels give account after account of people coming to Jesus haunted by their sin and seeking a new way out, and not one time do we see Jesus condemn or say, "I told you so." If moralism isn't the way and progressive Christianity isn't the way, how do we help people walk like Jesus in this world?

There is this idea in Judaism that one doesn't just obey the commands of God, but one beautifies them. This is called *"Hiddur Mitzvah."* The concept comes from Exodus 15:22, "This is my God, and I will beautify him with my praise."

The intention behind Hiddur Mitzvah is to look beyond the temptation of moralism as the means to please God. As Dallas Willard would say, "Grace is not opposed to effort, it is opposed to earning. Earning is an attitude. Effort is an action."[277]

Hiddur Mitzvah is also an attempt to avoid the progressive ideology that "you can do as you please and God is okay with it," by believing you can honor God by the beauty of your actions and devotion to Him. Hiddur Mitzvah is about expressing your commitment to Jesus and declaring with your body what your heart feels!

The way of scandalous grace doesn't dismiss holiness for rights. The way of scandalous grace elevates people to live out their God-given identity, creating paths for holiness to captivate the heart of the believer, that ultimately shouts the truth of old, "I will be your God, and you will be my people."[278]

BLESSED OR HAPPY?

What comes to mind when you think of the "Christian life?"

Would you describe Christians as happy, blessed, sad, deprived, repressed, or . . . boring?

For many of us, and definitely for people who are outside of the faith, they would describe the Christian life in various ways, but beautiful, blessed, or satisfied probably aren't any of them.

We just celebrated my wife's 30th birthday, and I surprised her with a nice dinner with all of her girlfriends. I love her friends; they are fun, intentional, and very Dutch... what I mean is they are direct!

During the dinner I was talking to one of her friends about me being a pastor and she straight up asked me, "Why are you a pastor? Isn't church boring? I think if church was more exciting more people would be interested." We ended up having a very good conversation about church and following Jesus, but even though I disagreed with her method on how to win people for Jesus, I agreed with the fact that something needed to shift.

In the greatest sermon ever preached, the Sermon on the Mount, Jesus lays out what it means to have the "good life."

Some of you guys are thinking, "Finally, now we get to talk about the good life!"

Does "the good life" mean a happy life or a blessed life? Is there a difference?

Happiness is something that is personal; what makes me happy might be something that makes you miserable! Jesus isn't offering His interpretation of what it means to be happy in life—He is offering us a counter-cultural framework of what it means to be *blessed*.

We throw that word around kind of loosely; "he was blessed with brains" or "he was blessed with generational wealth" as if being blessed is left up to chance.

In Jesus's teaching, the blessed life is for everyone.

What is the blessed life?

The blessed life is the second half of each beatitude.[279]

> You will possess the Kingdom of Heaven.
> You will inherit the earth.
> Those who mourn are comforted.
> Those who are hungry are satisfied.
> You will receive mercy.
> You see God.
> You are called God's child.

For Jesus these blessings come as a single package. The blessings aren't like a fast-food restaurant where Jesus is your server and you say, "I'll take the inherit the earth, with a side of being satisfied, leave off the mercy."

No, it's a package deal. Just like the eight characteristics are a package deal.

> Blessed are the poor in spirit.
> Blessed are those who mourn.
> Blessed are the meek.
> Blessed are those who hunger and thirst for righteousness.
> Blessed are the merciful.
> Blessed are the pure in heart.
> Blessed are the peacemakers.
> Blessed are those who are persecuted.

Yup, now you're thinking, "That's what I thought, that's the same self-deprecating Christianity I know." But if we overlook what Jesus is saying, we will miss out on how God intends to bring healing to the world.

For Jesus this isn't about human depravity. It's actually about reinforcing the order that we see in Genesis 1, where God blesses humanity before giving them instruction. In the same way, Jesus begins with blessing before He gives commands, reinforcing the idea that God's grace comes before obedience.

Each of the beatitudes is about cultivating a counter-intuitive identity that is relatable and attractive for those who hurt and mourn. That is why many of us have at some point in time related to all eight traits of the beatitudes.

Have you ever been poor in the spirit? Check! We know what it feels like to search for meaning and significance to only come up empty.

Have you ever mourned? I wouldn't be writing a book on pain if this wasn't part of my story.

Are you desperate to see the world as a better place? We all want to see our world and our personal lives be in a better place.

And the list goes on and on and on.

Jesus makes the point that for those who have experienced pain, rejection, and hurt and continue to search for meaning and have a heart to see the world a better place, there is good news! Because those who enter God's Kingdom first are those who hunger for righteousness and suffer as peacemakers.[280]

Jesus goes on to make a point that speaks to our role in restoring the world. He calls us "the salt of the earth."[281] In the Old Testament salt is a symbol of God's lasting covenant with Israel. Jesus makes the point that when we come to follow Him, we are carrying that covenant to its ultimate fulfillment.

We play a major role in the perfecting of the world, and we are only able to take on this role because Jesus has already overcome sin, death, and pain!

What used to be the authoritative voice in our story is now washed away because Jesus is ruling in our world here and now as the Messiah.

Some of you may be asking, "Why do bad things happen if Jesus is still ruling?"

The answer is found in Jesus's Sermon on the Mount.

When God is expected by people to sort things out, right all wrongs, rid the world of all pain, people want God to send in the metaphorical "tanks" and blast everything that is wrong with society away. But we see that is not the way of the Kingdom of God. When God wants to transform the world, He sends in the weak, meek, mourners, the broken-hearted, the pure in heart, the humble, and the hungry-for-justice people. By the time the tyrants, Caesars, the ruling powers of our time figure out what is going on, the weak, the meek, the mourners, the broken-hearted, the pure in heart, the humble, and the hungry-for-justice people have been looking after the poor and the hurting, they have been setting up schools, hospitals, and other means of hope for people, all while telling people that following Jesus is the way into a new way of life. A life that starts here and now because Jesus is already reigning.

The present rule of King Jesus is the rulership of the gospel, the rulership of the gospel is the way of love, love with skin on it, love people are drawn to, love that makes people become more alive, and Jesus will continue to rule until all injustice and pain are dealt with.

He sends in the wounded to save the wounded.

He sends those who have experienced pain to save those who are trapped in their pain.

He sends those who have been broken to help restore the broken.

This is the Christian purpose! You have been placed here and now to bring wholeness to the world around you—don't let pain stop you from entering into the fight.

Jesus concludes the Sermon of the Mount by offering us a choice.[282]

We can either follow Jesus on the narrow path or follow the world's trends and way of living that lead to the same cycle of brokenness. When we read about the narrow path, we often think it's about salvation or "who goes to heaven vs who goes to hell." But I don't think this was Jesus's point.

The narrow path is a lot like the wardrobe in C.S. Lewis's fiction novel, *The Lion, the Witch, and the Wardrobe*. Think back to the moment where Peter, Edmund, Susan, and Lucy run and hide from the professor. They all climb into the wardrobe and at first, they are squished tight, all attempting to fit, and as they each continue to move farther back into the wardrobe all of a sudden there is more space and freedom.

This is the way of Jesus's teaching. At first it will seem tight and restrictive, but the more you rest in His trust you will find that His teaching will lead you into a life of wonder, freedom, and excitement.

Pain, your pain, plays a vital role in the world's healing. It may not be the way we would do things, but we need to trust that Jesus sees the bigger picture.

BY HIS WOUNDS WE ARE HEALED

Loss and recovery, breakage and restoration, tragedy and the ability to overcome it. This is what Jesus offers us and invites us into.

Our hearts, in some ways, are most familiar with the reality that the brokenness of the world is not how it's supposed to be, and more often than not we feel like sojourners, people who are lost with no home. We know that home is somewhere in which we feel whole and safe.

People often say, "Home is where the heart is." This is true; take a moment and look at where your heart is.

Whether you're an artist, musician, pastor, police officer, schoolteacher, or influencer, your heart and vocation are an attempt to make the world a better place and to help people find their way in this life. More often than not our dreams are attached to the brokenness of the world.

Athletes speak of using their platform for a greater cause.

Fashion designers believe clothes give a voice to the voiceless.

Chefs help people forget about a hard day through a transcendent meal.

Musicians attempt to use raw elements of sound and words to bring together groups of hurting people.

My point is, I think Jesus's teaching on the Sermon on the Mount is a lot more familiar in our hearts than we even realize. We often know that when we set out goals and vision for our life, we are going to face opposition, whether that opposition is within ourselves or others. Either way, we know it's coming.

That is often what makes achieving our goals so satisfying! We know what we had to overcome in order to achieve our desired outcome.

All Jesus is doing is putting words to what we already feel, know, and want. Jesus's words remind us, before we go and attempt to reconstruct the world, *we are blessed*!

How are we blessed?

Well, a scar doesn't form on the dying!

Living "the blessed life" (mourning, peacemaking, broken-hearted, hungry, thirsty, merciful, pure in heart, and meek) is an indicator that you are fully alive! Being able to feel those emotions, being able to continue to believe and hope in the midst of a broken and fractured world are all indicators that you are alive!

In his book, *The Virtues of War*, Steven Pressfield portrays Alexander the Great as a leader who "bore his wounds on the front." He replays a moment when Alexander's army was struggling to continue fighting and wanted to turn around and go home.[283]

Pressfield describes Alexander's response to his army like this, "Alexander called an assembly. When the army had gathered, the young king stepped forth and stripped naked. 'These scars on my body,' Alexander declared, 'were got for you, my brothers. Every wound, as you see, is in the front. Let that man stand forth from your ranks who has bled more than I, or endured more than I for your sake. Show him to me, and I will yield to your weariness and go home.'

"Not a man came forward. Instead, a great cheer arose from the army. The men begged their king to forgive them for their want of spirit and pleaded with him only to lead them forward."

This is how we are called to live! Our leader isn't Alexander the Great, our leader is Jesus Christ, the risen King. What we see from Jesus after His resurrection is that He still bore His wounds.[284] When Jesus appears to His disciples, they are unsure who He is. He is unrecognizable. (Paul later tells us when we resurrect from the dead we will be "our truest selves," that we will be unrecognizable.[285])

In order for them to know who He is, Jesus reveals the wounds "on his hands and side, and the disciples recognized him and were overjoyed."[286] However, when the disciples shared with Thomas that they saw the risen Jesus, he didn't believe. Thomas didn't say, "unless I see his face" or "unless you show me a selfie with the correct time stamp." No, Thomas said, "I won't believe it unless I see the nail wounds in his hands, put my fingers into them, and place my hand into the wound in his side."[287]

Think about that for a minute, why the wounds?

Honestly speaking, if my wife were to die by a gunshot, and somehow come back from the dead, my first thought wouldn't be "show me the bullet hole." I would probably ask her a trick question that only she would know. I would probably ask 1,000 different questions, but asking to see the wound wouldn't be one of them. But for Thomas, the wounds that were on Jesus were the defining marks of His identity. Why was Jesus the Messiah? Not because He claimed Himself to be, not because He was the strongest or most intelligent, but because He conquered the one thing that no human on this earth could.

Death.

For Thomas, the wounds Jesus bore were attached to His Messiahship.

When Jesus approaches Thomas, He shows Thomas His wounds and says, "Go ahead, look and put your finger inside." Scripture doesn't say that Thomas ever put his finger inside Jesus's wounds, it tells us that because he *saw*, he believed. [288]

Jesus bore His scars in His resurrected body because He was alive! More alive than He ever was!

There are three temptations that we face when wounded:

First, we can ignore them, act like they don't matter, and continue to move forward without contemplating the implications of what happened. This presents Jesus in a negative light, displaying Him as a God who is emotionally distant and someone who doesn't care about your pain.

Second, we can over-celebrate them. Use them as badges for our own self-glorification. This is about self-righteousness, in a way condemning others for not sharing in your zeal.

The third way, which we see in Jesus's life, is that we make our wounds a part of who we are, we accept them. Our wounds are not a means for self-righteousness, but they are a witness to a story.

Paul Bunyan says this, "My marks and scars I carry with me, to be a witness for me that I have fought His battles who now will be my Rewarder."[289]

Our wounds are pointers to a different reality.

Our wounds are the reason people will invite us into their lives.

Our wounds are how we draw near into the depths of other people's pain.

Our wounds are our testimony that Jesus is more real, near, and satisfying than anything we could ever imagine.

16
REAL, NEAR, AND SATISFYING

There is one point that I have failed to make.

We all wrestle with a question that shapes our worldview more than we realize—a doubt rooted in the soil of secularism: *What if they're right, and Christianity is fake, and Jesus isn't Lord?*

What if Salvation, Heaven, and Hell really are made up ideologies in a way to control and manipulate people?

What if I have been lied to?

Because of the time and the culture we live in, at some point in our faith journey we all find ourselves at this crossroad.

Is Christianity real?

Is Jesus really near?

Can He provide a more satisfying life than the secular story?

This crossroads isn't new.

It's the same tension that has haunted souls for centuries—the desire for truth but the fear of what finding it might mean.

Take C.S. Lewis, for example. He was a committed atheist, convinced that Christianity was wishful thinking for the weak. Yet, the more he studied, the more he saw that Jesus wasn't just a historical figure or a religious leader—He was either everything He claimed to be or nothing at all. Lewis called himself "the most dejected and reluctant convert in all England,"[290] but he couldn't ignore the reality that Jesus was real, near, and compellingly good.

In the words of Lewis himself, "Jesus is either a liar, lunatic, or Lord."[291]

The implications for these questions are huge. If Jesus is a liar, then there's no point, we can do what we want and feel what we want because the secular narrative is true and provides the best way for flourishing. If Jesus is a lunatic, well, I think that question answers itself.

But if Jesus is Lord, then that means He is true and not just true about some things, but true about everything.

REAL AND TRUE

Truth in our modern world is fluid, subjective. We hear it all the time: "Live your truth." But what does that even mean? Truth, by definition, is that which corresponds with reality. Yet, society wrestles with it just as Pontius Pilate did when he stood before Jesus and asked, "What is truth?"[292]

Jesus's response wasn't a philosophical argument but a claim about Himself: "The reason I was born and came into the world is to testify to the truth."[293] The Greek word here, "*martureō*," means to *reveal evidence*.

In other words, Jesus wasn't just *speaking truth*—His *entire life* was the evidence of it.

That's the thing about Jesus.

He didn't just present an idea or moral philosophy. He made an exclusive claim: "I am the way and the truth and the life."[294] The weight of this statement forces us to decide—either Jesus is right about everything He said or He's completely mistaken. And if He's right, then it changes everything.

Blaise Pascal, the 17th-century philosopher, recognized this dilemma and framed it as a wager: If God is real and we choose to follow Him, we gain everything. If He's not, we lose nothing. But if we reject Him and He is real, we lose everything.[295]

Pascal saw faith in Jesus not as blind optimism, but as the most rational choice one could make.

But Jesus doesn't just ask us to believe in Him theoretically. He invites us into an experiential reality—one where He proves Himself near and satisfying.

Take Dietrich Bonhoeffer, the German theologian who stood against Nazi ideology. His life was marked by deep suffering, yet in the face of death, he spoke of the nearness of Christ as his only true comfort. He once wrote, "He who is alone with his sin is utterly alone. But it is the grace of the gospel that confronts us with the truth and says: You are a sinner, a great, desperate sinner. Now come as the sinner that you are to God who loves you."[296]

Even in prison, awaiting execution, Bonhoeffer experienced a peace and satisfaction that no worldly freedom could offer.

This is the paradox of following Jesus. At first, it feels like giving up control. But in surrender, we find something better—real peace, real joy, real love.

Saint Augustine, who once chased every pleasure the world had to offer, finally found rest in Christ and wrote, "You have made us for Yourself, O Lord, and our hearts are restless until they rest in You."[297]

The realization that Jesus is real is one thing. But discovering that He is good? That's what changes everything. It's not just about intellectually assenting to truth—it's about encountering a person who satisfies the deepest longings of the soul.

If Jesus is who He says He is, why wouldn't we trust that His way is best? The invitation is always open. The question is, how will we respond?

NEAR AND GOOD

I've never been one for physical touch. It's always felt a bit awkward. I am not a fan of people being that close to me, I mean, what if they forgot to put on deodorant or had a meal drenched in garlic. No thanks.

But when you're married to someone whose love language is physical touch, you learn to accept it as a part of life.

That's maybe part of the reason I thrived in Covid. "Six feet, please!" I would often tell Bren.

But as time stretched on, I realized how much I missed hugs. There's something about physical presence that speaks to the soul in a way words never could. It made me think: what must it have been like for the lepers in Jesus's day?

Leprosy was devastating—not just because of its physical effects but because it made people untouchable. (Not in the superior kind of sense unfortunately.)

Because of the Torah, those with leprosy were required to live outside the village, shouting "Unclean! Unclean!" whenever they came near others.

Worse, leprosy numbed the nervous system, leaving people unable to feel anything. A person could place their hand in a fire and not know it was burning.

With all this in mind, we see something beautiful about Jesus in Mark 1. A leper comes to Jesus, desperate: "If you are willing, you can make me clean." Not healed. *Clean*. He longs for more than restored health—he longs for restored connection, he misses the physical touch.

Jesus could have healed him with a word, He could have clicked His feet and . . . Bam! Healed. He could have done whatever He wanted to.

Instead, He reaches out and touches him.

Before the man is healed, Jesus does what no one else would do—He draws *near*. This is what sets Jesus apart. He doesn't just heal; *He enters into pain*. He moves toward the suffering, not away from it.

Think of Mother Teresa in the slums of Calcutta. She didn't just serve from a distance; she touched the sick, held the dying, embraced the untouchable. She once said, "Being unwanted, unloved, uncared for, forgotten by everybody, I think that is a much greater hunger, a much greater poverty than the person who has nothing to eat."[298]

That's the kind of nearness Jesus offers.

When He draws near to us, He truly can take what was meant for evil and turn it into good.[299]

SATISFYINGLY BEAUTIFUL

St. Augustine famously prayed, "Lord, give me chastity and self-control, but not yet."[300] His story mirrors the tension we all feel—wanting the joy of God but fearing we'll miss out on something better.

We often think of Christianity as restrictive.

Something to embrace later, once we've had our fun.

I remember talking to a friend who wasn't a Christian about faith, and his response to me about following Jesus was, "Nice, man, yeah I'll become a Christian when I'm older and ready to settle down." I remember thinking he was talking about following Jesus in the same way he would talk about putting a downpayment on a house.

But the problem with this worldview isn't the fact that my friend thinks Christianity won't help him here and now. He would probably even concede to the fact that living like Jesus would make the world a "better place."

The problem is that his worldview assumes that Jesus is holding out on us—that true satisfaction is found elsewhere.

Augustine once believed that, too. But later, he wrote, "You cast out my desires and entered yourself to take their place. You, who are more delightful than all pleasure."[301]

We see this in Luke's Gospel with the woman who anoints Jesus's feet. A woman, known for her sin, enters a Pharisee's house uninvited. Weeping, she washes Jesus's feet with her tears, dries them with her hair, and anoints them with perfume. Everything about this moment is scandalous—her presence, her touch, her gesture. The Pharisee is horrified, but Jesus isn't.

"Do you see this woman?" Jesus asks.

He doesn't rebuke her.

He honors her.

Because He understands what the Pharisee doesn't—she isn't just acting out of emotion. She's responding to something deeper. Her desires led her down a broken path, but at their core, they were never wrong. They were just misplaced. Jesus redirects them.

The problem with our culture and even within the church is that we don't know what to do with desire.

Religion tries to repress desire.

Secularism tells us to release desire.

Jesus redeems and redirects desire.

We often misdiagnose our longings. We chase pleasure, not realizing that what we're actually craving is intimacy. We seek success, not understanding that what we really want is to be seen and valued. We drown ourselves in distraction when what our souls need is rest.

Jesus meets a woman at a well and tells her, "Everyone who drinks this water will be thirsty again, but whoever drinks the water I give them will never thirst."[302]

The amazing part is that Jesus doesn't deny that the world offers satisfaction. But He knows that without Him, it never lasts.

The beauty of Jesus isn't that He demands we abandon desire—it's that He offers us something better. He knows what we value, what we chase, what we long for most. And rather than stripping it away, He invites us to place it in His hands, where it can finally bring life instead of destruction.

To help people heal, we must understand the sacred core of desire. Not shame it. Not indulge it. But, like Jesus, call it toward something greater.

THE SACRED CORE

The Sacred Core is a non-negotiable belief or value that a person or community has. In order for us as Christians to effectively share Jesus and present Jesus in a more compelling way, we need to first seek and understand what people's Sacred Core is.

Jesus was brilliant at this; He understood that the rich young ruler loved possessions! Yes, Jesus challenged the rich young ruler to give up his earthly possessions so that . . . what?

He would receive heavenly treasure![303]

Jesus didn't condemn the fact he had possessions or wealth; He just made the point that his earthly wealth was a hindrance to his formation.

We often take Jesus's command of, "Whoever wants to be my disciple must deny themselves and take up their cross and follow me"[304] as "self-denial." Rid yourself of things that give you pleasure, happiness, and satisfaction, but that's not Jesus's command. Jesus isn't talking about self-denial; He more so means to not let your desires be the ultimate goal in your life. It's about giving your desire to Him and pursuing what is good.

As John Mark Comer says, "We are to deny our 'self' not ourselves."[305]

Failing to understand the Sacred Core of people is what has led many people in our culture to lose interest in Jesus. Just think about the moments you have heard pastors or church leaders say, "If you really want to do God's work then you have to get into ministry or become a missionary."

Or an example that Jon Tyson uses is, how many people of the LGBTQIA+ community believe that Christians just want to "pray the gay away" and that they must become heterosexual in order to be loved by God? Jon understands that for many in the LGBTQIA+ community their sexuality is the most sacred part of who they are. Jon's response to the LGBTQIA+ community is that the gospel of Jesus isn't the gospel of heterosexuality, it's the gospel of the Lordship of Jesus ruling and reigning in our lives.[306]

Jesus understood what the Sacred Core was for each of His disciples, and He used each other's Sacred Core for one another's formation.

Do you think it was by accident Jesus chose a zealot and a tax collector to be His disciples? One was a "Make Israel Great Again" kind of person, and the other would have been a "socialist democrat."

Do you think it was by accident that He chose Judas (the one who seemingly loved money the most) to be in charge of the money?

No!

Jesus understood that the zealots believed Rome was the enemy and by choosing a tax collector to be part of His Kingdom meant that Simon the Zealot would have to learn how to love those he hated most—the same goes for Matthew.

And for Judas, Jesus understood that he was greedy and by placing him over the money it forced Judas to grow in generosity and gain wealth in spiritual and more lasting ways.

If we want to help people find healing in their life, then we need to be intentional in knowing people's stories, learning what their Sacred

Core is, and then humbly and gently presenting the way of Jesus to them. We need to show that Jesus doesn't just know what their Sacred Core is, but He can provide a more lasting and satisfying Sacred Core. As you can see, the way of Jesus and the way of culture are so vastly different! This isn't a declaration to stay away from culture. It's actually the opposite. Jesus calls us to run to culture and to present a different way of living that will truly be lasting and satisfying.

Jesus gives us the invitation, and we give the invitation to the world.

THE INVITATION

Perhaps the most compelling case for Jesus that we can offer this world comes from His invitation, "Come to me, all of you who are weary and carry heavy burdens, and I will give you rest."[307]

We live in a generation of weary and heavily burdened people.

For many of us we feel anxious, tired, and burdened from the troubles of the world. No amount of rest or sleep seems to allow us to catch up from the exhaustion we face. In a research study done by Pew Research, they found that 66% of Americans were suffering from "news fatigue."[308]

In other words, they were heavily burdened by the news of the world.

Burnout has gone viral; it has become the unwanted follower of our lives.

The World Health Organization defines burnout as, "A syndrome resulting from chronic work-related stress marked by fatigue and detachment."[309] In the U.K 79% of people say they have experienced a season of burnout, in the United States 51% of people say that they have experienced a season of burnout, and 34% of all suicides in Japan can be traced back to vocational burnout.[310] This is the unspoken pandemic of everyday life.

What about the church? Surely the people who value things like rest, sabbath, silence, and solitude must not struggle from burnout. Well unfortunately the church is just as bad. According to the Barna group only 35% of pastors are considered "healthy."[311] What they determined as "healthy" was overall well-being: spiritual, physical, emotional, and financial.

We are the exhausted generation.

How many of you know what it feels like to get a full 8 hours of sleep but wake up feeling exhausted?

How many of you know what it feels like to go on vacation and come back even more run down?

When you're struggling with exhaustion the last thing you want to do is go to church; the last thing in the world that sounds restful is going to place where you have to sit by a complete stranger, stand and awkwardly raise your hands, greet and awkwardly hug the people in front of you and behind you, and listen to some preacher who is telling you that you need to give more money, volunteer more time, and adopt this spiritual practice so that you can truly find rest and happiness.

If we are honest, Jesus's invitation to rest seems like an impossible reality.

After Jesus gives His first invitation to come to Him when weary and tired, He offers us a second invitation with a gift, "Take my yoke upon you and learn from me."[312] What is a yoke? A yoke was a wooden beam used to keep two animals close together, typically oxen, so together they could work in pulling a plowing cart.

Jesus is saying that we have a choice, we can either take on His yoke, or the yoke of something else. Some of you are thinking, "Do we have to take on any yoke?" it seems like we do, especially with the second half of Jesus's statement, "and learn from me." The yoke represents a way of life, and as we already talked about, everyone is being formed into something based on their way of life.

Jesus then goes on to describe His character for us, "For I am gentle and humble in heart."[313]

What is Jesus saying about Himself? Him being gentle means that He is non-threatening, approachable, kind and understanding. He gets you! That point becomes clear when He says that He is humble in heart. Though being God, He came to be a human, so He knows the weight which you carry. Doesn't that just sound amazing? How many of you wish to work for a boss who is gentle and humble? Or how many of us wish that life would be gentle and humble?

I remember once when I was bartending, my shift was incredibly slow, probably because it was a Sunday morning, and my manager, in order to keep me busy, told me to clean the keg room. The keg room is gross, it smells like a bunch of different spilled beer, the floors are sticky, and it's freezing cold. So I grabbed a mop and some towels and the next thing I knew my manager was waiting for me next to the keg room.

I said, "What's up?"

He smiled and said, "You ready?"

"You're going to help?" I replied.

"Yeah, let's knock this out," he said.

Confused as to why he was helping me out, I finally asked, "Why are you doing this?" He said, "I would never ask you to do something that I wouldn't do myself."

There was something about his humility and his understanding of what it meant to be the "low man on the pole" that inspired me to work harder. I started to look for things to clean, to go above and beyond at work. Why? Because there was something about him coming down to my level that elevated me to rise to his.

This is what Jesus did for us.

His invitation to take on His yoke and learn from Him is only possible because He came down to our level so that we could elevate up to His level.

What does the way of Jesus give us? "You will find rest for your souls."[314]

The exhaustion that we feel isn't purely physical exhaustion, it's spiritual fatigue.

We are wandering and wandering around the wilderness of life looking for anything that will satisfy our thirst to be whole. We dive headfirst into our careers, school, sex, partying, social justice movements, and consumerism, and we are left exhausted! The physical pursuit to satisfy a spiritual need leads to soulful exhaustion.

Jesus's final statement is, "For my yoke is easy and my burden is light." Here He is making a contrasting statement between His yoke and the yoke of the world (remember having a yoke isn't optional). The Greek word for "easy" (*chrēstos*) doesn't mean simple—it more so means "good or gentle." Interesting that the yoke of Jesus matches His character.

That's the point!

Jesus, who is gentle and humble, offers a yoke that is gentle and humble and walks alongside us, bearing the yoke with us. Remember, a yoke always requires two! God puts Himself next to us under His yoke by sending He His son Jesus to walk side by side with us, but the yoke of God is one that matches His character—one that is good, easy, and gentle that will lead to a life that is safe and full of rest.

Whereas the yoke of culture matches the character of culture. Which means, you are all alone, you must carry the weight all by yourself. The character and values of culture are rooted in the individual: You are responsible for determining what is right, wrong, good, true, and beautiful. Therefore, you must carry your own yoke. The tragedy in all this is that we don't have the ability to find true rest within ourselves.

Jesus's point is that the yoke of moralism and secularism will only lead you to one place: an anxious, weary, and burdensome life.

But His yoke is an invitation into a more lasting, satisfying, and rested life.

To cap it all off, when we come to Jesus, the Bible attests to the fact that we become a new creation,[315] and in our new self not only do we have the mind of Christ,[316] but we are like Christ;[317] which means we can now offer His yoke to people, and by humbling ourselves like Christ, we submit ourselves under Christ's yoke once again to help people carry the weight of the world, ultimately leading them to find true rest for their souls and their wounds.

Praise be to God the Father, who sent His Son to become our Salvation, and thanks be to the Holy Spirit who incorporates us into the life of the Trinity, praise be to God, forever and ever amen.

17

SACRED WOUNDS

Everybody loves a good comeback story.

There's just something about it—against all odds, the long wait, the heartbreak along the way—that makes victory taste even sweeter.

My dad is a die-hard Chicago Cubs fan. If you know anything about baseball, you know that the Cubs were historically more "Bad News Bears" than "New York Yankees." Winning just wasn't their thing.

I still remember the night of the Steve Bartman incident. And if you're a Cubs fan, I'm sorry for bringing up this ancient wound. But for those of you who don't know—October 14, 2003. A night that still haunts many. At that point, the Cubs hadn't won a World Series in *ninety-five years*.

2003 was supposed to be the year. The team was stacked: Mark Prior and Kerry Wood throwing heat from the mound, Sammy Sosa and Moisés Alou crushing baseballs. The Cubs had the lead and were five outs away from breaking the curse and heading to the World Series.

Then it happened.

A Marlins batter hit a pop-up down the third base line. Moisés Alou sprinted toward the wall, ready to make the out. But in the same moment, a fan named Steve Bartman—just a regular guy in the stands, wearing headphones and a Cubs hat—reached out, trying to snag the ultimate souvenir. His hand knocked the ball away from Alou's glove.

Alou lost it. He jumped, slammed his glove, shouted at the ump. He wanted fan interference. The umps didn't call it. The Marlins got another chance. And the Cubs? Well, they unraveled. The Marlins came back, won the game, forced a Game Seven, and—just like that—the Cubs were out.

And just like that, Steve Bartman became the guy everyone blamed.

(I mean, sure, maybe the team's meltdown played a tiny role. But nope—Bartman took the fall.)

I remember watching my dad, heartbroken. Another year, another heartbreak.

Fast forward to 2016. The Cubs finally had another shot. This time, they made it to the World Series against the Cleveland Guardians (back then, still called the Indians). *One hundred and eight years* since their last championship. It felt like the entire world was rooting for them—except Cleveland, obviously. But even they had to admit, it would be kind of beautiful.

But, of course, the Cubs did Cubs things.

They fell behind 3-1 in the series. Three losses, just one more and they were out. The same old story. But then—game by game—they clawed their way back. They tied the series 3-3. And suddenly, it was Game Seven. Winner takes all.

I wasn't even a die-hard Cubs fan, but I was nervous—not for me, but for my dad. He had waited his whole life for this.

That night, I was working at a bar, ironically surrounded by my dad's friends. Worst employee of the night? Hands down, me. But no one cared. They knew what this meant.

And then—it happened...

The Cubs won.

I ran to the breakroom, called my dad, and I could hear it in his voice—crackling, breaking, tears of joy. The Cubs had done it.

And just like that, all the painful moments of Cubs history seemed to vanish. Not erased, not forgotten, but *redeemed*. Because all of that pain, all the heartbreak—it led to this.

Victory.

I celebrated that night with fans of all teams—Dodgers fans, Padres fans, Yankees fans. We hugged, laughed, and one guy patted me on the back and said, "Your dad can wait another 108 years for the next one—because next year is the Dodgers' year. I was only a Cubs fan for one night!"

I hate to keep the sports analogy going, but I need to make my point: Christians in this world? We're *not* the Yankees. We're the Cubs.

We will experience pain, disappointment, and loss. We'll have our fair share of heartbreak. But one day—the whole world will see the *victory* that's coming.

Paul says it in Romans: "The whole creation has been groaning together in the pains of childbirth until now."[318]

That's our reality. Not just us, but creation itself—aching, longing, groaning. But here's the thing about childbirth: the pain *is leading somewhere*.

New life is coming.

So how do we, as the church, respond to these pains?

CONTROL, COERCION, OR INFLUENCE?

There's a long-standing debate on how Christians should usher in this *new age* that the New Testament speaks of.

Some believe the way forward is through legislation and government. That if we can just elect the *right people* and pass the *right laws*, then God's Kingdom will fully reign.

But honestly? That sounds a lot like the Pharisees.

They believed that if Israel could just *get it together*—obey the Torah *perfectly* for a single day—then the Messiah would come and overthrow Rome. They saw the Kingdom as something to be forced into existence by human effort, by control.

Jesus saw it differently.

He never told His followers to seize political power and enforce His way of living on the world. Rome already *tried* that. Spoiler alert: it didn't end well.

In his book *You Are Not Alone*, my friend Phil Manginelli writes, "Christians often fail to honor that there is a difference between Christianity and Christendom . . . Christianity is the true nature of Jesus and his way, while Christendom is the structures humans have built in the name of Jesus within society."[319]

In other words, Jesus didn't come to establish *Christendom*.

He came to establish *the Kingdom*.

Others take a different approach. They see the Kingdom as a *battle*—a war between good and evil that we need to *fight* our way through. But this sounds more like secularism than Jesus.

Paul is crystal clear: "Our struggle is not against flesh and blood."[320]

Yet when election season rolls around, it's like we forget. We slander, we divide, we tear each other down—all in the name of *righteousness*.

But Jesus never called us to *control* or *coerce* culture.

He called us to *influence* it.

The Latin word for *influence* is "*influere*," which means *to flow into* or *to flow in*. It's this effortless movement—like a gentle stream, water finding its way, shaping the landscape over time.

But let's be honest, sometimes we present Jesus more like a crashing wave than a quiet stream. We hit people over the head with truth, knock them off their feet with arguments, sweep them away with rhetoric.

I remember as a kid, my family went to the beach. My brother got caught in a riptide. One moment he was there, the next he was *gone*. We searched for what felt like forever. The panic. The helplessness. The overwhelming force of the water.

Don't worry, he made it out alive.

That's how some people feel about the church.

Like they got sucked into a riptide of moralism and self-righteousness. Like they were pulled under, gasping for air, unable to find solid ground.

But here's the thing about a stream—it carries just as much power as a crashing wave.

I've never been to the Grand Canyon, but do you know how it was formed?

Not by earthquakes. Not by explosions. Not by sudden force.

By water.

Years and years of slow, steady erosion. Water moving, rubbing, gliding over the hard edges of rock. Over time, the landscape shifted. What was once jagged and harsh became smooth and breathtaking.

People are *drawn* to the beauty of a stream. There's something about it—gentle, inviting, calming—that makes you *want* to step in. A stream creates space. It invites reflection. It silences the noise.

A crashing wave? It's thrilling, sure. But it's not *welcoming*.

This is the invitation: to be a *stream*, not a storm.

So many people in our culture see Christianity as *the problem*—because, in many ways, we've tried to *control* and *coerce* culture. But if we *influence* it? If we move through it like water, shaping it over time with quiet, consistent love?

The sharp edges people feel toward Jesus will begin to soften.

And maybe, just maybe, they'll step into the water themselves.

PRACTICED HEALING

How do we influence culture?

It's not going to be through a sermon, though I love a good sermon.

It won't be through a book, though I love a good book.

It's going to be through our practice. Our everyday lives. Dallas Willard gives us a good starting point, "We must arrange our days so that we are experiencing deep joy, confidence, and hope in God."[321]

In this section I want to give you some practical application in how you can participate in the healing of your life, others' lives, and the world. These practices are not limited to the specific category in which I placed them; they are all interchangeable.

Like anything, these are practices; they will only be useful to you through repetition. Think of the picture of erosion; doing this practice will not change your life in a day, week, or year. But if you stay consistent over time, you will be surprised by what God has done through you.

PRACTICES FOR PARTICIPATING IN THE WORLD'S HEALING

1. **Prayer**: This seems obvious. Of course we should pray for our world. If we are honest, prayer is one of the hardest things to do. Tim Keller says, "They often say the best things for us are often the hardest things–therefore prayer must be the hardest thing in the world."[322] It's true prayer is hard, but prayer is key to the renewal of the world.

   Prayer is the place where heaven and earth merge together. It's the place where God gives us insight into the heavenly places and we declare back to God, "On earth as it is in heaven."

   The practice is this, every time you offer a critique of the world, pray for the world. You will notice two things: your critique of the world will decrease and your love for the world will increase. If you don't know what to pray for, ask God, and He will put it on your heart. But don't let your complaints outnumber your prayers.

2. **Celebration**: Jesus loves a good celebration! Again, people rarely associate celebration and Christianity together. But God commanded His people to celebrate! Deuteronomy 14:26 says, "Use the silver to buy whatever you like; cattle, sheep, wine or other fermented drink or anything you wish. Then you and your household shall eat there in the presence of the Lord your God and rejoice."

   Everyone loves a good party! If we don't celebrate good things, then the world will celebrate evil things. Find a reason to celebrate! Celebrate your birthday, your spiritual birthday, a good grade on an exam, the completion of a project, or even cleaning your room. In a world full of despair, celebration will be the light on the hill people are drawn to.

3. **Generosity**: I'm not talking about money; I understand not everyone is in a place to give money. But what is something that you, me, Elon Musk, and the Pope have equal amounts of?

Time.

I would even argue that money is easier to give to people than your time. After all, "Time is money." People respond to intentionality. When you are generous with your time, it makes a huge impact on people's lives. The time which you give to someone will have more of an impact on their life than any sermon, song, or teaching you can offer.

Instead of binge-watching Netflix on a Friday night, go to In-N-Out, buy the homeless person who sits outside of it a burger, and talk to him or her about their story.

Live an interruptible life. The Gospels give several examples of how Jesus lived an interruptible life. He was often having a quiet time, drinking His flat white, reading His Bible, and people would interrupt Him because of a need. Jesus wouldn't freak out at them; He was generous with His time.

Let the one thing people say about you at your eulogy be, "They were a generous person."

4. **Blessing**: One of the most neglected and misunderstood concepts in the Bible is the idea of blessing. When we think of blessing, we tend to think of material blessings and inheritance.

But one of the things humans are called to do is bless the world. This is more than a "wish you well" moment. This is leaving a lasting presence of yourself behind for others to glean on. We are called to bless people with our smile, our laughter, our tears, our wounds, and our stories.

We can see how prestigious families' financial blessings carry over from generation to generation. The same happens when we bless the world around us with how God made us. We should, as the saying goes, "Be the gift that keeps on giving."

Take what you have, even if it's just a smile, and bless the world with it.

5. **Participation**: In order to bless people, you need to be around people. All the introverts are squirming.

Join a pickleball league, join a book club, poetry club, or a wine tasting community. Wherever people are at you should be. Not to "evangelize," but to just be a part of society.

One of the best people I've ever seen at this is a friend of mine, Ansley. She was a fellow missionary with my wife and I in Amsterdam. The second Ansley settled in Amsterdam, she joined a church and would go from restaurant to restaurant making friends. Ansley is a trusted voice for Jesus for many people.

I often joke with her that I get my social life through her. I'm not saying we all have to be Ansley, but maybe we take 10% of her intentionality and adopt it into our daily lives and see how much people begin to open up to us about their pain and needs.

Participation also brings an awareness to the needs of your community, creating space for you to pray intentionally into the world's pain.

6. **Invitation**: Who doesn't love to get invited to places? Sometimes my heart breaks when I know people are doing something and I wasn't invited—even if I really wouldn't have wanted to attend, I still want the invite.

Charles Finney has this amazing line, "If the presence of God is in the church, the church will draw the world in. If the presence of God is not in the church, then the world will draw the church out."[323]

We have looked at the power of invitation in the last chapter, and this is something we need to practice. As Jesus would say, "It's easy to invite people who you like, but what good is that? Even the secularists do that! Invite those who you don't like, and you will be blessed." (My personal modern-day twist.) Yes, invite your neighbors to church, that's important, but also invite your neighbors into your lives. Your next game night, invite someone you don't know or don't per se get along with. Invitation gets us out of our own way and creates space for empathy, healing, and transformation.

As you know, rejection is something that most people struggle with, and oftentimes rejection is the driving force for our pain that leads us into more pain. Inviting people into your life is the simplest, most practical way to heal that wound.

PRACTICES FOR PERSONAL HEALING

1. **Rest**: One of the best ways to heal in our modern world is to practice rest. Often, we take this to mean sit around and do nothing all day. I am not per se talking about rest for your bodies, I mean rest for your soul.

   Everyone is different, so I can't say what will work for you. But for me, especially after teaching, I have a rest day. Oftentimes this will look like me waking up early, enjoying the silence of the morning over a good cup of coffee, preferably a flat white (if you hadn't caught the hints). I will typically pick up a book to read slowly, go for a walk, or sit in the sauna and reflect. After a peaceful morning, I love playing with my daughter, and then in the evening my wife or I will try to make a special dinner and enjoy that over a nice glass of wine and finish the night with a good movie.

   For you, working out might be restful or painting the fence. I know some who like to go on long hikes for their rest. This is about rejuvenation; how did God make you?

   If you don't know what you find restful, a simple way to find out is what is something that makes you excited? Do that: fill your day with excitement and wonder.

   For those who like to sleep all day, that's okay, too.

2. **Worship**: Practicing worship is one of the best ways to find healing because worship is an offering of oneself to God. In worship we become like the One that we worship. This is the divine mystery—the more we worship and praise God, the more we heal.

This doesn't just mean putting on music—it means directing your attention and focus to Him.

When we worship the One who is whole, we become whole.

Brother Lawrence in his book, *The Practice of the Presence of God*, gives insight into how even the most mundane tasks, like changing a diaper, can be direct acts of worship to God.

One of the things I used to do was set an alarm every hour of the day (the hours I was awake, I didn't mess up my sleep) to remind myself to turn my attention to God. Often, I would pray the John 3:30 prayer, "You are the Christ, I am not the Christ, You must increase, and I must decrease."

Maybe you just need to set reminders of worship throughout your day.

3. **Practice Saying No**: This isn't about placing boundaries on others; this is about placing boundaries on yourself!

   Before you want something or indulge in something, tell yourself no! This will help you to discern between a want and a need. I struggle with self-control. I love to eat, and I love to eat until I am REALLY full! As I aged, I noticed that overeating took a toll on my body. So often when I finish dinner and I desire seconds, I stop and tell myself no!

   I ask myself, "Am I really hungry? Or was that dinner just bomb and I want more?"

   One thing that is important to remember, the validity of relationships is never defined by their "yes," but by their "no." When you get married, it does no good if you do marital things with everyone else—what kind of marriage would you have? Your marriage is defined by your "no" to others. In the same way, our formation and healing are attached to our willingness to forsake all things and trust Jesus for our healing.

4. **Memorization**: We live in a time of lost memories. I remember growing up we would memorize people's phone numbers and addresses.

We don't do that anymore because our beautiful cell phones do the work for us. Remember, God told Israel that remembrance was an important aspect to formation and avoiding sin.

Our brains are remarkable, you can practice the art of memorization. Healing takes time and often our trauma arises out of nowhere—the memorization of scripture helps us to speak truth over our pains and our wounds.

Memorize key verses that God has spoken over your life and use them as a reminder of God's faithfulness in your life.

5. **Replacement**: Catholics have this practice of replacing their thoughts and temptations with actions of blessings. For example, if you are struggling with pornography, when faced with temptation, stop and write a letter to your mother, sister, or wife and bless them.

If you struggle with greed, take the money you would have used for shopping and give it to someone in need. It's about replacing the thought with the opposite action. Eventually, the temptations that you face begin to fade.

6. **Fasting**: Jesus says that fasting should be a regular practice in our lives.[324] Fasting brings perspective, we rid our bodies from depending on food for our happiness, convenience, and pleasure to depend on God for them.

You don't have to start off with a 40-day fast. Just start off by skipping a meal to go and pray. If that feels good, try two meals and so on. Fasting isn't about trying to manipulate God into answering your prayer—instead, fasting is about getting in touch with the truer reality and then living that reality in your life.

Fasting will always shift our perspectives. Sometimes we need to shift our perspective of our pain.

7. **18 minutes**: These practices are not about intensity but consistency. Jesse Itzler, a notorious entrepreneur, suggests that consistent daily practice can lead to significant improvement, potentially placing you above 95% of the population in that area.

How do you do this?

Itzler says that investing just 18 minutes daily will eventually add up to 109 hours a year. You can do anything for 18 minutes a day! That's less than half of a Netflix show. Try it! If you want to grow in prayer, knowledge of the Bible, memorization, or worship, just set your iPhone timer for 18 minutes and do those things. In one year, see where you are at!

You can read the entire Bible in 70 hours; that leaves you 39 hours left over to practice reading in Greek!

Na, I'm just playing, but you get the point. These practices are not about intensity but consistency—be faithful and He will be faithful.

PRACTICES FOR PARTICIPATING IN OTHERS' HEALING

1. **Listening**: All people want their voices to be heard. One of the key lessons I have learned in pastoring is that most people aren't looking for an answer to their problems, they are just looking for someone who will listen and attempt to understand them. Jesus also taught the importance of listening and how listening creates space for transformation.[325]

   Sometimes the best way to help people find healing is to just listen to their story. One of the hardest things for me is to not offer my advice or what I would do, but what I have learned the hard way is that offering unwanted advice only leads to people not coming back to you.

   As James tells us: It's better to listen than to speak.[326]

2. **Hospitality**: The Greek word for hospitality is "*philoxenia.*" It's a compound word combining "*philo*" which means love of a friend and "*xenos*" which means foreigner. Literally, hospitality is the love of a stranger. If you were to trace hospitality through the Gospels you would find Jesus practicing hospitality over 10 times.[327]

   Jesus's hospitality to sinners, outcasts, strangers, and the broken was the way He drew people to Himself. When was the last time you turned down a free meal? Don't underestimate the power of food. They often say the way to a person's heart isn't the brain, it's the stomach.

3. **Encouragement**: Encouragement can change the dynamic of any situation. One of my closest friends is an encourager. He can find the good and beautiful in anything. He has breathed kindness into some of the most wounded places in my life.

   Encouragement will build bonds that hate, jealousy, and envy can't overcome.

4. **Submission**: This is about preference. In 1 Corinthians, Paul challenges the church in a way that makes most of us uncomfortable. He says, it is better for you to take fault for something you didn't do than it is for division to arise in the church.[328]

   We often misjudge submission; we think it means blind obedience or a matter of value. But that's not the case. Submission is an attitude towards another person. Often, it's about laying down your need to be correct for the benefit of the relationship.

   You know the saying, "Hurt people, hurt people." This is a true statement, but Jesus asks us to forgive people even without them offering an apology. This practice is about not harboring offense but learning how to put ourselves underneath people for their sake.

5. **Confession**: This is about transparency. Some of the best sermons ever spoken are by those who are willing to show what is inside their heart. Transparency, or confession as I named the practice, creates pathways of trust with other people.

   One of the lies of the Devil is that if you really share what your shadow is, they are going to "judge you or use it against you." The book of Hebrews says that Jesus has already "scorned the shame of sin." That means your weaknesses and wounds are not something you need to be ashamed of. They are the means through which other people will find healing as well.

6. **Thankfulness**: As I have mentioned a couple times already, St. Ignatius believed that the root of all sin stemmed from a lack of gratitude.

This simple practice is, in the morning, before your day starts, write out 5 things that you're grateful for. Then at the end of your day, do the same thing, write down 5 things you are grateful for that happened that day.

See what will happen to your perspective on life.

These practices are not a means to an end; they are just helpful practices that will create space for God to touch your wounds and lace them with gold.

There is one more practice that I believe is most important, so important that it needs its own section.

Forgiveness.

Forgiveness is everything. It's the way that we find healing, and it's the way that the world will find healing. Often people will say that "love trumps all," but what people fail to realize is that forgiveness and love go hand in hand. You can't have one without the other.

No?

How do we know that God loves us?

He sent His Son Jesus to take our place on the cross to *forgive* our sins.

How do we know that God forgave us?

He sent His Son Jesus to the cross to do away with our sin so that we can *love* Him.

No matter how much we try, we can't divorce forgiveness from love.

Practicing forgiveness is essential in the healing of the world, in others, and ourselves. Do you offer forgiveness to the world when it hurts you? Do you offer forgiveness to people when they hurt you? Or even more controversial, do you offer forgiveness to the Devil for waging war against you?

The biblical picture of forgiveness is to "release."

But what are you releasing?

Forgiveness is about releasing your right to hold offence, the need to be right, and the need to get even, so that healing and restoration can start taking place.

When we fail to forgive the world and people, we rob ourselves of our own healing.

As a pastor, people will often say to me,

"But you don't know what they did to me,"

or

"They aren't even sorry, why should I forgive them,"

or my personal favorite,

"Forgiveness is overrated."

Forgiveness isn't something Christians do; it's something Christians are!

We are a forgiven people. Jesus offered forgiveness to us without us even asking for it, and it is by His forgiveness that we know we are loved, and it is by His wounds we know we are healed.

I can't promise you that after you offer someone forgiveness you will immediately feel better. You may have to offer forgiveness to someone thousands of times. But what I can promise you is that when you practice forgiveness, your deepest wounds will begin to heal.

LACED WITH GOLD

Much of the beauty in kintsugi is the gold.

After all, who doesn't love gold?

But the beauty of kintsugi is that it's so counter-cultural in our Western world. We typically try to hide our wounds and fragmentations from people, but in kintsugi it's the wound and the fragmentation that is highlighted, drawing the eyes of the beholder to the broken places.

As I mentioned before, the gold isn't what holds the broken pieces together; that's the urushi, which is the blood of the lacquer tree. The gold, however, is what makes the kintsugi more valuable than it was once before. The gold in kintsugi represents the transformation of brokenness into beauty.

That is what you are; you are something beautiful, you are a wonderful work of art in the making, and the very things that were meant to break you are the very things that God is lacing with gold right now.

You don't have to be anyone but yourself. All you need to do is allow Jesus, the most perfect kintsugi master, to behold you, contemplate you, and gently put you back together.

Kintsugi acts as a visual for hope in the midst of an anxious generation. "*Tsugi*" has the meaning of "connecting the generations." Kintsugi connects the generations by giving hope to those in the present that the future is bright. The metaphor doesn't attempt to negate the past, actually quite the opposite. The gold is the reminder to the present generation that those in the past have also experienced pain, suffering, and brokenness, but there is hope because the kintsugi is the reminder that new beauty comes from broken places.

We see a similar picture in the Bible. Hebrews 11 lists names of the people of faith who have come before us. This is often labeled the "Hall of Faith" chapter. This chapter highlights various people who exemplified faith in some of the most challenging circumstances.

Remember, faith isn't an inner feeling towards God; it's about an unwavering commitment to God in the midst of trial and hardship. Hebrews 11 highlights figures like Moses, who chose to endure hardship rather than enjoy the fleeting pleasures of sin in Egypt,[329] and the Israelites who crossed the Red Sea by faith.[330]

The author of Hebrews makes the point that faith is not always rewarded on earth. As a matter of fact, people like Abraham didn't get to experience the full promise God gave him, which was ultimately fulfilled in Jesus. Yet, in heaven, after his death, Abraham realizes that you and I are a part of His promise, and even though he died on earth, he is still collecting on God's promise in heaven, and he is celebrating!!!

Many of those heroes faced significant pain, various trials, and persecution, but because of their unwavering commitment to Jesus, their reward is beyond comprehension.

In the same way kintsugi connects the past generations to the present, so too our faith is connected to those who came before us. Jesus made a fascinating statement in the Gospel of Matthew, "I tell you the truth, of all who have ever lived, none is greater than John the Baptist. Yet even the least person in the Kingdom of Heaven is greater than he is!"[331]

There is no one greater than John the Baptist in the Old Testament, but He goes on to make the point that even the most insignificant person in His Kingdom is greater than John ever was.

We live in the time of God's Kingdom reigning; you are the greatest thing that this world has ever seen! Jesus's invitation to us is to maintain and hold fast to what our spiritual ancestors have started for us.

Like them, we will have pain and hardship, but like them, we will enter into glory and our wounds will shine brighter than ever.

RICH WOUNDS

Matthew Bridges, who was an Anglican minister, wrote the famous hymn, "Crown Him with Many Crowns." There is one aspect of the hymn that I would like to highlight which I believe summarizes the theme of this entire book.

> "Crown him the Lord of love;
> Behold his hands and side,
> Rich wounds, yet visible above,
> In beauty glorified;
> No angels in the sky
> Can fully bear the sight,
> But downward bends his burning eye
> At mysteries so bright."

The very scars and wounds that we most want to hide will one day become the most glorious and most radiant thing about us.

Rich wounds—what a pregnant phrase!

In eternity, in God's Kingdom, wounds will be seen, and in beauty, wounds will be glorified and they will be beautiful! Our wounds will be so magnified, not even angels can bear the sight of them. In the same way that we try to look at the sun but are overwhelmed by its glory, in the same way the angels will not be able to comprehend the beauty of our Sacred Wounds.

Jesus took His Sacred Wounds into eternity, and so will we!

The Sacred Wounds of Jesus are the starting place for the healing in our life and the world; our Sacred Wounds are the starting place for others to find healing for their wounds.

My prayer for you is that in this life, your faith wouldn't waiver, that you would be rooted and established in the love of Jesus, and that you would come to know how deep and wide His love is for you. That no matter what you face in this life, you cling to Him and be filled with His lasting presence. I pray that whenever you experience pain, trials, and temptations you would stand strong with perseverance, faith, hope, and love. I pray that the deep things of God would be revealed to you, so that your life would be a living story of beauty, goodness, and truth of God! Now to the King eternal, immortal, invisible, the only God, be honor and glory for ever and ever. Amen.

May your Sacred Wounds shine bright!

Grace and peace to you as you navigate this life of pain and beauty.

With love,

Dakota

THANK YOUS

First and foremost, I give thanks to Jesus. Without His mercy, kindness, and unwavering love, I would not be here. May this book be a small act of worship, a reflection of the grace You have poured into my life.

To Bob Goff—thank you for challenging me to dream beyond my limits, to embrace whimsy, and to believe in what's possible. Your encouragement guided me through one of the biggest transitions of my life, and without your wisdom and generosity, this book would not exist.

Kimberly Stuart, my first editor—you have been more than an editor; you have been a friend. We have laughed, cried, and shared some of the deepest moments of this journey together. Your whisper-yells, grammatical debates, and even the gifts of chapter titles have shaped this book in ways I cannot fully express. My writing would not be what it is without you. I am beyond grateful for you.

Rob and Paula De Vries, your belief in me has been a light in moments of doubt. Thank you for your unwavering encouragement, for urging me to pursue my dreams, and for investing in my writing with such generosity. (*Rob en Paula De Vries, jullie geloof in mij was een licht in momenten van twijfel. Dank jullie wel voor jullie onwankelbare bemoediging, voor jullie aansporen om mijn dromen na te jagen, en voor jullie genereuze investering in mijn schrijven.*)

To the entire team at Blue Hat Publishing—thank you.

Jodi, you have made this process seamless, lifting burdens so I could focus on writing. Your care and attention to detail have meant more than you know. Raechel, your thoughtful edits shaped this book, but more than that, your encouragement made me believe I could actually do this. Your words have left a lasting imprint on my heart. Brandon, you may technically be my boss, but more than that, you have become a true friend. Your belief in me and this project has been a gift, and I hold it deeply.

Uncle Jon—You have been a constant figure in every significant moment in my life; it is only fitting for you to do the art on my first book. Your gifting is more than just creating beautiful things; your art operates as a signpost that points beyond yourself to Jesus. Long before I wrote a single word, this was the cover I saw in my heart, and you brought it to life perfectly. It has been an honor to create alongside you.

To the many people who have shaped my faith and lifted me in prayer—Pastor Dan, Shane Carroll, Dan Snead, Joel Sanchez, Phil & Emily Manginelli, Dr. Fairbairn, Don Stewart, Mom & Dad, Stephen & Justine Ashworth, Reinier Terblanche, and so many others—thank you. Your guidance and prayers have carried me through seasons of both struggle and joy.

And finally, Bren. There are no words that could fully capture what you have done to make this book possible. You have given me the time, space, and grace to write—even in the midst of a chaotic season. From moving across the world **twice**, birthing our son, caring for two little ones under two while I hid away upstairs writing, to being my first editor, to holding me in moments when my insecurities felt overwhelming—your love has been my foundation. You believed in me when I couldn't believe in myself, and for that, I am endlessly grateful. I love you.

END NOTES

1. Romans 8:28
2. Romans 8:29
3. Comer, John Mark. *Live No Lies: Recognize and Resist the Three Enemies That Sabotage Your Peace*. Zondervan, 2021
4. Yancey, Philip. *Where Is God When It Hurts?* Zondervan, 1990
5. John 10:10 (ESV)
6. Comer, John Mark. "*The Four American Gospels*" Sermon
7. Hebrews 2:10, Philippians 2:8-9, Colossians 2:15
8. "Analgesic" *The Oxford English Dictionary*, 3rd ed., Oxford UP, 2005
9. Zaki, Jamil. *Hope For Cynics*. Grand Central Publishing. 2024
10. Isaiah 40:31
11. Romans 15:13
12. Hebrews 10:23
13. Zaki, Jamil. *Hope For Cynics*. Grand Central Publishing. 2024
14. Yancey, Philip. *Where Is God When It Hurts?* Zondervan, 1990
15. "Pleasure, Pain Activate Same Part of Brain." *Harvard Gazette*, 23 Jan. 2002, news.harvard.edu/gazette/story/2002/01/pleasure-pain-activate-same-part-of-brain/. Accessed 24 Feb. 2025
16. Lewis, C. S. *The Problem of Pain*. HarperOne, 2001.
17. Yancey, Philip. *Where Is God When It Hurts?* Zondervan, 1990
18. Smith, James K. A. *You Are What You Love: The Spiritual Power of Habit*. Brazos Press, 2016
19. Bradford, M. E. *"Faulkner, James Baldwin, and the South."* University of Alabama Press, 1989
20. Manginelli, Phil. *You Are Not Alone*. Resistance & Renewal. 2024
21. Genesis 11:4
22. Hume, David. *Dialogues Concerning Natural Religion*. Edited by Norman Kemp Smith, Hackett Publishing, 2007
23. Voltaire. *Candide*. Translated by Theo C. H. N. B. H. H. E., Penguin Classics, 2005
24. Freud, Sigmund. *The Future of an Illusion*. Translated by W. D. Robson-Scott, W. W. Norton & Company, 1961
25. Smith, Jacob. "Nietzsche on God and Suffering." *Well-Read Christian*, 9 Mar. 2020, wellreadchristian.com/nietzsche-on-god-and-suffering/
26. Taylor, Charles. *A Secular Age*. Belknap Press of Harvard University Press, 2007
27. Schelsky, Helmut. *Die skeptische Generation* "The Skeptical Generation," 1957
28. Spelman, Elizabeth. *The Impulse to Restore in a Fragile World*. Oxford University Press, 2001
29. Matthew 16:25

30. Ezekiel 34:16
31. Ezekiel 34:2 (emphasis added)
32. Matthew 23:15
33. Matthew 23:37
34. (For example, in Exodus 3 when God calls Moses from the burning bush, "Moses, Moses . . . I am the God of your father Abraham, Isaac, and Jacob." God is telling Moses that he knows Moses. Moses may be running from Egypt, filled with shame, guilt, and identity issues, but God sees him, knows him, and affirms his identity by saying "I am the God of your fathers . . ." In other words, you are part of the covenant promises, you may have identity issues, but I know you and you belong.)
35. Isaiah 56:7
36. Matthew 23:38
37. Luke 21:5
38. John 16:33
39. Frank Llyod Wright quote - I stumbled across this during research
40. Nietzsche, Friedrich. *The Gay Science*. Translated by Walter Kaufmann, Vintage Books, 1974
41. Nietzsche, Friedrich. *The Gay Science*. Translated by Walter Kaufmann, Vintage Books, 1974
42. Pearcey, Nancy. *"Sex, Lies, and Secularism: A Call to Truth and a Return to Reason."* Crossway, 2020
43. Trueman, Carl R. *Strange New World: How Thinkers and Activists Redefined Identity and Sparked the Sexual Revolution*. Crossway, 2022
44. Patrikarakos, David. *War in 140 Characters: How Social Media Is Reshaping Conflict in the Twenty-first Century*. Basic Books, 2017
45. Willard, Dallas. *Hearing God: Developing a Conversational Relationship with God*. InterVarsity Press, 1999
46. Lowry, Todd. "Title of the Article." *Music for Life*, Date of Publication, www.musicforlife.com/article-url
47. Vrtz, Kevin. "John Lennon's 'God': A Declaration of Self-Belief and the Quest for Authenticity." *Medium*, 23 Jan. 2020, Medium.com/@vrtzkf/john-lennons-god-a-declaration-of-self-belief-and-the-quest-for-authenticity-71a5f-55d68ca
48. "Why Was John Lennon So Anti-Religion?" *Quora*, 10 Mar. 2018, www.quora.com/Why-was-John-Lennon-so-anti-religion
49. 1 Corinthians 15:32
50. Sayers, Mark. *The Vertical Self: How Biblical Faith Can Help Us Discover Who We Are in An Age of Self Obsession*. Thomas Nelson, 2010
51. "What Is Secular Humanism?" *Secular Humanism*, Center for Inquiry, secularhumanism.org/what-is-secular-humanism/
52. "What Is Secular Humanism?" *Secular Humanism*, Center for Inquiry, secularhumanism.org/what-is-secular-humanism/
53. "What Is Secular Humanism?" *Secular Humanism*, Center for Inquiry, secularhumanism.org/what-is-secular-humanism/
54. Wells, David. *No Place for Truth: or Whatever Happened to Evangelical Theology?* Eerdmans, 1993

55. Kirkey, Jason. *Salmon in the Spring: The Ecology of Celtic Spirituality*. Wild Goose Publications, 2007
56. Matthew 3:17
57. Hesiod. *Theogony, Works and Days, and Testimonia*. Translated by Glenn W. Most, Harvard University Press, 2006
58. Watkin, Christopher. *Thinking Through Creation: Genesis 1 ad 2 as Tools of Cultural Critique*. InterVarsity Press, 2017
59. Genesis 1:29 (ESV)
60. Genesis 1:27-28
61. Genesis 1:28
62. Genesis 1:28
63. Ignatius - This quote was referenced in Seminary
64. Plantinga, Cornelius. Not the Way It's Supposed to Be: A Breviary of Sin. Eerdmans, 1995
65. Genesis 3:17-19
66. Genesis 3:14-15
67. Genesis 3:17
68. Ecclesiastes 3:11
69. Plantinga, Cornelius. *Not the Way It's Supposed to Be: A Breviary of Sin*. Eerdmans, 1995
70. Matthew 15:11, Psalm 51:5
71. 1 Corinthians 5:6-8
72. John 3:6
73. Ephesians 1:11-14, Colossians 3:24, Hebrews 9:15
74. Genesis 6:11-12 (ESV)
75. Genesis 6:5
76. Romans 12:1-2
77. Kübler-Ross, Elisabeth. *On Death and Dying*. Macmillan, 1969
78. 2 Corinthians 5:21 (ESV)
79. Matthew 6:33
80. Luke 17:21
81. Matthew 12:24
82. Mark 8:27, 9:33-34, 10:17, 10:32, 10:52 (ESV)
83. Mark 9:31
84. Mark 10:48
85. Mark 10:52 (ESV)
86. Mark 2:17
87. Tyson, Jon. "Controversial Faith: The Exclusivity of Jesus" Sermon
88. Ephesians 6:12
89. Interview leading up to a fight against Buster Douglas
90. Lewis, C. S. *Surprised by Joy: The Shape of My Early Life*. Harcourt, 1955
91. *The Usual Suspects* Movie
92. Comer, John Mark. *Live No Lies: Recognize and Resist the Three Enemies That Sabotage Your Peace*. Zondervan, 2021
93. Matthew 4:1-11
94. Matthew 4:1-11
95. Luke 22:31-32

96. Luke 10:18
97. "God's Divine Council." *Truth or Tradition*, www.truthortradition.com/articles/gods-divine-council. & Isaiah 14:12-13
98. Comer, John Mark. *Live No Lies: Recognize and Resist the Three Enemies That Sabotage Your Peace*. Zondervan, 2021
99. 1 John 5:19, Matt 4:3, Rev 12:10
100. Comer, John Mark. *Live No Lies: Recognize and Resist the Three Enemies That Sabotage Your Peace*. Zondervan, 2021
101. James 1:13, Matthew 4:1-3, Revelation 2:10, Luke 22:31-33
102. Isaiah 14:12
103. Harper, Simon. "'Sympathy For The Devil': The Story Behind The Rolling Stones Classic." *Discover Music*, 6 December 2024. www.udiscovermusic.com/stories/the-rolling-stones-sympathy-for-the-devil-feature/.(emphasis added)
104. Revelation 12
105. Revelation 20
106. Revelation 20
107. Wells, David. *Losing Our Virtue: Why the Church Must Recover Its Moral Vision*. Eerdmans, 1998
108. Revelation 13, Daniel 11
109. Revelation 12
110. John 8:44
111. John 10:10
112. 1 Peter 5:8
113. 2 Corinthians 12:9
114. Rohr, Richard. "Richard Rohr on the Age of Outrage: 'Even Those Who Think They Are Angry Are Really Sad.'" *National Catholic Reporter*, 26 Aug. 2021
115. Psalm 27:1
116. 2 Corinthians 10:4-5
117. John 10:10
118. Luke 22:31-32
119. Tozer, A. W. *The Knowledge of the Holy: The Attributes of God: Their Meaning in the Christian Life*. Harper & Row, 1961
120. Tozer, A. W. *The Knowledge of the Holy: The Attributes of God: Their Meaning in the Christian Life*. Harper & Row, 1961
121. Job 1:1
122. Luke 6:38
123. Proverbs 11:25 (MSG)
124. Job 8:5-7, 11:14-20, 22:21-30
125. Zechariah 7:9
126. Job 3
127. Job 1:1. Now you may be thinking, Job was human, of course he sinned, the Bible says all have fallen short. That's not the point here. The story of Job isn't answering the question if Job is perfect like Jesus, it's addressing the way God rules the world. So the author of the book of Job is using a "perfect" person to make his point.
128. Job 38:4 (NLT)
129. Yancey, Philip. *Where Is God When It Hurts?* Zondervan, 1990

130. Job 38
131. Genesis 1:28
132. Matthew 5:45
133. Job 40:8
134. Job 38-41
135. Micah 6:8
136. Nouwen, Henri J. M. *The Wounded Healer: Ministry in Contemporary Society*. Doubleday, 1972
137. Nehemiah 1:2-3
138. Nehemiah 1:4-7
139. Lewis, C. S. *Mere Christianity*. HarperCollins, 2001
140. Mark 10:17-22
141. Mark 10:22
142. Mark 10:21
143. John 16:33
144. Sacks, Jonathan. *To Heal a Fractured World: The Ethics of Responsibility*. Schocken Books, 2005
145. Job 42:3 (NLT)
146. Job 42:7-9 (NLT)
147. John 9:1-4
148. Romans 8:19-21 (NLT)
149. Barro, Josh. "Candidate Trump Attacked Obama's Executive Orders. President Trump Loves Executive Orders." *The Washington Post*, 17 Oct. 2017, www.washingtonpost.com/news/monkey-cage/wp/2017/10/17/candidate-trump-attacked-obamas-executive-orders-president-trump-loves-executive-orders/.
150. Hickey et. al. "Here are the executive actions Biden signed in his first 100 days." *CNN*, 30 April 2021, edition.cnn.com/interactive/2021/politics/biden-executive-orders/
151. Herodotus. *The Histories of Herodotus*. Translated by A. D. Godley, Harvard University Press, 1920
152. Sayers, Mark. *The Vertical Self: How Biblical Faith Can Help Us Discover Who We Are in an Age of Self Obsession*. Thomas Nelson, 2010
153. Sayers, Mark. *The Vertical Self: How Biblical Faith Can Help Us Discover Who We Are in an Age of Self Obsession*. Thomas Nelson, 2010
154. Sayers, Mark. *The Vertical Self: How Biblical Faith Can Help Us Discover Who We Are in an Age of Self Obsession*. Thomas Nelson, 2010
155. Jon Tyson referenced it in a Sermon, Tyson was mentored by Tim Keller
156. Trueman, Carl R. *The Rise and Triumph of the Modern Self: Cultural Amnesia, Expressive Individualism, and the Road to Sexual Revolution*. Crossway, 2020
157. Taylor, Charles. *A Secular Age*. Belknap Press of Harvard University Press, 2007
158. Taylor, Charles. *A Secular Age*. Belknap Press of Harvard University Press, 2007
159. The Art of Teaching Podcast: Season 2 Episode 6
160. Judges 21:25 (ESV)
161. Judges 17:6, 21:25 (ESV)
162. Judges 17:5, 10
163. The Art of Teaching Podcast: Season 2 Episode 6
164. "The Constitution of the United States of America." US Government Printing Office, 1787 (emphasis added)

165. Brownstein, Barry. "What Thomas Jefferson Meant by 'Pursuit of Happiness.'" *Foundation for Economic Education*, 15 Apr. 2017, fee.org/articles/what-thomas-jefferson-meant-by-pursuit-of-happiness/
166. Harrison, Stephanie. The New Happy: Getting Happiness Right in a World That's Got It Wrong. TarcherPerigee, 2022
167. "Thomas Jefferson: The Meaning of Life — Liberty & Happiness." *Excellence Reporter*, 20 May 2014, www.excellencereporter.com/thomas-jefferson-the-meaning-of-life-liberty-happiness/
168. Taylor, Charles. *A Secular Age*. Belknap Press of Harvard University Press, 2007
169. Taylor, Charles. *A Secular Age*. Belknap Press of Harvard University Press, 2007
170. "How Words Enter the OED." *Oxford English Dictionary*, Oxford University Press, www.oed.com/information/editorial-policy/how-words-enter-the-oed/?tl=true
171. Klemperer, Victor. *Language of the Third Reich: LTI: Lingua Tertii Imperii*. Translated by Martin Brady, Continuum, 2000
172. Klemperer, Victor. *Language of the Third Reich: LTI: Lingua Tertii Imperii*. Translated by Martin Brady, Continuum, 2000
173. Churchill, Winston. "The Gift of the Common Tongue." *The Collected Works of Winston Churchill, Volume 16*. Houghton Mifflin, 1976
174. Rachel Zeger Interview
175. Boroditsky, Lera. "How Language Shapes Our Thoughts: A Study on the Influence of Language on Cognition" *Frontiers in Psychology*, vol. 10, 2019, article 885, http://lera.ucsd.edu/papers/sci-am-2011.pdf
176. JFK. First Inaugural Address. 1961
177. Furedi, Frank. "Wokeness–a top-down project to re-socialise the world." *Substack*, 11 April 2023, frankfuredi.substack.com/p/wokeness-a-top-down-project-to-re
178. Jung, Carl. *Aion: Researches into the Phenomenology of the Self*. Translated by R. F. C. Hull, Princeton University Press, 1969
179. Ecclesiastes 3:11
180. Hebrews 10:23, Revelation 2:10
181. Philippians 2:3
182. 1 Corinthians 11:24
183. Romans 8:18, Colossians 1:27
184. Philippians 1:6
185. Hebrews 12:10, 2:10
186. Term coined by Pastor Jon Tyson
187. Genesis 2:25
188. Naugle, David. *Reordered Love, Reordered Lives: Learning the Deep Meaning of Happiness*. Baker Academic, 2008
189. Bavinck, Herman. *Reformed Dogmatics*. Translated by John Vriend, edited by James T. Dennison, Baker Academic, 2003
190. Romans 5:12-21; 1 Corinthians 15:22, 44-49
191. Augustine. *The City of God*. Translated by Marcus Dods, Modern Library, 2000
192. Naugle, David. *Reordered Love, Reordered Lives: Learning the Deep Meaning of Happiness*. Baker Academic, 2008
193. Deuteronomy 4:28
194. Galatians 5:19-21
195. Psalm 115:8

196. "16 Employee Burnout Statistics You Can't Ignore." *EveryoneSocial*, 11 June 2024, www.everyonesocial.com/blog/employee-burnout-statistics/
197. Dickson et. al. "First sexual intercourse: age, coercion, and later regrets reported by a birth cohort." *National Library of Medicine*, www.ncbi.nlm.nih.gov/pmc/articles/PMC2665316/
198. Romans 1:25
199. Romans 1:19-20
200. Romans 1:24, 26
201. Naugle, David. *Reordered Love, Reordered Lives: Learning the Deep Meaning of Happiness*. Baker Academic, 2008
202. Lewis, C. S. *The Weight of Glory*. HarperOne, 2001
203. Marshall, Bruce. *The World, the Flesh, and Father Smith*. Sheed & Ward, 1949
204. Essay by C.S. Lewis
205. Read Ezekiel 16 & 23. See how the Lord is jealous over you.
206. Exodus 33:11
207. Psalm 27:4
208. Psalm 27:2
209. Mark 5:1-20
210. Mark 5:9
211. Sayers, Mark. The Horizontal Self: How Our Search for Identity in the Digital Age is Leading Us Away from True Fulfillment. Multnomah, 2020
212. Genesis 3:7
213. Luke 4:18-19
214. Luke 4:19, Isaiah 61:2
215. Deuteronomy 32:10, Psalm 17:8, Zechariah 2:8
216. 2 Corinthians 3:17-18; Psalm 27:4-5
217. Hwee Hwee Tan Quote
218. Luke 2:30
219. Hebrews 4:15, 2 Corinthians 5:21, 1 Peter 2:22
220. Colossians 1:16
221. Luke 2
222. Mark 6:3
223. Mark 6:3; Matthew 13:55
224. Matthew 3:13-17. Jesus' baptism was a way of identifying himself with humanity. Scripture says that Jesus lived a perfect life, and so in theory, there would be no need for him to have been given the sinners baptism. But his baptism was a way to identify himself with the human condition.
225. Matthew 3:17
226. Matthew 4:3
227. Matthew 26:42, my own paraphrase
228. Ezekiel 20:8-9
229. Mark 3:21
230. John 6:26
231. John 21:25
232. Matthew 26:50
233. Luke 23:34
234. Matthew 5:48

235. Hebrews 2:10
236. John 1:1
237. John 1:14
238. John 6:35
239. John 8:12 & 9:15
240. John 10:7
241. 1 Corinthians 4
242. John 10:11
243. John 11:25
244. John 14:6
245. John 15:1
246. John 15:2
247. John 8:16
248. John 14:26 (KJV)
249. John 8:23
250. John 16:33
251. John 8:50
252. John 1:39
253. Genesis 1:1-3
254. Romans 12:1-2
255. Isaiah 49:16
256. 1 Corinthians 15:20-22
257. John 11:22-35
258. John 11:25-26
259. John 1:39; 11:34
260. 1 Corinthians 15
261. Wright, N.T. *Surprised by Hope: Rethinking Heaven, the Resurrection, and the Mission of the Church*. HarperOne, 2008
262. Wright, N.T. *Surprised by Hope: Rethinking Heaven, the Resurrection, and the Mission of the Church*. HarperOne, 2008
263. Revelation 2:17
264. Luke 22:18-20
265. Exodus 12:14 (NLT)
266. Deuteronomy 8:11
267. Jeremiah 29:11
268. Mulholland Jr. M.R.. *Invitation into a Journey: A Road Map for Spiritual Formation*. IVP Academic, 2016
269. Mark 2:17
270. Ortberg, John. "Become New." Podcast.
271. Job 1:6
272. Job 1:7 (CEV)
273. Willard, Dallas. *The Divine Conspiracy: Rediscovering Our Hidden Life in God*. HarperCollins, 1998
274. Leviticus 20:10
275. John 8:11
276. Keller, Tim. *Counterfeit Gods: The Empty Promises of Money, Sex, and Power, and the Only Hope that Matters*. Dutton, 2009

277. Willard, Dallas. *The Divine Conspiracy: Rediscovering Our Hidden Life in God.* HarperCollins, 1998
278. Leviticus 26:12
279. Matthew 5:1-12
280. Matthew 5:3-12
281. Matthew 5:13
282. Matthew 7:13-27
283. Pressfield, Steven. *The Virtues of War: A Novel of Alexander the Great.* Doubleday, 2004
284. John 20:20-29
285. 1 Corinthians 15:50-58
286. John 20:20
287. John 20:25 (NLT)
288. John 20:29
289. Bunyan, John. *The Pilgrim's Progress.* Edited by C. H. Simpkinson, Oxford University Press, 2010
290. Lewis, C. S. *Surprised by Joy: The Shape of My Early Life.* Harcourt Brace Jovanovich, 1955
291. Lewis, C. S. *Mere Christianity.* HarperOne, 2001
292. John 18:37
293. John 18:38
294. John 14:6
295. Pascal, Blaise. *Pensées.* Translated by A. J. Krailsheimer, Penguin Classics, 1995
296. Bonhoeffer, Dietrich. *Life Together: The Classic Exploration of Christian Community.* Translated by John W. Doberstein, Harper & Row, 1954
297. Augustine. *Confessions.* Translated by R. S. Pine-Coffin, Penguin Classics, 1961
298. Famous quote of Mother Teresa
299. Genesis 50:20
300. Augustine. *Confessions.* Translated by R. S. Pine-Coffin, Penguin Classics, 1961
301. Augustine. *Confessions.* Translated by R. S. Pine-Coffin, Penguin Classics, 1961
302. John 4:7-37
303. Mark 10:21
304. Matthew 16:24
305. Comer, John Mark. *Live No Lies: Recognize and Resist the Three Enemies That Sabotage Your Peace.* WaterBrook, 2021
306. Carey Nieuwhof Podcast. "CNLP 363: Jon Tyson on What the Future Church Needs to Do Post-COVID, What Leaders Missed in Rushing Back to Normal, and How to Rest Deeply in an Exhausting Era"
307. Matthew 11:28 (NLT)
308. Gottfriend, Jeffery. "Americans' news fatigue isn't going away – about two-thirds still feel worn out." *Pew Research Center*, 26 Feb. 2020, www.pewresearch.org/short-reads/2020/02/26/almost-seven-in-ten-americans-have-news-fatigue-more-among-republicans/
309. Burch, Audra. "Seeing Workplace Misery, Burnout Coaches Offer Company." *The New York Times*, 9 July 2024, www.nytimes.com/2024/07/09/business/work-stress-burnout-coach.html

310. Gonzales, Matt. "Here's How Bad Burnout Has Become at Work." *Society for Human Resource Management (SHRM)*, 2024, www.shrm.org/mena/topics-tools/news/inclusion-diversity/burnout-shrm-research-2024
311. Barna Group. "38% of U.S. Pastors Have Thought About Quitting Full-Time Ministry in the Past Year." *Barna Group*, 2024, www.barna.com/research/pastors-well-being/
312. Matthew 11:29
313. Matthew 11:29b
314. Matthew 11:29
315. 2 Corinthians 5:17
316. 1 Corinthians 2:16
317. 1 John 4:17
318. Romans 8:22 (ESV)
319. Manginelli, Phil. *You Are Not Alone*. Resistance & Renewal. 2024
320. Ephesians 6:12
321. Willard, Dallas. *The Divine Conspiracy: Rediscovering Our Hidden Life in God*. HarperCollins, 1998
322. Keller, Tim. *Prayer: Experiencing Awe and Intimacy with God*. Penguin Books, 2014
323. Charles Finney Quote
324. Matthew 6:16-18
325. Matthew 15:10 & Luke 8:18
326. James 1:19
327. Luke 5 Jesus eats with sinners and tax collectors, Luke 7 Jesus is anointed at the home of Simon the Pharisee during a meal, Luke 9 Jesus feeds 5,000, Luke 10 Jesus eats with Martha and Mary, Luke 11 Jesus condemns the Pharisee and teachers of the law at a meal, Luke 14 Jesus is at a meal when he urges people to invite the poor to their meals rather than friends, Luke 19 Jesus invites himself to dinner with Zacchaeus, Luke 22 the Last Supper, Luke 24 the risen Christ has a meal with two disciples in Emmaus, and then later eats fish with the disciples in Jerusalem.
328. 1 Corinthians 6:7
329. Hebrews 11:24-26
330. Hebrews 11:29
331. Matthew 11:11

www.ingramcontent.com/pod-product-compliance
Lightning Source LLC
Chambersburg PA
CBHW070320010526
44107CB00004B/366